THE PREDICTORS OF SUCCESSFUL
VERY BRIEF PSYCHOTHERAPY

THE PREDICTORS OF SUCCESSFUL VERY BRIEF PSYCHOTHERAPY

A Study of Differences by Gender, Age, and Treatment Variables

By

JOSEPH E. TALLEY, PH.D.

Psychologist and Coordinator of Research
Program Evaluation and Testing
Counseling and Psychological Services
Clinical Faculty, Department of Psychiatry
Duke University, Durham, North Carolina

With Contributors from
Counseling and Psychological Services
Duke University
Durham, North Carolina

With a Foreword by
Hans H. Strupp, Ph.D.

CHARLES C THOMAS • PUBLISHER
Springfield • Illinois • U.S.A.

Published and Distributed Throughout the World by

CHARLES C THOMAS • PUBLISHER
2600 South First Street
Springfield, Illinois 62794-9265

ISBN 0-398-05758-3

Library of Congress Catalog Card Number: 91-24231

With THOMAS BOOKS *careful attention is given to all details of manufacturing
and design. It is the Publisher's desire to present books that are satisfactory as to their
physical qualities and artistic possibilities and appropriate for their particular use.*
THOMAS BOOKS *will be true to those laws of quality that assure a good name
and good will.*

Printed in the United States of America
SC-R-3

Library of Congress Cataloging-in-Publication Data

Talley, Joseph E.
    The predictors of successful very brief psychotherapy : a study of
differences by gender, age, and treatment variables / by Joseph E.
Talley ; with contributors from Conseling and Psychological
Services, Duke University, Durham, North Carolina ; with a foreword
by Hans H. Strupp.
        p.   cm.
    ISBN 0-398-05758-3
    1. Brief psychotherapy—Evaluation.   I. Duke University.
Counseling and Psychological Services.   II. Title.   III. Title: Very
brief psychotherapy.
    RC480.55.T34   1992
    616.89'14—dc20   91-24231
                                                                         CIP

CONTRIBUTORS

John C. Barrow, Ed.D., ABPP, Assistant Director for Career Development and Outreach Services and Staff Psychologist, Counseling and Psychological Services, Duke University. Assistant Clinical Professor, Division of Medical Psychology, Department of Psychiatry, Duke University Medical Center, Durham, North Carolina.

A. Timothy Butcher, M.Div., Project Research Assistant, Counseling and Psychological Services, Duke University. Data Technician, Division of Medical Psychology, Department of Psychiatry, Duke University Medical Center, Durham, North Carolina.

Lisa D. Hinz, Ph.D., former Psychology Intern, Counseling and Psychological Services, Duke University, Durham, North Carolina. Currently, Staff Psychologist, Psychological and Counseling Services, University of California at San Diego, San Diego, California.

Melinda A. Maguire, former Undergraduate Research Assistant, Counseling and Psychological Services, Duke University, Durham, North Carolina. Currently, Ph.D. candidate in Clinical Psychology, University of Texas Southwestern Medical Center at Dallas, Dallas, Texas.

Jane Clark Moorman, M.S.W., BCD, Director and Clinical Social Worker, Counseling and Psychological Services, Duke University. Associate, Division of Psychiatric Social Work, Department of Psychiatry, Duke University Medical Center, Durham, North Carolina.

Rolffs S. Pinkerton, Ph.D., ABPP, Director, Psychology Internship Program and Staff Psychologist, Counseling and Psychological Services, Duke University, Durham, North Carolina.

W. J. Kenneth Rockwell, M.D., FAPA, Staff Psychiatrist, Counseling and Psychological Services, Duke University. Assistant Professor and Director, Eating Disorders Program, Department of Psychiatry, Duke University Medical Center, Durham, North Carolina.

Joseph E. Talley, Ph.D., ABPP, Coordinator of Research, Program Evaluation and Testing Services and Staff Psychologist, Counseling and Psychological Services, Duke University. Assistant Clinical Professor, Division of Medical Psychology, Department of Psychiatry, Duke University Medical Center, Durham, North Carolina.

FOREWORD

The search for briefer and more cost-effective methods of psychotherapy has gathered momentum in our time and is receiving growing attention from practitioners as well as researchers. In this forward-looking study Dr. Joseph Talley and his collaborators have turned the spotlight on "very brief psychotherapy," a treatment approach lasting from one to seven sessions. Although they disclaim that the approach is a competitor to long-term or even brief psychotherapy, the study presents clear evidence that the approach is helpful to a sizable proportion of intelligent and well-educated patients. The findings are consistent with the results of psychotherapy outcome studies in general. The treatment produced notable symptom reduction and client satisfaction.

The study was executed with meticulous care and attention to the limitations that apply to any piece of research. The author is fully conversant with the pertinent psychotherapy research literature and places the study firmly within the framework of contemporary psychotherapy research. The reporting is clear and notably free of exaggerated claims. Perhaps most valuable, from the standpoint of therapist, patient, and researcher is another demonstration that even a limited amount of psychotherapy can be helpful to a good many people.

HANS H. STRUPP, PH.D.
Distinguished Professor of Psychology
Vanderbilt University
Nashville, Tennessee

PREFACE

It is the purpose of this book to present the findings and many exploratory statistical analyses from what is to our knowledge the first formal study of very brief psychotherapy. For our purposes, very brief psychotherapy is defined as lasting from one to seven sessions. The effectiveness of very brief treatment is documented here as measured by the recipient's satisfaction with services received and symptom reduction as reported on psychometric measures. Findings with regard to the treatment "process" variables or ingredients of the treatment that are predictive of successful very brief psychotherapy are presented and compared by different gender and age groups. Analyses of the effects of factors studied in the general psychotherapy outcome literature are likewise reported. These factors include the gender and experience level of the therapist, the gender, age, and affect severity level of the person receiving treatment, and the number of sessions attended. Relevant interactions of these variables are also explored. Finally, data relevant to the use of the psychometric measures employed as screening devices and as outcome measures are reported and new modified briefer forms of these scales are proposed for experimental use.

The claim is made and supported with the data that very brief psychotherapy, while not competing with brief or long-term psychotherapy, is efficacious in meeting the goals of this type of intervention. It is proposed that these goals are to have a positive experience with the psychotherapist and at least the initiation of some change in the presenting dysphoria. This change may consist of beginning to look at self, others, or one's life circumstances at least somewhat differently or beginning to feel at least somewhat differently. No pretense is made that the more complete work done in brief or in long-term psychotherapy is necessarily accomplished, but rather the assertion is made that a commencement on this road is, in and of itself, of value by virtue of the improved subjective feeling state of those receiving treatment and by virtue of the positive experience with the psychotherapist thus leaving the door open for further treatment if needed in the future. However, often very brief psychotherapy is itself sufficient to result in a different perspective on the problem and alter the dysphoria or the accompanying symptoms.

J.E.T.

ACKNOWLEDGEMENTS AND DEDICATION

The work of Melinda Maguire on the data collection and data organization for this study is greatly appreciated. The presentation of this study in written form would not have been possible without the diligent efforts of Timothy Butcher being applied to the manuscript preparation. Gratitude is extended to Jane Clark Moorman, Director of Counseling and Psychological Services of Duke University, for her continued support of our contributing to the professional literature.

Finally, this volume is dedicated to William J. Griffith, Vice-President for Student Affairs of Duke University, who, after over forty years of affiliation with the University, has recently retired. Deepest appreciation is felt for the many years of his affirming the work of Counseling and Psychological Services at Duke. He has encouraged and supported the scientific study of our practice, thus allowing us to contribute not only to students themselves and to the larger mission of the University, but also to the knowledge base of our profession.

J.E.T.

CONTENTS

THE PREDICTORS OF SUCCESSFUL
VERY BRIEF PSYCHOTHERAPY

Chapter I

INTRODUCTION: THE CASE FOR INVESTIGATING VERY BRIEF PSYCHOTHERAPY

Joseph E. Talley

THE CONTEXT

Many excellent studies have persuasively demonstrated the efficacy of psychotherapy of limited duration (Strupp, 1980a; Luborsky, Mintz, Auerbach, Christoph, Bachrach, Todd, Johnson, Cohen, and O'Brien, 1980; Koss and Butcher, 1986). The theories and techniques of brief psychotherapy by Mann (1973), Malan (1963), Sifneos (1972), and Strupp and Binder (1984) have been popular for quite some time. Brief psychotherapy has been generally defined as lasting from eight to twenty-six sessions (Mann, 1973; Malan, 1976; Flegenheimer, 1982; Pinkerton, 1986). However, "the median number of visits for all mental disorders treated in organized outpatient psychiatric services in the United States" has been found to be 3.7 sessions (Pardes and Pincus, 1981, p. 15). Thus, the practice of psychotherapy as it is most often done is actually briefer than brief therapy. Nevertheless, these authors do allow that, "the average number of visits in private psychiatric practice is somewhat larger (26 visits for non-analysts)" (Pardes and Pincus, 1981, p. 15).

This briefer than brief therapy has been called *ultra-brief psychotherapy* (Hersh, 1988), and a body of literature exists concerning what has been called *single-session psychotherapy* (Talmon, 1990), or *very brief interventions* (VBI's) (Pinkerton and Rockwell, 1982; Rockwell and Pinkerton, 1982). Furthermore, many of the new and now popular company sponsored Health Maintenance Organizations, Preferred Provider arrangements, and Employee Assistance Programs, in addition to community mental health centers, university counseling centers, and student mental health centers offered a limited (usually less than eight) number of psychotherapy sessions. Finally, Howard, Kopta, Krause, and Orlinsky (1986) in their meta-analysis, "The Dose/Effect Relationship in Psychotherapy," have concluded that the greatest amount of improvement effect due to

3

therapy occurs during the first eight sessions. Thus, taking all of these points together, studies in very brief psychotherapy (interventions lasting for less than eight sessions) appear to be not only warranted, but a necessity.

As Howard, Kopta, Krause, and Orlinsky (1986) examined differential effects of psychotherapy by diagnosis, so too, other patient/client characteristics such as gender, age, and initial level of disturbance have been shown to be relevant in assessing psychotherapy outcome (Luborsky, Auerbach, Chandler, Cohen, and Bachrach, 1971). It is quite possible that client gender or age serves as a moderator variable for the predictors of a successful outcome. The work of Gilligan (1977) and her conclusion that males and females taken as groups seem to differ as to *modus operandi* in making moral decisions suggest that gender differences may exist with regard to values relating to other issues. Gilligan (1977) found that with regard to decisions of moral choice females would choose to act in such a way as to reflect the value of preserving relationships over the value of implementing a particular principle for action. Males, on the other hand, seemed to value the preservation of a principle more highly than the preservation of a relationship. It must be emphasized that neither need be superior, rather males and females simply appear to be different in this way. Likewise, it was hypothesized in the present investigation that males and females may differ with regard to what they value in a psychotherapeutic contact. An earlier investigation (Talley, Roy, and Moorman, 1986) prompted the consideration that age may interact with gender concerning what is found most helpful in treatment and which ingredients are more likely to result in a successful intervention with a given group of people.

To further make the case for the relevance of the present study, it might be contrasted to the genre of psychotherapy research which appears to maintain that in order for a study to be of value, videotapes of all sessions must be made, judges whose inter-rater reliability has been established must view the tapes and rate the occurrences of certain phenomena concerning what the therapist and the patient are doing, the therapists must have all been found to successfully deliver therapy in a manner very closely prescribed in a training manual and patients must be found homogeneous according to diagnostic criteria. This does not even address the host of other variables that the researcher is expected to control. When such a psychotherapy study is completed, the investigators may conclude that intervention X works better than intervention Y and/or better than nothing at all in treating subjects carefully screened to be of a given diagnosis. It is arguable that what has in fact been demonstrated is that patients being treated under the most desirable of circumstances by very well to excellently trained therapists at a major medical center in a heavily funded and closely watched NIMH study will report changes and changes will be observed by judges and the therapists. Such a study may say little about psychotherapy as it is delivered by the typical practitioner under more usual conditions.

The problem of assuming that we can in any way control for or measure a sufficient number of the plethora of intervening variables in psychotherapy is made clearer in a comment by Alan Kazdin who has written that the goals of comparative psychotherapy outcome research, "may push the limits of information that can be legitimately expected from a single type of research" (Kazdin, 1986, p. 102). Hans Strupp addressing the same issue has noted that it is unlikely that one can identify specific techniques or attribute to them specific effects and that the isolation of technique from the therapist's personality is impossible suggesting that all technique must be analyzed in the context of the therapist's personality (Strupp, 1986).

If this is the case, the same intervention actually never happens twice as no two therapists have the same personality and even the approximations of similarity among therapists' personalities can only be but so close. When one considers the combined complexity of the therapist's and patient's personalities, each with numerous traits and all to varying degrees interacting with each other and moderating each other, with some traits masking others, the true gravity of Kazdin's and Strupp's comments is underscored. It is most unlikely, if not impossible, that all of the most salient and critical variables can be controlled, measured, or accounted for. Even if this were possible the results would be of questionable generalizability with regard to psychotherapy as conducted by general practitioners in a setting that is primarily practice-oriented. Thus, the naturalistic, but measured, observations and findings from a setting that is primarily practice-oriented might have some merit as a help to the psychotherapist who practices in a similar setting despite the lack of random assignment of subjects to treatment, therapists trained in a manually based intervention, videotaped sessions, and the employment of judges' ratings.

A final note concerning the setting is directed to the population samples. While all subjects in the present study were enrolled in a university, the age spectrum is quite broad because many were graduate or professional students. Thus, the findings should be relevant to most young adults seeking psychotherapy services as all are going through the same developmental demands of that period of life. However, since our samples were in all probability brighter than average, more likely to be single and from a family of higher than average annual income, and diagnostically included no subjects with a known, serious thought process disorder or psychosis, the generalizability of the findings is constrained by these and perhaps other factors. Nevertheless, there is much in common between university young adults seeking psychotherapeutic services and their nonuniversity peers due primarily to their age and related developmental tasks as noted by Erik Erickson (1968) and Chickering (1976).

Thus, although the procedures, interventions, and population may differ in ways from those found in traditional psychotherapy research, there is a robust case to be made for the inclusion of studies such as this in the literature and in meta-analytic reviews. Moreover, given the unusual circumstances under which most published psychotherapy data are gathered, a case for the actual superiority of more naturalistic studies can be made in light of the phenomena of demand characteristics (Orne, 1962) and the now age old Hawthorne Effect (Roethlisberger and Dickson, 1939).

SOME NOTES ON TERMINOLOGY

The question of language for the phenomena under investigation and its components might be debated. The term *therapy* is more associated with the remediation of a disorder while the terms *counseling* and *consultation* have the connotation from other usages of the giving of advice and may convey that the essence of psychotherapeutic treatment is exclusively cognitive. Describing the process as an *intervention* or a *treatment* may come closest to accuracy, although the former term may suggest a power of action by the intervening party as if an action is to be controlled, maintained, or prevented primarily by this intervening party. The term *treatment* may suggest that there is a more specific technique for a given situation than is the case. However, it does acknowledge that there is a treatment with some specific guidelines. To call the process an *encounter* seems to deprofessionalize it almost entirely and to gloss over the fact that one party seeks out the other party for a particular service that presupposes the mastery of a body of knowledge that when applied can bring about a result desired by the seeker.

Prefacing whatever the term of choice is with *very brief* admittedly has its problems as it is likely to convey the notion that it produces the same effect, in the same manner, as the more protracted version. Thus, the term *very brief psychotherapy* certainly has its limitations as does the term *brief psychotherapy*. However, given the limitations of all of these descriptors, it seems that from a technical viewpoint either the phrase *very brief psychotherapeutic intervention* or *very brief psychotherapeutic treatment* captures the essence of the activity, with the appropriate modifier, in that it is psychotherapeutic activity, but not psychotherapy proper in which the goals can be of greater magnitude with a longer period of time in which to work. Nevertheless, there are many principles and modifications of the treatment of psychotherapy that are incorporated into brief psycho-therapy and very brief psychotherapeutic treatment. The argument as to the inadvisability of shortening *very brief psychotherapeutic treatment* to *very brief psychotherapy* can be made in that nonpractitioners might assume that very brief psychotherapy can provide the same ends as brief or extended psychotherapy. However, taking all of these matters into account, the appeal of brevity and the acknowledgement that the term psychotherapy has to date been readily applied to such very brief forms of treatment seem to coalesce and compel the acknowledgement of the term *very brief psychotherapy*. Nevertheless, it is accepted that *very brief psychotherapeutic treatment* or *very brief psychotherapeutic intervention* is probably more accurate. However, if we are to use the term very brief psychotherapy as we use the term brief psychotherapy it must be made explicit by treating professionals that this treatment cannot be expected to produce the effects of longer-term treatment.

Just as more profoundly troubled persons who have been so for many years are less likely to benefit from brief psychotherapy, as is the general consensus (Pinkerton, 1986), it might be assumed that these profoundly troubled persons are even less likely to benefit from very brief psycho-therapy. Therefore, this treatment will be of most benefit to those who are or who generally have been within the normal range of human functioning. They probably do not warrant a diagnosis from the *Diagnostic and Statistical Manual III-R* (American Psychiatric Association, 1987) other than a V code understood to be for a condition that is the focus of attention or treatment but is not attributable to a mental disorder.

Yet the treatment of very brief psychotherapy may be extremely helpful and beneficial, it can be argued, with a person of any diagnosis when the technique is tailored to that individual's needs by determining an adequate formulation and making an accurate assessment. The seeker need not be in crisis although that would be permissible. The seeker must have a dilemma of sufficient importance to create from within a containable drive for relief and sufficient motivation to contact one who can provide psychotherapeutic treatment. Thus, the seeker must have the belief that a provider of psychotherapeutic services can be of benefit. It might also be argued that for the intervention to be productive the seeker must be mentally and to some extent emotionally accessible to the therapist (i.e., the seeker must be open to receiving something). This same process might be described in terms of the therapist being permitted to have impact sufficient to modify the seeker's thought processes to a degree. Preferably the seeker adopts a stance with some vulnerability *vis à vis* the therapist. Thus, a productive intervention is unlikely with a person in a psychotic state or whose faculties are otherwise impaired at the time, and a productive encounter is less likely with a person whose personality traits or character is tightly defended and inaccessible to emotional contact.

The delineations of who may benefit most and least from briefer forms of psychotherapy have been set forth by many, and the criteria are usually quite specific and exclusive. It is assumed here that more flexible criteria with regard to who might benefit from services, such as those proposed by Strupp and Binder (1984), are most useful and might also be applicable to very brief psychotherapy if the outcome expectations are modified. Nevertheless, most persons for whom such treatment will be sufficient, in and of itself, are generally in the normal range of functioning. However, persons with other diagnoses may benefit from very brief psychotherapeutic treatment if it is designed to treat a relatively circum-scribed problem that is not tightly bound to a larger problem. Yet even in a situation in which the presenting concern is symptomatic of a more fundamental nemesis, it is possible that very brief psychotherapy with a well defined focus can yield results that, although initially minimal, begin to generalize to other parts of the personality and lead to a larger therapeutic effect on overall functioning and subjective distress (Erickson, 1980).

If the individual does not meet the criteria for any *DSM-III-R* diagnosis other than a V-code, it is probably erroneous to use the referent *patient* as an identifier for the person receiving treatment. The term *client* has strong associations to the practice of business and law and thus, with such practices the cognitive component resonates with the term as clients are given *advice, consultation,* or *counsel.* Likewise, to refer to such an individual as a *student* (in a nonacademic setting) suggests the educative process is most salient in the treatment. The term *seeker* is probably accurate, but this seems unnecessary if such seekers can simply be *persons.* Further, if the majority of those utilizing very brief psychotherapy are to be called *persons,* the question may then follow, why not the rest? Let it first be stated that the use of the term person in this context is not meant to endorse a Rogerian or Humanistic theory of personality with what appears to be at times the assumptions of some basic or inherent all goodness of persons and the ability of persons to heal themselves alone in a supportive and safe environment. Rather, the term *person* is suggested as a noun of respect and the expression of a stance endorsing the fundamental equality of the treatment provider and the person receiving services in the realm of the core of one's innermost being. In this manner it is useful as a term by way of reminding both the receiver and the provider of services of this stance, which at times appears forgotten, if it was indeed accepted at the outset.

Finally, then, what are we the providers of very brief psychotherapy to persons to be called? While the term *counselor* has the same problems as the term *counseling* already described, it is nevertheless palatable and commonly used. Therefore, it may be the best compromise for use with the population receiving services. Although it may seem both more accurate and less unnecessarily complicated to simply term the service providers according to their discipline as a *psychologist, clinical social worker,* or *psychiatrist,* etc., these terms are more technically accurate and therefore, in some sense are preferable. Yet, they do not allow one term for generic use as is often needed in order to avoid becoming unnecessarily cumbersome, for example, in a research study or in the office. The term *psychotherapist* would appear to summarize the activity most accurately and also would allow credit for technical expertise while providing a generic term applicable to various disciplines. Nevertheless, the term may be incongruent with how some receivers of the service wish to see themselves. At such times the term *counselor,* despite the connotations noted, may be a better choice in order to allow users to feel comfortable seeking services.

In this volume the terms very brief psychotherapy, very brief psychotherapeutic treatment, very brief treatment, very brief psychotherapeutic interventions, and very brief interventions are all used to refer to the same phenomenon. The term very brief psychotherapy appears to be the best compromise although the term very brief psychotherapeutic treatment is in all probability the more accurate. When the context has made it clear the modifier *very brief* may be omitted for the sake of readability. Likewise, for the sake of readability and clarity the person receiving services is at times, depending on the context, referred to as the client, the patient, the client/patient, the receiver of services, the seeker of services, etc. However, the term person is found to be most philosophically compatible with the model of treatment described. The service provider is most often referred to as a therapist. In reference to data from the Client Satisfaction Index the term counselor is used in order to continue the use of the generic and palatable term chosen for research with the satisfaction questionnaire. The terms counselor and provider of services are meant to convey to the reader of this study the exact same meaning as the term therapist used in the text.

PURPOSE AND HYPOTHESES OF THE STUDY

All of the data reported in this volume were gathered in one study with the same subjects, procedures and instruments as described in the methodology section of the second chapter. All subsequent chapters are reports of various aspects of this one study. The general purposes of the investigation were as follows:

1. To determine whether very brief psychotherapy resulted in improvement in degree of reported symptoms of anxiety and depression. Very brief psychotherapy is defined as lasting from one to seven sessions. (The phrase one to seven sessions in this text is meant to *include* those attending seven sessions.)

2. To determine whether those receiving very brief psychotherapy were satisfied with this treatment.

3. To determine whether outcome varied as a function of therapist gender, therapist experience level, therapist gender x experience level interaction, the gender, age, or gender x age interaction of the client/patient or the number of sessions attended. The variable of age was divided dichotomously such that those eighteen through twenty-two years of age were in one group and those twenty-three years of age and older were in

the other group. This division allowed those of late adolescent/young adult age (usual undergraduate age) to be compared to those of young to middle age adulthood (usual graduate and professional school age).

4. To determine the components of the treatment process that were predictive of symptom reduction and satisfaction with treatment and to determine whether these predictors differed by the age and gender of those receiving very brief psychotherapy.

5. To explore the utility of the psychometric measures used as both screening devices and as outcome measures and to determine whether there were differences by gender and sample group manifested on the inventories.

6. To examine related aspects of the above findings with exploratory statistical analyses. The partial r^2 and percentage of the variance calculations from the stepwise regression analyses and the stepwise discriminant function analyses must be interpreted with caution as stepwise procedures were employed. Thus, it is possible that "shared" or "common" variance may be added to the variance uniquely attributable to the first predictor. All *Beta* weights reported are unstandardized parameter estimates.

endnote: Given that this is an exploratory study, the hypotheses are implied in the purpose statements rather than being stated formally.

Chapter II

THE EFFECTS OF VERY BRIEF PSYCHOTHERAPY ON SYMPTOMS OF DYSPHORIA

Joseph E. Talley, A. Timothy Butcher, Melinda A. Maguire,
and Rolffs S. Pinkerton

REVIEW OF THE PSYCHOTHERAPY OUTCOME LITERATURE

The search for the factors that govern the outcome of psychotherapy has been undertaken with much interest since Rosenzweig (1936) and Freud (1937) published their benchmark papers on the subject. Rosenzweig (1936) observed that diverse methods in psychotherapy produced equally positive results and argued that different methods had certain implicit factors in common that led to success. He hypothesized that even more important than the methods being purposely employed were certain unrecognized factors that exist in any therapeutic situation, e.g., the "indefinable effect of the therapist's personality" (Rosenzweig, 1936, p. 413). Subsequent studies of the efficacy of psychotherapy sought not only to show that psychotherapy was in fact capable of producing positive change in clients, but also to delineate the specific factors in therapy that led to favorable outcome.

Among the most important studies to investigate the specific factors resulting in positive outcome were the studies by Rogers (1957) and Wallerstein, Robbins, Sargent, and Luborsky (1956). Rogers (1957) postulated that six conditions in psychotherapy were essential if "constructive personality change" (p. 95) was to take place, including most importantly, the existence of at least a minimal relationship between therapist and client. Wallerstein, Robbins, Sargent, and Luborsky (1956) listed various qualities of both patient and therapist hypothesized to affect the outcome of psychotherapy.

Although these studies seemed to reveal some of the factors that led to success in psychotherapy, it was, as we know from the literature, by no means clear in the early years of psychotherapy research that psychotherapy was in fact effective or capable of producing positive change in clients (i.e., positive change that could surpass the improvement produced by the passage of time alone). Eysenck (1952) attempted to show, in a review of a portion of the literature on psychotherapy, that two-thirds of all people with a neurotic disorder would improve within two years whether or not they entered psychotherapy. However, when the studies that Eysenck used were analyzed more carefully it was demonstrated that Eysenck's methods of assigning subjects to different improvement categories were flawed and this error largely accounted for his findings (Rosenzweig, 1954). The rates of improvement that could be attributed to the passage of time alone were in fact, much lower than Eysenck had reported. Also, Eysenck's critics went a step further and maintained that the use of a no-treatment control group would be superior to spontaneous remission data in the evaluation of psychotherapy outcome (Bergin, 1971; Lambert, 1976; Bergin and Lambert, 1978).

Meta-analytical studies (Smith, Glass, and Miller, 1980; Howard, Kopta, Krause, and Orlinsky, 1986) have done much to confirm the overall effectiveness of psychotherapy in producing positive change in clients and have shown that rates of improvement for those in psychotherapy are significantly higher than for those who never enter psychotherapy. In their meta-analysis of 475 controlled studies of the effectiveness of psychotherapy, Smith, Glass, and Miller (1980) found an average effect-size of .85 (std. err. = .03). When this effect-size is represented graphically with the psychotherapy and untreated control groups viewed side by side, it can be seen that "the average person who receives therapy is better off at the end of it than 80 percent of the persons who do not [receive treatment]" (Smith et al., 1980, p. 87). Further, Howard, Kopta, Krause, and Orlinsky (1986) analyzed the data of fifteen studies covering a thirty-year span that included a total of 2,431 patients in weekly outpatient psychotherapy. Their meta-analysis indicated that, depending on the diagnosis, up to 58 percent of clients showed measurable improvement by the eighth session, and that about 75 percent of clients showed some improvement by the twenty-sixth session (Howard et al., 1986). Thus, the evidence for the effectiveness of psychotherapy in producing positive change in clients is considerable.

Patient/Client Variables And Outcome In Psychotherapy

In a comprehensive review and evaluation of the quantitative research, Luborsky, Auerbach, Chandler, Cohen, and Bachrach, (1971) cataloged predictive factors from the literature that led to success in psychotherapy. Patient, therapist, and treatment variables were all found to be noteworthy, but by far the most impressive predictors of outcome were patient variables. Among the patient factors most significantly associated with improvement were adequacy of personality functioning, motivation, intelligence, anxiety, education, social class, and previous experience in psychotherapy. Additionally, in a report based on twenty-five years of research on brief psychotherapy (of approximately 2½ months to six months duration) at the Johns Hopkins Psychotherapy Research Unit, Frank (1974) concluded that "the weight of the evidence . . . supports the view that the most important determinants of long-term improvement lie in the patient" (p. 339). Frank (1974) delineated a number of patient variables that influenced outcome in therapy including social class, perseverance, suggestibility, social integration, attractiveness (which subsumed age and education), locus of control, and most significant for long-term prognosis, coping capacities and the modifiability of the presenting dysphoria. Thus, a multiplicity of client variables have been found to influence the outcome of psychotherapy. While some of these client variables are more significantly related to outcome than others, it would nevertheless be beneficial to briefly review some of the primary client variables as found in the literature.

Client social class is one such variable, yet there are relatively few studies that have considered the social class of clients and its relationship to outcome. Those studies that have evaluated client social class and outcome have found no consistent relationship between social class and psychotherapeutic outcome. Five early studies addressing social class variables (also reviewed by Luborsky et al., 1971) are as follows: McNair, Lorr, Young, Roth, and Boyd (1964) found that social attainment was significantly associated with favorable change in patients at three-year follow-up; Rosenbaum, Friedlander, and Kaplan (1956) found higher social class to be correlated with positive outcome; Brill and Storrow (1960) found a significant relationship between a prospective patient's social class and whether or not the person was even accepted for treatment with higher social class being associated with greater acceptance; Katz, Lorr, and Rubinstein (1958) found that occupational level and annual earnings were not significantly related to improvement in psychotherapy; and finally, Gottschalk, Mayerson, and Gottlieb (1967) conversely found that patients of lower socioeconomic status showed more improvement in therapy than patients of higher socioeconomic status. These studies have been critiqued by Luborsky et al. (1971), who found that the conclusions of the investigations appeared warranted. Lorion's (1973) extensive review of the literature addressing client social class and psychotherapy corroborated the findings that socioeconomic status was significantly related to a presenting client's being accepted for psychotherapy.

Frank (1974) reported that patients of lower socioeconomic status dropped out of treatment more often than patients of middle or upper socioeconomic status, yet the general conclusion that there is no consistent relationship between client socioeconomic status and psychotherapy outcome was supported by the findings of Schmidt and Hancey's (1979) evaluation of therapy rendered at a military psychiatric outpatient clinic. In their study no differences were found on the basis of client social class for diagnosis, number of sessions attended, or psychotherapy outcome.

The relationship between client education and outcome in psychotherapy has been found to be somewhat more significant than the relationship between client social class and outcome. Seven studies that investigated the effects of this variable were evaluated by Luborsky et al. (1971), and our review of these studies resulted in similar conclusions with regard to their findings. Five of the seven studies (Bloom, 1956; Casner, 1950; Hamburg, Bibring, Fisher, Stanton, Weinstock, and Haggard, 1967; McNair, Lorr, Young, Roth, and Boyd, 1964; Sullivan, Miller, and Smelser, 1958) found higher education in clients to be associated with some increased success in psychotherapy. Two of these studies (Knapp, Levin, McCarter, Wermer, and Zetzel, 1960; Rosenbaum, Friedlander, and Kaplan, 1956) found no significant relationship between client educational status and psychotherapeutic outcome. The data is sparse and by no means definitive, but taken as a whole it does suggest the likelihood of some relationship between client education and outcome in psychotherapy with more educated clients doing better in psychotherapy.

Client intelligence level has also been found to be related to outcome in psychotherapy (Barron, 1953; Barry and Fulkerson, 1966; Casner, 1950; Fiske, Cartwright, and Kirtner, 1964; McNair et al., 1964; Miles, Barrabee, and Finesinger 1951; Rioch and Lubin, 1959; Rosenberg, 1954; Sullivan, Miller, and Smelser, 1958; Zigler and Phillips, 1961), but the nature of the relationship is unclear. Luborsky et al. (1971) found a positive relationship between client intelligence and outcome in ten of thirteen studies reviewed, while Meltzoff and Kornreich (1970) found no relationship between client intelligence and outcome in eight of fifteen studies. Garfield (1986), in his excellent, comprehensive review of the literature on client variables and psychotherapy, states that it is not clear whether a certain minimum level of intelligence is required for successful outcome in psychotherapy. Further, Garfield (1986) states, "if we were to take a correlation of around .30 as indicating the possible relationship of intelligence to outcome, intelligence would still account for less than 10 percent of the variance" (p. 239).

The client variable that Luborsky et al. (1971) found to have been studied most frequently was the "adequacy of general personality functioning" (p. 147), or client level of initial disturbance. The authors found that fourteen of twenty-eight studies addressing this variable showed a significant correlation between a patient's initial personality functioning and psychotherapy outcome. These studies " . . . indicate that the healthier the patient is to begin with, the better the outcome—or the converse— the sicker he is to begin with, the poorer the outcome" (Luborsky et al., 1971, p. 148). For example, among these earlier studies Barron (1953) found that "level of integration" (p. 241) is positively related to success in therapy, while Kirtner and Cartwright (1958) found that clients who had success in short-term therapy (less than twelve sessions) generally demonstrated higher levels of personality integration. Also, Rogers, Gendlin, Kiesler, and Truax (1967), of the Wisconsin Project on Psychotherapy, found that a patient who "showed more awareness of his inner feelings and . . . more ownership of his own reactions . . ." (p. 87) in the initial interview was more likely to have success in psychotherapy. However, Stone, Frank, Nash, and Imber (1961) found that patients who experienced the greatest decrease in discomfort at five-year follow-up were sicker initially. This may in part be an artifact of the method used to measure improvement. Specifically, if pretreatment *vs.* posttreatment difference scores are used, then there is a greater possibility for clients scoring higher on the initial measures of pathology or distress to show a greater difference in pre- and post-treatment scores.

Subsequent studies of client level of initial disturbance and its relationship to outcome have similarly yielded inconsistent results. Kernberg, Burstein, Coyne, Applebaum, Horwitz, and Voth (1972) of the Menninger Foundation's psychotherapy research project found that ego strength correlated positively with overall improvement. Moreover, Luborsky, Mintz, and Christoph (1979) of the Penn Psychotherapy Research Project, found that clients who were rated higher by clinical observers on an adequacy of functioning assessment did slightly better in therapy. Steinmetz, Lewinsohn, and Antonuccio (1983) found that patients who were initially more depressed as rated by the Beck Depression Inventory tended to be more depressed at the conclusion of psychotherapy, and the findings of Rounsaville, Weissman, and Prusoff (1981), in a study of short-term (sixteen weeks) interpersonal psychotherapy, indicated that patients who were judged to be more emotionally healthy initially were more likely to improve in psychotherapy. However, Gelso, Mills, and Spiegel (1983), in a study of time-limited counseling, concluded that therapists' initial assessments of client functioning did not influence success in time-limited therapy, but nonetheless concluded that "tested initial adjustment" (p. 111) may predict success or failure in time-limited therapy.

In a recent study addressing the issue of the client's initial level of personality functioning, Piper, Azim, McCallum, and Joyce (1990) found that patients who were rated high on quality of object relations at intake did better in short-term, dynamically-oriented, individual psychotherapy than patients who were rated as low on quality of object relations. Thus, those patients who obtained the best results in therapy were rated as more capable of participating in "equitable relationships characterized by love, tenderness, and concern for objects of both sexes" (Piper et al., 1990, p. 477). In an outcome study of psychiatric outpatients at the two-year posttreatment follow-up point, Harder, Greenwald, Strauss, Kokes, Ritzler, and Gift (1990) found that general social competence factors, including health-sickness ratings and social competence ratings, were the best predictors of outcome.

Client expectation in psychotherapy is another variable that has received attention. Frank, Gliedman, Imber, Nash, and Stone (1957) concluded that a client's willingness to persevere, presumably indicating expectancy of change, could influence his/her continuation in therapy. Rosenthal and Frank (1956) argued that the "placebo effect" (p. 300), or a patient's belief that therapy will produce change may exert considerable influence on the outcome of therapy. Other studies (Goldstein, 1960; Lennard and Bernstein, 1960; Lipkin, 1954) have similarly concluded that clients who anticipate success and gratification in therapy experience more symptomatic change than those who enter therapy with reservations.

Luborsky et al. (1971) found that patient expectation of change was predictive in three of the above five studies. However, Wilkins (1973) in his review and critique of the literature on client expectancy and outcome found conflicting reports of the importance of client expectations and outcome. Six studies were found to show a positive relationship, eight studies to show no relationship, and one study was found to show mixed conclusions concerning client expectations and outcome (Wilkins, 1973). Nevertheless, subsequent findings have shown that client expectations may considerably influence outcome in psychotherapy. For instance, Steinmetz et al. (1983) found that clients who expected to be the least depressed after therapy improved the most.

In later years a considerable amount of attention has been devoted to the nature of the therapeutic alliance between client and therapist. Various client characteristics have been highlighted in these studies as having particular importance for the therapeutic alliance and outcome. Gomes-Schwartz (1978) noted that patient involvement appeared to be the best predictor of outcome. Consistent with Gomes-Schwartz's findings (1978), O'Malley, Suh, and Strupp (1983) found that, "the process dimension of Patient Involvement showed the strongest and most consistent relationship to outcome" (p. 585). Garfield (1986) noted that the client's subjective experience of being helped to change by the therapist and the client's feeling that the therapist felt concerned, could be the essential variables with regard to the therapeutic alliance. Hartley and Strupp (1983) of the Vanderbilt Psychotherapy Project found that even in the early phases of the therapeutic relationship it is possible to discriminate between more and less successful therapeutic alliances, and that "strengthening of the alliance ... predicted good outcome, whereas weakening of the alliance predicted poor outcome" (p. 23). In a more recent evaluation of theory-based research on dynamic psychotherapy, Luborsky, Barber, and Crits-Christoph (1990) found that in five of six studies evaluated therapeutic alliance measures proved to be signfiiant predictors of outcome.

Garfield (1986), in reviewing the effects of client age on outcome in psychotherapy, addresses the difficulty in forming general conclusions from the studies that address client age and outcome. The difficulty arises in part from the fact that age is a continuous variable with definitions and cut off points varying from study to study. Thus, the older subjects in one study are not the same age as the older subjects in another study. Therefore, it is difficult to draw meaningful conclusions as to whether "older" subjects do better or worse in psychotherapy than "younger" subjects. Garfield (1986) notes that this difficulty has limited the findings concerning age and its relationship to outcome in psychotherapy.

Luborsky et al. (1971) found that of eleven studies that addressed the variable of age in relation to psychotherapy outcome, four found a positive relationship between age and outcome such that younger patients had somewhat more success, five revealed no significant results, and two found that older patients did better. Luborsky et al. (1971) concluded that younger patients tended to have a better chance of positive outcome than older clients. Smith et al. (1980) in their meta-analytical analysis found a .00 correlation between client age and outcome in psychotherapy. Yet, in a study of psychotherapy outcome for major depression, Sargeant, Bruce, Florio, and Weissman (1990) found that females over thirty years of age showed considerably higher rates of depression persistence than females under thirty years of age. Sargeant et al. (1990) noted that this higher persistence is consistent with increased rates of depression among females who are between thirty and fifty years of age.

To date, client gender has not been shown to have a strong relationship to outcome in psychotherapy. Several studies (Cartwright, 1955; Gaylin, 1966; Knapp et al., 1960) have reported no significant relationship between gender of the client and outcome. Luborsky, Mintz, and Christoph (1979) found no consistent relationship between gender of client and outcome in psychotherapy, and other studies (Gomes-Schwartz, 1978; Siegel, Rootes, and Traub, 1977; Steinmetz, Lewinsohn, and Antonuccio, 1983) have found either inconsistent or conflicting results when client gender and outcome were assessed. However, Jones and Zoppel (1982) did find that female therapists appeared to form more effective therapeutic alliances with clients than did male therapists, but they, nonetheless, concluded that client gender was not a dominant influence on outcome.

Therapist Variables and Outcome in Psychotherapy

Therapist variables found to be most significantly associated with improvement include experience, interest patterns, empathy, and the match between patient and therapist (Luborsky et al., 1971). Therapist level of experience and training is a variable that has received considerable attention in the research. The studies in which the influence of therapist level of experience upon psychotherapy outcome has been examined have generated contradictory findings. Haccoun and Lavigueur (1979) concluded that more experienced therapists showed greater tolerance for their patient's anger, rated angry clients more favorably, and showed more self-confidence and less discomfort in dealing with anger than less experienced therapists did. Luborsky et al. (1971) found that eight of thirteen studies that investigated this variable reported a positive relationship between therapist level of experience and outcome. However, in an analysis of comparative studies of experienced vs. inexperienced therapists, Auerbach and Johnson (1977) found twelve studies of which only five supported the conclusion that the more experienced therapist had greater success in psychotherapy. Auerbach and Johnson (1977) noted that three of the five studies supporting the conclusion that more experienced therapists have more success were flawed in design. Parloff, Waskow, and Wolfe (1978) found that in only four of thirteen studies did the more experienced therapists produce significantly greater success at the $p. < .05$ level of probability. Yet, Auerbach and Johnson (1977), in their comprehensive evaluation of the literature, found no studies that favored inexperienced therapists over experienced ones.

Therapist age is another variable for which the research findings are inconclusive. Luborsky, Crits-Christoph, Alexander, Margolis, and Cohen (1983) assessed the importance of age similarity of client and therapist and found that age similarity attained the highest correlation of the variables studied with their helping alliance measure. Luborsky et al. (1983) state, "the presence of certain basic similarities between patient and therapist apparently facilitates the formation of the patient's experience of a helping alliance with the therapist" (p. 488). Karasu, Stein, and Charles (1979) investigated age differences between therapist and client and concluded that the therapy process is more productive and beneficial when the therapist and the client are of similar age. The therapists in their study preferred to treat younger patients and tended to evaluate younger patients more favorably than they did the older patients. In cases where the therapist was younger than the client the dropout rates increased despite statements from clients of their need for more treatment. Further, in the Getz and Miles (1978) and Lasky and Salomone (1977) studies, adolescents were found to prefer therapists or counselors who were closer to their own age when the interaction focused on personal problems.

Other variables may moderate the way therapist age affects therapeutic process and outcome. For instance, Donnan and Mitchell (1979) and Simons and Helms (1976) found that female clients would rather work with therapists who are older than they are. Also, therapist age is correlated with therapist experience. Conclusions about the effects of therapist age on outcome are difficult to draw, but there does seem to be empirical support for favoring the matching of therapist and client on the basis of age similarity.

The literature on therapist gender and its relationship to therapy process and outcome is more prolific, especially in more recent years, than is the literature on the therapist variables of age and level of experience. Nevertheless, conclusions about the influence of therapist gender on outcome in psychotherapy are still elusive. Meltzoff and Kornreich (1970), in their review of twenty studies concluded that the research revealed no difference between male and female therapists with regard to effects on outcome. Parloff, Waskow, and Wolfe (1978) found and reviewed fifteen studies from the mid-1970s that investigated the effects of therapist gender and came to the similar conclusion that there is very little support for the hypothesis that therapist gender significantly influences outcome in psychotherapy. Goldenholz (1976) also found no significant differences in outcome between various gender matchings of client and therapist. In their review of the literature Orlinsky and Howard (1980) state:

> We are left to echo the conclusions of other commentators: not much directly relevant research, not much consistent quality, and not much by way of results. The impression thus far sustained is that gender, by itself, is not a powerful or consistent predictor of therapeutic outcome. (Orlinsky and Howard, 1980, p. 23)

Nevertheless, Orlinsky and Howard (1976) have found that female therapists were more successful with younger female clients than were male therapists and that female clients perceived male therapists as more distant and demanding than female therapists. Yet, Orlinsky and Howard (1976) did not conclude that male therapists produced inferior therapeutic outcomes as opposed to female therapists. In a follow-up to their earlier study, Orlinsky and Howard (1980) found that in treating schizophrenic women, female therapists had significantly more success than male therapists to the extent that 89 percent of patients working with female therapists improved while only 43 percent of those with male therapists were improved. It was similarly found that female therapists were more successful than male therapists, particularly with younger female clients (mean age thirty years). Jones and Zoppel (1982) found that female clients reported having gained more from therapy than males did and that male and female clients "agreed that female therapists were more effective in terms of the actual behavior that constitutes psychological intervention" (Jones and Zoppel, 1982, p. 270). Moreover, Jones, Krupnick, and Kerig (1987) concluded that gender influenced process and outcome in their study of brief, twelve-session, psychodynamic psychotherapy. Patients who had female therapists reported more symptomatic improvement and more satisfaction with treatment than patients who had male therapists. Jones et al. (1987) are quick to point out that these results are moderated by the fact that "patient age accounted for twice and patient pretreatment level of disturbance more than three times the outcome variance contributed by gender" (p. 348). Jones et al. (1987) conclude that the role of therapist and client gender as well as patients' pretreatment adequacy of personality functioning, and their effects on the therapeutic process, need to be accounted for more adequately.

Process Variables and Outcome in Psychotherapy

In the Luborsky et al. report (1971) the only treatment variable producing a noteworthy effect was the number of sessions attended. In twenty of twenty-two studies reviewed "the length of treatment was found to be positively related to outcome; the longer the duration of treatment or the more sessions, the better the outcome" (p. 154). Orlinsky and Howard (1986), in their comprehensive evaluation of process and outcome variables in psychotherapy, found that 74 of 114 studies revealed a significantly positive correlation between length of therapy and outcome. Orlinsky and Howard (1986) conclude, "the evidence rather consistently indicates that patients who have more therapy get more benefit from it" (p. 361).

However, length of intervention and its relation to outcome in psychotherapy continues to be evaluated with much interest as more emphasis has been placed on briefer forms of psychotherapy (Beck, 1979; Budman and Gurman, 1983; Butcher, Stelmachers, and Maudel, 1984; Klerman, Weissman, Rounsaville, and Chevron, 1984; Strupp and Binder, 1984). Research on brief psychotherapy has supported the efficacy of this treatment modality. Weber and Tilley (1981) found that 34 percent of college students returning evaluations of brief psychotherapy (ten sessions or less) reported that the treatment was at least "moderately helpful," 40 percent found it "very helpful," and 15 percent found it "extremely helpful" (p. 193). Thus, nearly 90 percent of the 174 students returning the questionnaire reported benefiting from short-term therapy (Weber and Tilley, 1981). These results support other studies that conclude that short-term therapy is beneficial (Dorosin, Gibbs, and Kaplan, 1976; Nigl and Weiss, 1977). Howard, Kopta, Krause, and Orlinsky (1986) have shown that within only eight sessions approximately 50 percent of clients experience measurable improvement.

In the literature on very brief psychotherapy (treatment lasting less than eight sessions) such treatment has been variously described as *extra-brief therapy* (Lewin, 1970), a *very brief intervention* (VBI) by Dorosin, Gibbs, and Kaplan (1976), and Haggerty, Baldwin, and Liptzin (1980), *five-session psychotherapy* (Bellack and Small, 1978), *productive brief encounters* (Hanfmann, 1979), *single session psychotherapy* (Talmon, 1990), and *one or two session psychotherapy* (Pinkerton and Rockwell, 1982). As early as 1946, references were made to very brief psychotherapy within a psychoanalytic framework (Alexander, 1946; Fuerst, 1946). Utilizing the restricting limit of one session, references include Freud's (1936) chance encounter with Katarina and his more formal session with Gustav Mahler (Jones, 1955). Successful single-session, psychoanalytic psychotherapies have also been described by Knight (1937), Grotjahn and Case (1946), Saul (1951), Rothberg (1955) and Springmann (1978). Utilizing an eclectic approach, the interventions of Spoerl (1975), Wolberg (1977), Scrignar (1979), and Bloom (1981) are noteworthy. For a more detailed discussion of the literature on single-session psychotherapy, the interested reader is referred to Rockwell and Pinkerton (1982).

Bellack and Small (1978) described a five-session psychotherapy model. The first session focuses on gathering a thorough history of the current problem and its historical connections. At the conclusion of the session it is advised to give the patient a summary, underscoring common denominators between current symptoms and past experiences. The authors recommend beginning the second session with the thoughts, feelings, and reactions to the first session. They advocate a review of recent dreams. It is recommended that some of the focus also be on further exploration of the initial intervention. In general relatively accessible, superficial problems are dealt with first followed by those that are more heavily defended. A similar process is prescribed for the third session at that time the patient often shows some improvement according to the authors. During the third session, time is spent focusing on anxiety with regard to impending separation from the therapist. The fourth session is spent on working through feelings that have already been discussed. The patient is encouraged to discuss the relationship with the therapist and related separation anxiety. The fifth and final session is described as a "mopping up" operation. This last session is to sum up and review and to leave the patient with a positive transference. At the conclusion of this session it is urged that the patient contact the therapist in a month for follow-up. It is noted that this five session model can be translated into six sessions.

Since feelings of discomfort or dysphoria in the form of anxiety or depression appear to be what most often motivates one to seek psychotherapy, a test of the efficacy of very brief psychotherapy in diminishing the symptoms of these unpleasant affective states is critical. It is the purpose of this portion of the investigation to ascertain whether very brief psychotherapy was effective in reducing symptoms of depression and anxiety and whether there were significant differences in improvement by client gender, age, number of sessions attended and related interactions or by therapist experience, therapist gender and therapist experience x gender interaction.

METHOD OF THE STUDY AT COUNSELING AND PSYCHOLOGICAL SERVICES OF DUKE UNIVERSITY

Setting

Duke's Counseling and Psychological Services is a multidisciplinary service with psychiatrists, psychologists, and clinical social workers on the staff at both the senior staff and intern/resident levels. It serves the entire student body including undergraduate, graduate, and professional schools of Duke University which has approximately 10,000 full-time, degree-seeking students. A full range of counseling and mental health services are provided from career counseling to psychiatric hospitalizations for suicidal or decompensating students, and thus the service functions as both the counseling center and the student mental health center for the university. Approximately 12 percent of the entire student population present for services each year. The senior staff consists of two half-time psychiatrists, two full-time and one three-fifths-time clinical social workers, and four full-time psychologists. In addition, there are three quarter-time psychiatry residents, three full-time psychology predoctoral interns, and one full-time master's degree candidate clinical social work intern. (For more detail on the setting see Moorman, 1985.)

Subjects

The initial testing condition subjects included a total of 609 students who were recruited from four samples as follows: 66 (91.67 percent) of 72 students approached while waiting for medical services at the Student Health Center of Duke University comprised the medical sample (66.7 percent female and 33.3 percent male; although the precise mean age of the medical sample was unknown, the subjects were randomly selected from the same population as the random sample, and thus, the mean age and standard deviation of the medical sample may be presumed to be approximately equal to that of the random sample); 168 respondents (44.09 percent, as 19 were returned by the postal service unable to be delivered) of a random sample of 400 Duke students stratified by race, school, age, gender, and marital status comprised the random sample (52.4 percent female and 47.6 percent male; mean age = 21.66, SD = 1.52); 306 (99.03%) of 309 clients seeking "personal" counseling or psychotherapy at Counseling and Psychological Services (CAPS) of Duke University comprised the clinical sample (64.6 percent female and 35.4 percent male; mean age = 21.35, SD = 3.85); and 69 (97.18 percent) of 71 clients seeking vocational counseling at CAPS comprised the vocational sample (60.3 percent female and 39.7 percent male; mean age = 19.78, SD = 2.43). During the four-month period of this study 114 others presented at CAPS for services. Some of the 114 came as couples or for other reasons (e.g., concern about a friend, a screening interview for a group or for a letter to their insurance company) and were not included in this study. These figures include all subjects responding to the initial testing. However, all of these subjects did not also respond to the follow-up testing.

At the time of initial assessment, subjects in the clinical group who completed treatment in 7 or fewer sessions and who responded to the follow-up assessment did not differ significantly on the BDI, SDS, or SAS from subjects in the clinical group who completed treatment in 7 or fewer sessions but did not respond to the follow-up assessment as demonstrated by the (MANOVA) overall multivariate effect for responders vs.

nonresponders, $F(3, 133) = .08$, $p. = .9714$. Likewise the (MANOVA) multivariate main effect for responders vs. non-responders on the VAS–D and the VAS–A showed no significant effect, $F(2, 105) = .57$, $p. = .5671$.

At the time of initial testing, subjects in the clinical group who completed treatment in 7 or fewer sessions did not differ significantly on the BDI, SDS, or SAS from subjects in the clinical group who attended 8 or more sessions as demonstrated by the (MANOVA) overall main effect for 7 or fewer sessions vs. 8 or more sessions, $F(3, 108) = 1.25$, $p. = .2937$. Again, the (MANOVA) multivariate main effect with the VAS–D and the VAS–A also showed no significant effect, $F(2, 91) = 1.78$, $p. = .1745$. Among those attending 7 or fewer sessions, responders to the follow-up assessment did not differ from nonresponders more than .6 of a point on any measure at the time of initial assessment. Although there were no significant differences at the time of initial assessment between those attending 7 or fewer sessions who responded to the follow-up assessment and those attending 8 or more sessions, the means of those attending 8 or more sessions were somewhat higher (i.e., BDI 3.1, SDS 3.1, SAS 2.1, VAS–D .1, and VAS–A .9 points).

Follow-up test completion response rates for each sample were as follows: medical sample, 38 (56.06 percent, 63.2 percent female and 36.8 percent male; mean age $\approx$ 21.65) of the 66 completing the initial assessment; random sample, 124 (73.81 percent, 50.8 percent female and 49.2 percent male; mean age = 21.65, $SD = 1.52$) of the 168 completing the initial assessment; vocational sample, 16 (26.66 percent, 60.3 percent female and 39.7 percent male; mean age = 20.93, $SD = 2.43$) of the 60 who completed the initial assessment; and the clinical sample, 95 (68.35 percent, 61.1 percent female and 38.9 percent male; mean age = 22.66, $SD = 4.17$) of 139 who completed from 1 to 7 sessions of very brief psychotherapy within the 4-month period studied and were able to be located by the postal service.

All subjects did not complete every item on every inventory and some subjects omitted an inventory or scale. In such instances the relevant n is specified. Usually this was an omission of the Visual Analogue Scales or the omission of items on the inventories. In the clinical group at the time of initial testing 4 clients omitted more than 3 items on the Beck Depression Inventory (BDI) and 3 omitted more than 4 items on the Zung Self-rating Depression Scale (SDS). Thus, enough items were omitted to invalidate these inventories. Of the 95 respondents to the follow-up testing and Client Satisfaction Index (CSI), 18 completed only the CSI leaving 77 (55.40 percent) of the 139 completing the other posttreatment measures. Therefore, some totals reported subsequently vary from the figures presented here.

Clients presented with a wide range of problems primarily consisting of anxiety, depression or dysphoria of a mild to severe degree in response to familial problems, academic adjustment or other interpersonal problems. Of the 95 respondents in the clinical sample 61 percent were female and 39 percent male. They ranged in age from 18 to 51 years with 65.26 percent being between 18 and 22 years of age and 34.74 percent being 23 years of age and older. However, only 6 of these were over 30 years of age. The mean age was 22.83 ($SD = 5.23$). The number of clients attending a given number of sessions were as follows: One ($n = 42$), two ($n = 22$), three ($n = 11$), four ($n = 9$), five ($n = 4$), six ($n = 5$), and seven ($n = 2$). The mean number of sessions attended was 2.31 ($SD = 1.63$).

Therapists

A total of twelve therapists treated these 95 clients who responded to the follow-up assessment packet. Of the twelve therapists, two were female psychiatry residents in their fourth year of post M.D. training, three were female psychologists doing their predoctoral internship, two were clinical social workers with seven and ten years of post-M.S.W. experience, one was a female M.S.W. student on internship, two were male psychologists with seven and seventeen years of postdoctoral experience, and two were male psychiatrists, one with three and one with twenty-four years of experience. Thus, females outnumber males two to one in the therapists group. The average number of years of post graduate experience was roughly comparable for each discipline. All therapists excepting the psychology interns acknowledged that psychodynamic therapy theories had a substantial influence on their treatment style. The psychology interns were more influenced by cognitive-behavioral and interpersonal schools of practice. Consequently, the treatment was not standardized or uniform. However, this may be viewed as an asset from one perspective in that the average practitioner of psychotherapy is not intensively trained, rated, and observed in the delivery of a strictly manual-based intervention.

Instruments

The Zung Self-rating Depression Scale (SDS)

The Zung Self-rating Depression Scale (SDS) is a twenty-item self-report scale designed as a screening device to measure both the psychological and physical symptoms of depression (Zung, 1965; 1967). Respondents rate the frequency of depressive features using a four point format indicating that symptoms are present as follows: 1 = none or a little of the time, 2 = some of the time, 3 = a good part of the time, 4 = most or all of the time (see Appendix A). Total scores are related to symptom severity with a scaled score of 59 (raw score of 40) or above indicating clinically significant depressive symptoms.

The SDS has been demonstrated to have high internal consistency and excellent inter-rater reliability (Zung, 1972a). In addition, it has good construct and predictive validity (Biggs, Wylie, and Ziegler, 1978). Schaefer, Brown, Watson, Plemel, DeMotts, Howard, Petrik, and Balleweg (1985) reported correlations of the SDS with the MMPI–D ($r. = .73$) and with the BDI ($r. = .81$) and with global rating ($r. = .75$) for male psychiatric inpatients. Zung (1969) has reported a correlation of $r. = .56$ with the Hamilton Depression Rating Scale. Brown and Zung (1972) have reported a correlation of $r. = .79$ with the Hamilton scale. Finally, the SDS has reportedly demonstrated adequate sensitivity and excellent specificity (McNair, 1974; Zung, 1973b). The SDS focuses more on the somatic aspects than the BDI and less on the cognitive aspects of depressive symptoms. Zung (1965; 1967) has reported the validity and reliability of the SDS. The scale has been most commonly employed within medical and psychiatric settings.

The Zung Self-rating Anxiety Scale (SAS)

Like the SDS, the Zung Self-rating Anxiety Scale (SAS) is a twenty-item, self-report screening measure designed to represent the psychological and physical manifestations of anxiety (Zung, 1971a). The SAS uses the same 4-point format as the SDS for assessing the frequency of anxiety symptoms (see Appendix B). The SAS has demonstrated excellent internal consistency, good reliability, and good construct validity (Sharply and Rogers, 1985). Zung (1971a) reported a correlation of $r. = .66$ between the SAS and the Anxiety Status Inventory (ASI) and a correlation of $r. = .74$ between the ASI and the SAS for patients with a diagnosis of anxiety disorder. He also reported a correlation of $r. = .30$ between the SAS and the Taylor Manifest Anxiety Scale. In addition, the SAS has demonstrated significant specificity in differentiating anxiety patients from those with other diagnoses (Zung, 1971b). Omitted items on both Zung scales are scored as a 2 and if more than four items are omitted an inventory is considered invalid.

The Visual Analogue Depression and Anxiety Scales (VAS–D and VAS–A)

Each scale was a ten centimeter line anchored at the polar extremes for depression (VAS–D) with "I am not depressed (down-hearted, blue, low) at all" at 0 and "I am as depressed (down-hearted, blue, low) as I have ever been" at 10. For the anxiety analogue (VAS–A) the 0 pole read, "I am not anxious (tense, nervous, uptight) at all," and at 10 it read, "I am as anxious (tense, nervous, uptight) as I have ever been." Subjects were asked to: "Please cross (with a pencil) each of the following lines once at the place which best represents how you feel now" (see Appendix C). Each scale was scored by laying a ten centimeter ruler by the line and scoring the mark from 0.0 to 10.0 centimeters. Visual analogue scales were originally proposed to assess affective states but have of late become widely used to assess pain. If they prove to be valid measures of affective states, visual analogue scales may be more economical and perhaps easier than questionnaires to administer as screening instruments. Folstein and Luria (1973) reported a correlation of $r. = -.46$ between the Visual Analogue Mood Scale and unhappiness as measured by the Clyde Mood Scale for psychiatric inpatients and a correlation of $r. = -.56$ for patients selected from major diagnostic groups. Luria (1975) found a correlation of $r. = -.77$ between a visual analogue scale for depression and unhappiness as measured by the Clyde Mood Scale. Faravelli, Albanesi, and Poli (1986) found that a visual analogue depression scale correlated $r. = .14$ with the Hamilton Depression Rating Scale and $r. = .37$ with the Zung Self-rating Depression Scale.

The Beck Depression Inventory (BDI)

The BDI (Beck, Ward, Mendelson, Mock, and Erbaugh, 1961) is a frequently employed measure of the severity of depressive symptoms. Its theoretical foundations and clinical applications have been widely accepted (Hammen and Padesky, 1977). Beck demonstrated that his original instrument correlated well ($r. = .65$ and $r. = .67$) with clinicians' ratings of depth of depression and that internal reliability was good (Pearson

$r. = .86$ and Spearman-Brown correlation $= .93$) (Beck et al., 1961). Subsequent studies (Bumberry, Oliver, and McClure, 1978; Davies, Burrows, and Poynton, 1975; Hammen, 1980; Lambert, Hatch, Kingston, and Edwards, 1986) have supported the validity and reliability of this 21-item self-report inventory. The revised self-report form of the BDI (Beck, Rush, Shaw, and Emery, 1979) has been found to correlate highly ($r. = .94$) with the original BDI (Beck, Steer, and Garbin, 1988). The BDI has also been reported to discriminate between depression and anxiety (Steer, Beck, Riskind, and Brown, 1986), although this has been called into question with some populations (Gotlib, 1984) and others (Carroll, Felding, and Blanshki, 1973) have concluded that the BDI and other self-report inventories do not discriminate well persons who are moderately depressed from those who are severely depressed.

Moran and Lambert (1983) found that the BDI reflected improvement in subjects' depression more frequently than did the Hamilton Rating Scale for Depression (Hamilton, 1960) and the Zung Self-rating Depression Scale. This finding may reflect a greater vulnerability of the BDI to experimental demand characteristics. However, a more recent study has found the BDI to be less sensitive to outcome changes (Lambert et al., 1986). If more than three items are omitted an inventory is considered invalid. Omitted items may be scored as a zero as in the present study or they may be prorated and assigned the mean score for all other items rated by the subject.

The publisher of the BDI did not wish to permit the full BDI to be presented as an appendix. However, the 21 items may be described as measuring the following: mood/sadness (item 1); pessimism/hopelessness (item 2); sense of failure (item 3); lack of satisfaction (item 4); guilty feeling (item 5); sense of punishment (item 6); self-disappointment/self-hate (item 7); self-accusations/self-criticism (item 8); self-punitive wishes/thoughts of suicide or self-harm (item 9); crying spells (item 10); irritability (item 11); social withdrawal/loss of interest in others (item 12); indecisiveness (item 13); body image/feeling old or unattractive (item 14); work inhibition/difficulty working (item 15); sleep disturbance (item 16); fatigability/tiredness (item 17); loss of appetite/appetite disturbance (item 18); weight loss (item 19); somatic preoccupation (item 20); and, loss of libido/interest in sex (item 21).

The Client Satisfaction Index (CSI)

The Client Satisfaction Index (see Appendix D) presented the respondent with sixteen items, each on a ten-point Likert scale with anchors of 1 = not at all true, 4 = somewhat true, 7 = quite true, and 10 = extremely true. Item content was drawn from Rogerian, Cognitive, Interpersonal Influence, and Psychodynamic theories of treatment. Although psychiatrists, psychologists, and clinical social workers were the service providers, they were generically referred to as "counselors" in part as an effort to normalize the seeking of psychotherapeutic services.

Ratings were sought with regard to the following: perceived increased self-understanding (item 1), assistance received in goal clarification (item 2), feeling comfortable with (item 3), and feeling understood by (item 4) the counselor, perceiving the counselor as authentic or real (item 5), assistance received in clarifying the coping styles of the client (item 6), accomplishing what was hoped for (item 7), assistance in breaking the problem down into smaller parts (item 8), the counselor seeming to be warm (item 9), and encouraging (item 10), counselor assisted client change in methods of dealing with problems (item 11), increased client certainty in decision making abilities as a result of counseling (item 12), the felt sense of working together with the counselor (item 13), counselor encouraged discussion of feelings about the counselor (item 14), the counselor seeming skilled (item 15), and in general satisfaction with the services received (item 16). Additionally, the rating of "same," "better," or "worse" with regard to postcounseling performance in academics and quality of relationships was sought as was information (no, yes/ self-initiated, yes/ at the suggestion of the counselor) concerning any subsequent treatment sought.

Procedure

All clients presenting for clinical services or "personal" counseling over a period of approximately four months from late October through February were given the Beck Depression Inventory (BDI), The Zung Self-rating Depression Scale (SDS), The Zung Self-rating Anxiety Scale (SAS), a depression visual analogue scale (VAS–D), an anxiety visual analogue scale (VAS–A), and an intake form (completed by the clinical and vocational groups only) for relevant demographic data before being seen by a therapist for the initial evaluation session. This group of 309 comprised the clinical pre-treatment sample.

All students presenting for vocational counseling were asked to complete the two Zung scales and the two visual analogue scales along with the intake form. This group of 71 clients was not given the Beck Depression Inventory as they were volunteering their time for an experiment that was not related to their reason for seeking services and, therefore, less was asked of these clients. They comprised the vocational pretreatment sample.

In late October, a stratified random sample of 400 students was selected by computer from the university registrar's roster of all full-time, degree-seeking students in local residence including those in undergraduate, graduate, and professional school programs. Materials were mailed out to those in the random sample gradually across the four-month period to parallel the rate and time that clients presented for treatment. This group completed the same instruments as the clinical sample excepting the intake form and comprised the initial testing of the random sample.

Likewise, students waiting to be seen for medical problems at the University's Student Health Center during these same months were approached and asked to participate in the study. Over 91 percent ($n = 66$) agreed and completed the same materials as did the random sample and the pretreatment clinical sample. They comprised the initial testing of the medical sample.

The materials in the packets included, a cover letter that explained the request for their help as part of a study of depression (the letter was signed by the Coordinator of Research and Program Evaluation at Counseling and Psychological Services), an informed consent form for the participant to sign and return with the other materials, a BDI, a Zung SDS, a Zung SAS, a VAS–D, and a VAS–A. Confidentiality was promised and all consent forms except those for the clinical sample advised that there would be no direct benefit to them for their participation. The clinical sample consent form noted that the information received would assist the therapist/counselor in understanding the client better. Mailed packets contained a stamped envelope addressed for return to Counseling and Psychological Services at Duke University, and all materials were plainly coded.

Four months from the beginning of the data collection (one month after the completion of gathering the pretreatment and initial-testing control group data) the follow-up assessment materials were mailed to all subjects in the random, medical, and vocational samples who had completed the initial testing and to all clients in the clinical sample who were no longer receiving services ($n = 151$), 12 of whom were unreachable by mail leaving an n of 139. All mailed packets included cover letters (again explaining the nature of the study and the importance of completing the follow-up testing) and a second copy of all forms completed at the initial testing. The clinical and vocational groups were also informed that their responses would be used in analyzing and improving service delivery. A Client Satisfaction Index was also sent to those in the clinical and vocational groups with the materials for follow-up assessment. Subjects who did not respond were sent an additional follow-up packet in two weeks and those still not responding were telephoned and offered an additional packet of materials.

RESULTS AND DISCUSSION

As there were no Beck Depression Inventory scores for the vocational sample, a repeated measures analysis of variance was done to compare the scores at the time of initial and follow-up testing on the Beck Depression Inventory alone by random, clinical, and medical groups. A multivariate repeated measures analysis of variance was also done using scores from the initial and the follow-up testing on the Zung Self-rating Depression Scale, the Zung Self-rating Anxiety Scale, the Visual Analogue Scale for depression and the Visual Analogue Scale for anxiety by the random, clinical, medical, and vocational groups. Given that two analyses were done instead of one in order to retain the data from the vocational sample the probability levels reported may be doubled (e.g., changing $p. < .0001$ to $p. < .0002$) so that a conservative estimate is achieved guarding against a Type I error. At this juncture, as at others, the increased probability of a Type I error as a result of conducting two analyses is accepted rather than a Type II error minimizing a significant finding.

With regard to the Beck Depression Inventory results, there was a significant overall effect due to differences by group, $F(2, 235) = 13.47$, $p. < .0001$. There was a significant effect for time of testing, $F(1, 235) = 52.85$, $p. < .0001$, indicating a significant difference in BDI scores between the first administration and the follow-up administration and there was a significant time of testing x group interaction effect, $F(2, 235) = 29.21$, $p.$

< .0001, indicating a significant difference among the groups with regard to the effects of time of testing. Scores from the first administration revealed significant differences by group such that the BDI scores from the clinical group were significantly higher than scores from the random sample ($p. < .0001$) and BDI scores from the clinical group were significantly higher than scores from the medical sample ($p. < .0001$) as was shown by *post hoc* pairwise comparisons with Tukey's Standardized Range (HSD) Test. However, at the initial testing the difference in scores between the medical and the random group was not significant ($p. < .3514$). At the time of the follow-up testing there were no significant differences among the groups on the Beck Depression Inventory, $F(2, 235) = .73, p. < .4849$.

Thus, prior to treatment the scores on the Beck Depression Inventory for the clinical group were significantly higher than the scores in either the random sample or the medical sample. Following treatment at the second administration of the BDI the scores from the clinical group were not significantly different from the scores produced by the medical group or by the random sample and scores for the clinical group were significantly lower following treatment than prior to treatment. This finding would seem to argue in favor of the efficacy of very brief psychotherapy in improving depressive or dysphoric symptoms as measured by the Beck Depression Inventory.

The multivariate repeated measures analysis of variance using the SDS, SAS, VAS–D, and VAS–A initial and follow-up test data from the clinical, random, medical, and vocational groups showed an overall multivariate effect due to group membership that was significant, $F(3, 215) = 9.01, p. < .0001$. Likewise, there was a significant effect due to time of testing such that there was a significant difference between the initial test scores and the follow-up test scores at the multivariate level, $F(1, 215) = 43.29, p. < .0001$. There was a significant group x time of testing interaction effect, $F(3, 215) = 11.94, p. < .0001$. There was a significant scale (dependent variables) effect at the multivariate level, $F(3, 213) = 1095.26, p. < .0001$, indicating that all measures were not equivalent concerning degree of sensitivity in measuring the magnitude of affective disturbance. There was a significant scale x group interaction, $F(9, 518.54) = 3.75, p. < .0001$, indicating that the differences by scale differed by group membership. A significant scale x time of testing effect was found at the multivariate level, $F(3, 213) = 8.91, p. < .0001$ indicating that the differences by scale varied by the time of testing. Finally, there was a significant scale x time of testing x group effect, $F(9, 518.54) = 3.37$, $p. < .0005$, indicating that differences among the dependent variables in their measure of the magnitude of the effect differed by group membership which in turn varied by time of testing.

The univariate analyses of scores on the dependent variables revealed a significant difference among the groups at the time of initial testing as measured by the SDS, $F(3, 215) = 14.33, p. < .0001$; the SAS, $F(3, 215) = 14.28, p. < .0001$; the VAS–D, $F(3, 215) = 12.33, p. < .0001$; and the VAS–A, $F(3, 215) = 6.57, p. < .0003$. Tukey *post hoc* pairwise comparisons indicated that at the time of initial testing, scores from the clinical group on the SDS were significantly higher than scores from the random sample $(p. < .0001)$, the medical sample $(p. < .0001)$, and the vocational sample $(p. < .0341)$. As measured by the SAS the clinical group had higher scores than the random sample $(p. < .0001)$, medical sample $(p. < .0001)$, and the vocational sample $(p. < .0065)$. There were no significant differences between any other groups on the SDS or the SAS.

Findings on the VAS–D at the time of first administration revealed significant differences as measured by the VAS–D between the clinical and random samples $(p. < .0001)$ and the clinical and medical samples $(p. < .0001)$. However, there were no significant differences between the clinical and the vocational samples as measured by the VAS–D $(p. < .9704)$ and the difference between the scores produced by the vocational and the medical samples was significantly different $(p. < .0038)$ as was the difference between the vocational and the random samples $(p. < .0155)$. Findings on the VAS–A showed the clinical sample to have significantly higher scores than the random sample $(p. < .0003)$, the medical sample $(p. < .0002)$, and the vocational sample $(p. < .0298)$ at the time of initial testing. The means and standard deviations by each group on each measure are presented in Table 2.1, by time of testing.

There were no significant differences among the groups at the time of follow-up testing as measured by the SDS, $F(3, 215) = 1.46, p. < .2269$; the SAS, $F(3, 215) = 2.00, p. < .1150$; the VAS–D, $F(3, 215) = .57, p. < .6343$; or the VAS–A, $F(3, 215) = 1.40, p. < .2426$. Thus, at the time of the follow-up testing there were no significant differences on any of these symptom measures (SDS, SAS, VAS–D, and VAS–A) in addition to the BDI as reported earlier.

From these data it appears that the effects of very brief psychotherapy as measured by the self-report, symptom oriented scales (the BDI, SDS, SAS, VAS–A, and VAS–D) produce significant pre- vs. posttreatment differences in the treated group. Moreover, following the intervention no significant differences among groups on these measures were present, whereas prior to treatment there were significant differences between the clinical group and the random, vocational and medical groups. Very brief psychotherapy appears to have been an effective intervention in reducing symptoms of dysphoria as defined by the measures utilized such that although the clinical group showed significantly higher scores on all measures at the time of initial testing, at the time of follow-up testing there were no significant differences among the groups on any of the measures (see Table 2.1). Given that this is a study with a random control group and with two comparison groups it would appear to demonstrate the efficacy of very brief psychotherapy.

Predictors of Dysphoria Percent Change Scores

A series of stepwise multiple regression analyses was done with all clients combined in the clinical sample who responded to the follow-up assessment and then with clients divided into the four gender/age groups as defined in the purposes of the present study in Chapter I. The percent change score on the BDI, SAS, or SDS was used as the dependent variable and the individual items of the same inventory as completed while waiting for the initial session were the potential predictors. Percent change scores were calculated by subtracting the score from the second administration of the inventory/scale from the score at the first administration and then dividing the difference by the first score to get a percent of net improvement.

For all clients combined using the BDI individual items to predict BDI percent change score, a model, $F(2, 72) = 5.63, p. < .0053$, emerged that accounted for 13.52 percent of the variance in BDI percent change scores. The model included self-disappointment (BDI item 7), which accounted for 8.57 percent of the variance, $F = 6.84, p. < .0108$, and sleep disturbance (BDI item 16) which accounted for 4.96 percent of the variance, $F = 4.13, p. < .0458$. Higher scores on these items and all items to follow were predictive of lower percent change scores for the specified group.

Using the SDS a model accounting for 24.31 percent of the variance, in SDS percent change score, $F(2, 72) = 11.56, p. < .0001$, emerged that included sleep disturbance (SDS item 4), which accounted for 15.95 percent of the variance, $F = 13.85, p. < .0004$, and personal devaluation

TABLE 2.1

MEANS AND STANDARD DEVIATIONS BY GROUP AND TIME OF TESTING ON
THE BECK DEPRESSION INVENTORY, THE ZUNG SELF-RATING DEPRESSION
SCALE, THE ZUNG SELF-RATING ANXIETY SCALE, AND VISUAL
ANALOGUE SCALES FOR ANXIETY AND DEPRESSION

	Initial Testing				Follow-Up Testing		
Group	BDI	SDS	SAS		BDI	SDS	SAS
Clinical	14.88	42.77	38.42		7.12	33.65	30.34
	SD=8.68	SD=9.40	SD=8.80		SD=7.20	SD=9.00	SD=7.02
	N=302	N=303	N=306		N=75	N=76	N=76
Random	7.78	34.59	30.94		6.1	33.01	29.16
	SD=7.25	SD=8.65	SD=7.07		SD=5.83	SD=7.90	SD=6.45
	N=168	N=167	N=167		N=124	N=124	N=124
Medical	6.03	33.61	30.62		6.18	32.32	28.38
	SD=4.71	SD=6.62	SD=5.83		SD=6.59	SD=7.17	SD=5.25
	N=66	N=66	N=66		N=38	N=37	N=37
Vocational	.	35.9	31.04		.	31.69	28.44
	.	SD=7.47	SD=5.87		.	SD=4.74	SD=4.73
	.	N=69	N=68		.	N=16	N=16

	Initial Testing				Follow-Up Testing		
Group	VAS-D	VAS-A	.		VAS-D	VAS-A	.
Clinical	5.72	6.34	.		2.9	3.57	.
	SD=2.75	SD=2.75	.		SD=2.87	SD=2.71	.
	N=246	N=251	.		N=59	N=59	.
Random	3.27	4.58	.		2.73	3.97	.
	SD=2.64	SD=2.84	.		SD=2.49	SD=2.83	.
	N=160	N=159	.		N=118	N=117	.
Medical	2.76	3.7	.		2.43	2.89	.
	SD=2.23	SD=2.54	.		SD=2.24	SD=2.12	.
	N=58	N=58	.		SD=35	N=35	.
Vocational	4.24	4.27	.		2.57	3.39	.
	SD=2.85	SD=2.57	.		SD=2.32	SD=2.88	.
	N=62	N=62	.		N=15	N=15	.

(SDS item 17), which accounted for 8.36 percent of the variance, $F = 7.96$, $p. < .0062$.

Using the SAS a model accounting for 47.77 percent of the variance, $F(4,71) = 16.24$, $p. < .0001$, in SAS percent change scores emerged and included anxiousness (SAS item 1), accounting for 35.83 percent of the variance, $F = 41.32$, $p. < .0001$; apprehension (SAS item 5), accounting for 5.93 percent of the variance, $F = 7.43$, $p. < .0080$; dizziness (SAS item 11), accounting for 3.05 percent of the variance, $F = 3.98$, $p. < .0499$; and, insomnia (SAS item 19), accounting for 2.97 percent of the variance, $F = 4.033$, $p. < .0484$.

With regard to the predictors by gender/age group, for females 18 to 22 years of age no BDI items met the $p. < .05$ significance level. Using the SDS, irritability (item 15), did account for 15.65 percent of the variance, $F(1, 30) = 5.57$, $p. < .0250$, in SDS percent change in score. Using the SAS, a model accounting for 47.21 percent of the variance, $F(2, 30) = 13.41$, $p. < .0001$, in SAS percent change scores emerged and included insomnia (SAS item 19), accounting for 37.70 percent of the variance, $F = 18.76$, $p. < .0001$, and anxiousness (SAS item 1), accounting for 9.51 percent of the variance, $F = 5.40$, $p. < .0271$.

For males 18 to 22 using the BDI, only self-disappointment (BDI item 7), emerged and accounted for 34.19 percent of the variance, $F(1, 15) = 7.79$, $p. < .0137$, in percent change scores on the BDI. Using the SDS with this group a model accounting for 53.04 percent of the variance, $F(2, 14) = 7.91$, $p. < .0050$, emerged and included sleep disturbance (SDS item 4), accounting for 31.44 percent of the variance, $F = 6.88$, $p. < .0192$, and indecisiveness (SDS item 16), accounting for 21.61 percent of the variance, $F = 6.44$, $p. < .0237$. Using the SAS only anxiousness (SAS item 1), emerged and accounted for 60.57 percent of the variance, $F(1, 15) = 23.04$, $p. < .0002$.

For females 23 and older no BDI, SDS, or SAS inventory items met the $p. < .05$ level of significance as predictors of percent change scores.

Concerning males 23 and older no BDI items met the $p. < .05$ level as a predictor of BDI percent change score. Using the SDS, sleep disturbance (SDS item 4), emerged and accounted for 51.08 percent of the variance, $F(1, 9) = 9.40$, $p. < .0135$. Using the SAS a model accounting for 85.02 percent of the variance, $F(2, 8) = 22.71$, $p. < .0005$, emerged with restlessness (SAS item 9), accounting for 67.32 percent of the variance, $F = 18.54$, $p. < .0020$, and (SAS item 1) anxiousness, accounting for 17.71 percent of the variance, $F = 9.46$, $p. < .0152$. Items on the BDI, SDS and SAS that appear to be the best predictors of percent change score differed by gender/age group. *Beta* weights are reported in Table 2.2 by all subjects combined and by gender/age group. Lower scores on all identified variables were predictive of higher percent change scores.

TABLE 2.2

BETA WEIGHTS FOR SIGNIFICANT ITEM PREDICTORS
OF PERCENT CHANGE SCORES BY INVENTORY AND GENDER/AGE GROUP

Females 18 to 22		Males 18 to 22	
Item	Beta Weight	Item	Beta Weight
SDS 15	-.09549197	BDI 7	-.96516998
SAS 1	-.05640297	SDS 4	-.10042976
SAS 19	-.08716590	SDS 16	-.11533599
.	.	SAS 1	-.14121618
All Groups Combined		Males 23 and Older	
Item	Beta Weight	Item	Beta Weight
BDI 7	-.34392593	SDS 4	-.22094143
BDI 16	-.20738302	SAS 1	-.12975620
SDS 4	-.07955606	SAS 9	-.19847474
SDS 17	-.08426060		
SAS 1	-.08581274		
SAS 5	-.04367520		
SAS 11	-.06911958		
SAS 19	-.03820171		

*No BDI, SDS, or SAS items were significant predictors
of percent change scores for females 23 and older.

The Effects of Therapist Experience and Gender on Symptom Improvement

Since the effects of therapist gender and experience have been reported in the general psychotherapy literature, a multivariate analysis of variance (MANOVA) was done to determine the effects of therapist experience, therapist gender, and therapist x gender interaction on BDI, SDS, and SAS percent change scores. There was no multivariate overall significant effect for therapist gender, $F(3, 68) = 2.12$, $p. < .1060$. However, the multivariate overall main effect for therapist experience approached significance at the $p. < .05$ level, $F(3, 68) = 2.70$, $p. < .0522$. The superior change scores, however, belonged to the less experienced therapists as measured by the Zung Self-rating Depression and Anxiety Scales such that the clients of less experienced therapists showed a gain of 18.68 percent on the SDS versus 14.47 percent improvement for clients working with more experienced therapists. Likewise, on the Zung Self-rating Anxiety Scale the clients of less experienced therapists manifested a 20.97 percent improvement whereas the more experienced therapists' clients showed a 13.42 percent improvement. With regard to the Beck Depression Inventory, however, the clients of the more experienced therapists showed a slight advantage. The mean improvement percentage of the clients of more experienced therapists was 37.18 percent and the mean BDI improvement percentage of the less experienced therapists was 36.37 percent. There was no significant multivariate effect due to therapist experience x gender interaction, $F(3, 68) = 1.88$, $p. < .1419$.

Further, since none of the individual dependent variable (BDI, SDS and SAS percent change scores) univariate analyses showed a level of significance approaching the $p. < .05$ level, no conclusions can be made from these data with regard to the effects of therapist gender, experience, or gender x experience interaction. The F values and probability levels for the overall individual dependent measures were as follows: BDI percent change score, $F(3, 70) = .45$, $p. < .7206$; SDS percent change score, $F(3, 70) = 1.01$, $p. < .3923$; SAS percent change score, $F(3, 70) = 2.14$, $p. < .1033$.

The only independent variable univariate factor under any dependent variable percent change score that itself showed a significance level of $p. < .05$ was the therapist gender x experience interaction for the SAS percent change score that showed more experienced female therapists to have a mean percent improvement of 18.30 ($SD = 15.51$) while the less experienced female therapists had a mean percent improvement of 16.80 percent ($SD = 23.89$). However, with regard to male therapists the less experienced male therapists' clients showed a mean percent change of 33.48 percent ($SD = 19.79$) on the SAS while the more experienced male therapist's clients had a mean percent improvement of 10.84 percent ($SD = 23.68$). Nevertheless, given the lack of significant multivariate effects and the lack of significant overall effects on the individual dependent variables, the finding with regard to the SAS and the univariate factor of therapist experience x gender interaction was in all likelihood due to chance.

A second multivariate analysis of variance was done with the depression and anxiety Visual Analogue Scales to test for differences by therapist experience, therapist gender, and therapist gender x experience interaction effects. A second MANOVA was done given that placing all dependent variables in the same MANOVA would have resulted in the loss of approximately one-third of the subjects who completed the BDI, SDS, and SAS posttreatment but who did not complete the Visual Analogue Scales. Consequently, the probability levels may be doubled to get the most conservative estimates possible if desired. There was no multivariate overall main effect due to therapist gender, $F(2, 50) = .54$, $p. < .5884$. Likewise, there was no multivariate overall main effect due to therapist experience, $F(2, 50) = 1.15$, $p. < .3256$. Neither was there any significant overall main effect due to therapist gender x experience interaction, $F(2, 50) = .82$, $p. < .4468$. The F values and probability levels associated with them for the VAS–D and VAS–A percent change scores were as follows: VAS–D, $F(3, 51) = .78$, $p. < .5112$ and VAS–A, $F(3, 51) = 1.39$, $p. < .2554$. Thus, the effects in very brief psychotherapy of therapist gender, therapist experience and therapist gender x experience interaction were not significant as measured by the BDI, SDS, SAS, VAS–D, or VAS–A.

The Effects of Client Gender, Age, and Number of Sessions Attended on Symptom Improvement

A multivariate analysis of variance was done to test for the effects of client gender, client age (18 to 22 *vs.* 23 and older), and number of sessions attended (1–7) on percent change scores (symptom reduction) as measured by the BDI, SDS, and the SAS since these variables have been shown to be associated with outcome differences (Talley, Roy, and Moorman, 1986). There was an overall multivariate main effect due to gender, $F(3, 50) = 4.46$, $p. < .0075$. There was no significant multivariate overall main effect due to age, $F(3, 50) = .52$, $p. < .6736$. Likewise, there was no significant multivariate main effect due to number of sessions attended, $F(18, 141.91) = .98$, $p. < .4867$. Further, there was no significant age x gender interaction multivariate effect, $F(3, 50) = 1.36$, $p. < .2665$. Nor was there a significant age x number of sessions attended interaction multivariate effect, $F(15, 138.43) = 1.24$, $p. < .2489$. The gender x number of sessions attended interaction multivariate effect approached statistical significance at the $p. < .05$ level, $F(18, 141.91) = 1.60$, $p. < .0675$.

The age x gender x number of sessions attended interaction multivariate effect was also not significant, $F(3, 50) = 1.60$, $p. < .2001$. Thus, although the results with regard to the individual dependent measures did not confirm it at the $p. < .05$ level (see below), the multivariate results suggested that females may show a greater percent improvement than males following very brief psychotherapy. There were no significant effects from very brief psychotherapy that appeared to be due to age, number of sessions attended, age x number of sessions attended interaction, gender x age interaction, gender x number of sessions attended interaction, or age x gender x number of sessions attended interaction as measured by the BDI, SAS, and SDS percent change scores.

The F values and probability levels of the overall individual dependent variables (univariate analyses) were as follows: BDI percent change score, $F(21, 52) = 1.70$, $p. < .0623$; SDS percent change score, $F(21, 52) = 1.24$, $p. < .2603$; and, SAS percent change score, $F(21, 52) = 1.35$, $p. < .1877$. Given the multivariates reported, the only factor that might be legitimately examined as univariate component factors of the BDI, SDS, and SAS percent change scores would be the effect of gender. The univariate effect due to gender did appear significant with regard to BDI percent change score, $F(1, 73) = 6.99$, $p. < .0108$. Mean percent change on the BDI was 49.50 percent ($SD = 67.95$) for females and 16.22 percent ($SD = 96.16$) for males. However, this difference was not statistically significant at the $p. < .05$ level according to a *post hoc* pairwise comparison with Tukey's Standardized Range (HSD) Test. There were no significant univariate effects found due to gender on the SDS or SAS. On the Zung Self-rating Depression Scale the mean percent change score for females was 17.35 percent and for males it was 13.82 percent. However, this difference for the univariate factor of gender was not significant at the $p. < .05$ level. On the Zung Self-rating Anxiety Scale females showed a mean percent change score of 17.23 percent while males showed a mean percent change score of 14.63 percent. Again, the difference was not significant at the $p. < .05$ level for the univariate factor of gender. Since the gender x number of sessions attended interaction approached the $p. < .05$ level of significance at the multivariate level it is noteworthy that the univariate factor of gender x number of sessions attended did reach significance with regard to the BDI percent change score, $F(6, 68) = 2.88$, $p. < .0170$. Females showed a significant increase in BDI percent change score as the number of sessions attended increased while males did not show a significant gain in BDI percent change score as the number of sessions attended increased.

A multivariate analysis of variance was done to test for the effects of client gender, age, and number of sessions attended on percent change scores for the Visual Analogue Scales. The multivariate overall main effect due to gender approached but did not attain the $p. < .05$ level of statistical significance, $F(2, 35) = 2.9343, p. < .0664$. The multivariate overall main effect due to age was also close to the $p. < .05$ level, $F(2, 35) = 2.7761, p. < .0760$. The multivariate overall main effect due to number of sessions attended was highly significant, $F(12, 70) = 4.1533, p. < .0001$ with more improvement being associated with attending more sessions. The overall multivariate main effect due to the gender x number of sessions attended, $F(8, 70) = 1.6464, p. < .1274$, and the age x number of sessions attended interaction did not reach the $p. < .05$ level, $F(4, 70) = 1.1736, p. < .3300$.

Finally, the gender x age x number of sessions attended overall multivariate main effect did reach significance at the $p. < .05$ level, $F(2, 35) = 3.7465, p. < .0335$. The subsequent correlational analyses should serve to clarify these results. These effects were not significant at the $p. < .05$ level for the VAS–A dependent variable mean percent change score, $F(18, 36) = 1.53, p. < .1351$ and no univariate factors were significant at the $p. < .05$ level for the VAS–A. However, the individual dependent variable measure VAS–D mean percent change score was highly significant, $F(18, 36) = 5.59, p. < .0001$. The significance level for the univariate factors with regard to VAS–D percent change scores were as follows: gender, $F(1, 53) = 5.57, p. < .0238$; age, $F(1, 53) = 5.68, p. < .0226$; gender x age interaction, $F(1, 53) = 7.35, p. < .0102$; number of sessions attended, $F(6, 48) = 4.94, p. < .0009$; gender x number of sessions attended, $F(4, 50) = 1.98, p. < .1181$; age x number of sessions attended, $F(2, 52) = 2.39, p. < .1058$; and, gender x age x number of sessions attended interaction, $F(1, 53) = 7.71, p. < .0087$. The gender x age multivariate interaction effect did reach the $p. < .05$ level of significance, $F(2, 35) = 3.8632, p. < .0305$. The gender x age differences on the VAS–D manifested such that females 18 to 22 years of age had a mean percent change score of 43.74 percent while males 18 to 22 years of age had a mean percent change score of 16.24 percent. Females 23 and older had a mean percent change score of 34.93 percent while males 23 years of age and older showed a mean percent change score of -182.86 percent.

Thus, all groups showed some positive change on this measure with the exception of the older males.

Thus, at the multivariate level the effects of age and gender were not significant at the $p. < .05$ level and at the univariate level the effects of gender x number of sessions attended and age x number of sessions attended interaction factors were not significant at the $p. < .05$ level as measured by the VAS–D. Therefore, the factors of number of sessions attended and the interaction effects of gender x age x number of sessions attended appear worth noting in more detail given their significance at the multivariate and univariate level (VAS–D) on the percent change scores.

Looking at the number of sessions attended by the gender/age categories, the VAS–D percent change score was correlated with number of sessions attended as follows: females 18 to 22 years of age, $r. = .14892$, $p. < .4585$ ($n = 27$); females 23 years of age and older, $r. = -.16823$, $p. < .6210$ ($n = 11$). However, males 18 to 22 years of age showed a significant correlation for number of sessions attended and percent change on the VAS–D, $r. = .64556$, $p. < .0234$ ($n = 12$) as did males 23 and older, $r. = .81406$, $p. < .0139$ ($n = 8$). Correlations of the BDI, SDS, and, SAS percent change score with number of sessions attended were not significant at the $p. < .05$ level for any of the gender/age groups.

SUMMARY AND CONCLUSIONS

In conclusion, these findings demonstrated the efficacy of very brief psychotherapy as other studies (Smith, Glass, and Miller, 1980; Luborsky et al., 1971; Bergin and Lambert, 1978; Howard, Kopta, Krause, and Orlinsky, 1986) have demonstrated the efficacy of psychotherapy in general. It is possible that this intervention was more effective with the population in this study than it would be with less intelligent and/or less educated young adults as the preponderance of studies have concluded that positive outcome in psychotherapy is affected by education and intelligence (Luborsky et al., 1971). The present finding that therapist gender had no significant effect on outcome is in accord with the findings of Meltzoff and Kornreich (1970), Parloff, Waskow and Wolff (1978), Goldenholz (1976), and Orlinsky and Howard (1980) and in contrast to the findings of Jones and Zoppel (1982) who did find gender effects as reported in the literature review. Our finding that therapist experience did not significantly affect outcome corroborates the preponderance of findings as reported by Auerbach and Johnson (1977), Parloff, Waskow, and Wolff (1978) and Beutler, Crago, and Arizmendi (1986) although the findings of Luborsky et al. (1971) and Haccoun and Lavigueur (1979) were less conclusive that therapist experience level was not a factor affecting significant differences in outcome. Since some studies (Luborsky et al., 1983; Karasu, Stein, and Charles, 1979) have found that clients work better with therapists of a similar age, and given that the present population was quite young, it is possible the similarity of age factor for less experienced therapists resulted in equally positive effects to those produced by experience level alone (if indeed any were) such that there were no apparent differences in the result of treatment provided by more experienced vs. less experienced therapists.

The present finding that client age was not a factor significantly influencing psychotherapy outcome, supports the same finding by Smith, Glass, and Miller (1980). In the present investigation client gender was found to have a significant effect on outcome at the multivariate level with females reporting greater change than males. However, only the BDI came close to the $p. < .05$ level of significance in confirming this on the dependent measures with a significant univariate factor for gender. Thus, our conclusion concerning gender is in agreement with Luborsky, Mintz, and Christoph (1979) who found no consistent relationship between gender of client and psychotherapy outcome.

The present findings did not show a positive linear relationship between number of sessions attended and symptom reduction as measured by the BDI, SDS, SAS, VAS–D, or the VAS–A, although Howard, Kopta, Krause, and Orlinsky (1986) and Luborsky et al. (1971) have shown such a finding of therapeutic gain over the course of up to seven sessions. This may be due to the measures employed as when looking at client satisfaction as a function of number of sessions attended, such a relationship did appear as will be described in the following chapter.

Chapter III

CLIENT SATISFACTION WITH VERY BRIEF PSYCHOTHERAPY

JOSEPH E. TALLEY, A. TIMOTHY BUTCHER, AND JANE CLARK MOORMAN

C lient satisfaction has been viewed as one of the important components of a comprehensive outcome study and satisfaction with psychotherapeutic services by the recipients has been held to be as good an indicator as any of the effectiveness of treatment as is evident from the studies cited below. Further, without at least a modicum of client satisfaction, services will not continue to be sought and funding will not continue for agencies to provide psychotherapeutic services.

REVIEW OF THE CLIENT SATISFACTION LITERATURE

Pinkerton (1986) has noted that the most popular method of assessing the outcome of brief counseling and psychotherapy has been client satisfaction. Client satisfaction has also been widely used as a measure of the success of psychotherapy in general (Sorensen, Kantor, Margolis, and Galano, 1979; Kalman, 1983; Tanner, 1981). Thus, a considerable body of literature exists that addresses a number of issues related to client satisfaction.

The role of client expectations as it pertains to client satisfaction with counseling has been investigated often, and the results are inconsistent. Wilkins (1973), in an analysis of the studies addressing client expectations, found that in eleven of seventeen studies client expectations had no significant relationship to therapeutic success. However, Hartlage and Sperr (1980) reported a consensus among clients that psychotherapy was more effective when therapists displayed characteristics that were compatible with clients' expectations of therapists. Friedlander (1982) concluded that college students' expectations for counseling were of major importance both in the decision to seek psychotherapeutic services and in subsequent satisfaction with psychotherapy. Friedlander (1982) also found that positive outcomes may have been more likely when initially low expectations were disconfirmed. Hansson and Berglund (1987) found that client satisfaction was mainly a result of global improvement, symptoms at termination, and a client's expectations of improvement. Conversely, Bordwell (1989), found that neither clients nor counselors reported higher global satisfaction ratings when their expectations were met in psychotherapy.

Both client and therapist demographic variables and their influence on client satisfaction have received attention in the literature. Studies addressing client age and its relationship to satisfaction have concluded that the two were not significantly correlated (Balch, Ireland, McWilliams, and Lewis, 1977; Denner and Halprin, 1974; Feifel and Eells, 1963; Larsen, 1978; Larsen, Attkisson, and Hargreaves, 1979). These studies report similar findings for the relationship of client socioeconomic status, income, and occupation with satisfaction (Balch et al., 1977; Larsen, 1978; Larsen et al., 1979). Larsen (1978), Larsen et al. (1979), and Dyck and Azim (1983) found no significant relationship between client satisfaction and previous psychiatric experience. However, Spencer (1986) found that clients who had previous counseling experience reported greater satisfaction than clients who had no such experience.

Tanner (1981), in an analysis of thirty-eight quantitative studies of client satisfaction, reported inconsistent results in eleven studies published between 1975 and 1979 that addressed client gender and satisfaction with a majority of studies finding no significant satisfaction differences by gender (Balch et al., 1977; Denner and Halprin, 1974; Frank, Salzman, and Fergus, 1977; Heubush and Horan, 1977; Larsen, 1978; Scher, 1975). Hibbs (1976) also concluded that client satisfaction was not related to gender dyads in counseling relationships among college students. McIntyre (1987) reported that female clients were more satisfied than males with higher levels of counselor nurturance. Bugge, Hendel, and Moen (1985) have called for more research on gender differences in the evaluation of psychotherapeutic services as they found that "women were slightly more satisfied than men with both the overall quality of therapy ... and the overall helpfulness of their therapists ... " (p. 143). Additionally, Jones et al. (1987) concluded (as noted in Chapter II) that gender had influenced process and outcome in their study of brief twelve-session psychodynamic psychotherapy. Patients who had female therapists reported more symptomatic improvement and more satisfaction with treatment than patients who had male therapists. Jones et al. (1987) also reported that female therapists generated less negative feeling and fewer interpersonal conflicts than did male therapists, and presumably, more satisfaction in female clients.

The studies that have addressed therapist experience (Feifel and Eells, 1963; Frank et al., 1977), and therapist profession (Bloom and Trautt, 1978; Feifel and Eells, 1963) have similarly shown no significant effects on client satisfaction. However, some studies have concluded that certain therapeutic relationship variables such as therapist warmth (Bent, Putnam, Kiesler, and Nowicki, 1976; McClanahan, 1974; Nigl and Weiss, 1977; Rudy, McLemore, and Gorsuch, 1985), therapist empathy/understanding (Anderson, Harrow, Schwartz, and Kupfer, 1972; Henry, Schacht, and Strupp, 1986; Hibbs, 1976; Lorr, 1965; McClanahan, 1974; McNally, 1973), therapist nurturance (McIntyre, 1987), therapist activity (Anderson et al., 1972; Bent et al., 1976; Rudy et al., 1985), and therapist interest (McClanahan, 1974; Bent et al., 1976) have significantly influenced client satisfaction. Moreover, Silove, Parker, and Manicavasagar (1990) found a strong association between "perceived therapist care" and patient satisfaction in a comparison of different modalities of psychotherapy—a finding which supports other literature that has emphasized the fundamental importance of the therapeutic relationship (Butler and Strupp, 1986; Greenberg, 1986; Heppner and Heesacker 1983; Lambert, 1983; Rudy et al., 1985; Strong, 1968).

As noted in Chapter II, Luborsky et al. (1971), and Orlinsky and Howard (1986) reported a significant positive correlation between length of therapy and outcome. However, the effect of length of treatment on client satisfaction has not been found to be significant by others (Denner and Halprin, 1974; Dyck and Azim, 1983; Larsen et al., 1979). In a study that compared single-session psychotherapy with multisession psychotherapy, Silverman and Beech (1984) found that client satisfaction ratings in both groups were quite similar and very positive with moderately more multisession clients reporting that they had been helped by treatment (79 percent for multisession vs. 68 percent for single-session).

In a study of intermittent brief psychotherapy, Siddall, Haffey, and Feinman (1988) reported that 77 percent of patients indicated satisfaction with previous treatment and that 61 percent of the total number of returning patients had had two to ten sessions in their previous psychotherapy. Siddall et al. (1988) also reported that the average number of visits has remained fairly constant at 6.5 since the inception of their clinic. Again, Howard, Kopta, Krause, and Orlinsky (1986) have noted in their meta-analysis of psychotherapy outcome studies that the greatest effect of psychotherapy occurs in the first eight sessions. Strupp and Binder (1984) consider the minimum duration for "brief therapy" to be eight sessions; nevertheless, client satisfaction with attending from one to seven psychotherapeutic sessions as the duration under study has not been reported. Thus, we are examining client satisfaction with less than brief (one to seven sessions) or very brief psychotherapy which is relatively uncharted ground. However, Silverman and Beech (1984) have reported that both single session clients and multiple session (five or more sessions) clients were satisfied with treatment.

The purposes of this portion of the study were to discern the degree of client satisfaction with psychotherapeutic interventions lasting from one to seven sessions and to investigate whether satisfaction with such interventions differed by the recipient's gender, age, number of sessions attended, the therapist's gender or experience level, or the specific components of the intervention as perceived by the client/patient. It was also our purpose to demonstrate the utility of a satisfaction index for the population attending less than eight sessions of psychotherapeutic treatment.

Subjects, as described in full in Chapter II, were the 95 (68.35 percent return rate) clients who completed the Client Satisfaction Index mailed to all clients who had sought and completed services for personal counseling/psychotherapy at Counseling and Psychological Services (CAPS) of Duke University during a four month period. These clients, their therapists, and the procedure eliciting their ratings are described in the method section presented in Chapter II of this volume.

RESULTS AND DISCUSSION

A factor analysis of the Client Satisfaction Index (CSI) revealed that items 1 through 16 loaded heavily on one factor that accounted for 66.67 percent of the variance. A second factor accounted for 7.21 percent of the variance with items 1, 2, 6, 7, 8, 10, 11, and 12 loading negatively on factor 2 and items 4 and 15 loading heaviest in the positive direction at .43644 and .46231 respectively. Thus, the two factors together accounted for 73.88 percent of the variance. These figures are summarized in Table 3.1. The findings suggest that the Client Satisfaction Index employed is useful to assess satisfaction with very brief psychotherapy since a primary factor most associated with satisfaction (item 16) emerged. The means and standard deviations for the ratings by all clients combined of the perceived prevalence of the various components of treatment and the clients' satisfaction with the intervention appear in Table 3.2. It is evident from these data that the mean response regarding satisfaction approximates a rating of 7 ("quite true") with regard to the clients being satisfied with the services received, suggesting that very brief psychotherapy can leave the recipient of services quite satisfied. This rating is not appreciably different from ratings in a similar study when the length of treatment ranged from one to twelve sessions (Talley, Roy, and Moorman, 1986).

Nevertheless, when taken as a whole, clients were more satisfied the more sessions they received within the one to seven session range as the correlation between satisfaction rating and number of sessions attended indicates ($r. = .21166, p. < .0428$). Mean satisfaction ratings and standard deviations by number of sessions attended were as follows: one session attended, $M = 6.54$ ($SD = 3.25, n = 41$); two sessions, $M = 6.10$ ($SD = 2.62, n = 21$); three sessions, $M = 6.36$ ($SD = 2.94, n = 11$); four sessions, $M = 7.38$ ($SD = 1.77, n = 8$); five sessions, $M = 9.00$ ($SD = 1.41, n = 4$); six sessions, $M = 8.00$ ($SD = 1.87, n = 5$); and seven sessions attended, $M = 9.00$ ($SD = 0.00, n = 2$). Three clients did not respond to the satisfaction item on the Client Satisfaction Index. Although clients were on the whole quite satisfied with one to seven sessions, those receiving four to seven sessions were as a group more than "quite satisfied" whereas, taken as a group those receiving one to three sessions were slightly less than "quite satisfied."

A multivariate analysis of variance (MANOVA) was done to test the hypothesis that there were statistically significant ($p. < .05$) differences in the ratings on Client Satisfaction Index items 1–16 (as the dependent variables) by client gender (male and female), age (18 to 22 *vs.* 23 years of age or older), and number of sessions attended (1 to 7) or the interaction of any of these factors. No significant multivariate main effects due to client gender, $F(16, 42) = .77, p. < .7089$; age, $F(16, 42) = 1.16, p. < .3349$; or number of sessions attended, $F(96, 244.77) = 1.26, p. < .0800$, were found. Although, the effect of number of sessions attended was strong. Likewise, the multivariate client gender x age interaction effect was strong but not significant at the $p. < .05$ level, $F(16, 42) = 1.74, p. < .0756$. The multivariate gender x number of sessions attended interaction,

Table 3.1

FACTOR ANALYSIS OF
CLIENT SATISFACTION INDEX

CSI Item Number	Loadings Factor 1	Loadings Factor 2
1	0.83152	- 0.21603
2	0.83152	- 0.16813
3	0.8314	0.115
4	0.77347	0.43644
5	0.8703	0.35001
6	0.84819	- 0.27217
7	0.86049	- 0.17854
8	0.78588	- 0.22622
9	0.78671	0.357
10	0.86228	- 0.16492
11	0.78677	- 0.32615
12	0.78671	- 0.29325
13	0.89635	0.11961
14	0.5458	0.09606
15	0.78382	0.46231
16	0.9288	0.00529
Variance Accounted for		
Factor 1	Factor 2	
66.67 percent	7.21 percent	

$F = (80, 206.51) = .84$, $p. < .8212$, showed no significant effect and neither was the multivariate client age x number of sessions attended interaction effect significant, $F(80, 206.51) = 1.23$, $p. < .1252$. However, the multivariate overall effect due to gender x age x number of sessions attended interaction was significant, $F(16, 42) = 2.17$, $p. < .0228$.

With regard to the individual dependent variables (CSI, items 1–16), there was a significant effect on item 1 (increased self-understanding as a result of counseling), $F(20, 57) = 1.78$, $p. < .0455$. The univariate factors

TABLE 3.2

MEAN RATINGS AND STANDARD DEVIATIONS
BY ALL CLIENTS COMBINED ON
CLIENT SATISFACTION INDEX ITEMS

CSI Item	Content	Mean (SD)	n
1	Increased self-understanding	5.07 (2.90)	95
2	Counselor assisted clarification of what was wanted	5.47 (2.85)	95
3	Counselor understood me	6.27 (2.76)	95
4	I felt comfortable with the counselor	6.88 (2.89)	95
5	Counselor seemed authentic/real.	7.12 (2.76)	94
6	Counselor assisted clarification of means of dealing with frustration.	5.84 (2.85)	92
7	I accomplished what I hoped to	5.60 (3.11)	94
8	Counselor assisted breaking of problem into parts	5.54 (3.10)	92
9	Counselor seemed to be a warm person	7.57 (2.61)	95
10	Counselor encouragement that I could improve situation	6.73 (2.85)	95
11	Methods of dealing with problems have changed	5.02 (2.96)	95
12	I have become more certain of my ability to make good decisions	4.78 (2.86)	91
13	I felt I was working together with the counselor	5.41 (2.91)	91
14	Counselor encouraged me to discuss feelings about him/her	4.68 (3.26)	88
15	Counselor seemed skilled	7.55 (2.40)	92
16	I am satisfied with the services received	6.73 (2.86)	92

*See Appendix D for complete item wordings.

of client gender, age, number of sessions attended, gender x age interaction, gender x number of sessions attended interaction, age x number of sessions attended interaction, and gender x age x number of sessions attended interaction accounted for 38.51 percent of the variance in ratings on item 1 although the only univariate factor to reach statistical significance on item 1 was the age x number of sessions attended interaction, $F(5, 77) = 3.19$, $p. < .0132$. Male and female clients 18 to 22 years old, in general felt more increased self-understanding with more sessions. This was less true of female clients 23 and older while males 23 and older reported variable increased self-understanding with more sessions. Females 18 to 22 attending only one session gave a mean rating ($M = 3.20$, $SD = 2.36$) lower than any other subgroup except for the 2 males 18 to 22 years of age attending three sessions ($M = 2.50$, $SD = 2.12$). With the standard deviation of 2.12 only 1 of these 2 male clients would have actually given a rating less than the mean (3.21) given by the 18- to 22-year-old female clients attending only one session ($n = 14$).

Significant overall differences were found on item 4 (feeling comfortable with the counselor), $F(20, 57) = 2.15$, $p. < .0126$, and the univariate factors as described for item 1 accounted for 43.01 percent of the variance. However, the age x gender x number of sessions attended interaction was the only univariate factor to reach significance for item 4, $F(1, 77) = 4.10$, $p. < .0475$. The females 18 to 22 attending only one session rated themselves as feeling less comfortable than any other subgroup ($M = 3.86$, $SD = 3.25$) except for the rating by the 18 to 22-year-old males attending three sessions ($M = 2.50$, $SD = .71$, $n = 2$). Given the size of each of these two subgroups, the mean of the fourteen females 18 to 22 attending one session appears more noteworthy than the mean of the two males 18 to 22 attending three sessions.

Significant differences were found on item 5 (the counselor appearing authentic/real), $F(20, 57) = 1.80$, $p. < .0430$. The factors previously noted accounted for 38.73 percent of the variance. No univariate factor reached the $p. < .05$ level for item 5. The gender x age x number of sessions attended interaction was the closest, $F(1, 77) = 2.77$, $p. < .1015$. Females 18 to 22 years of age attending one session had the lowest mean rating ($M = 4.00$, $SD = 3.06$). The closest mean to this was a rating of 5.00 given by males 18 to 22 attending three sessions ($SD = 0$, $n = 2$) and also given by the one male in the 23 and older subgroup attending five sessions.

A significant overall effect on item 9 (the counselor seeming to be a warm person) was found, $F(20, 57) = 1.89$, $p. < .0313$, with the only significant univariate factor being the gender x age x number of sessions attended interaction effect, $F(1, 77) = 6.36$, $p. < .0145$. The univariate factors for item 9 accounted for 39.91 percent of the variance in ratings. Females age 18 to 22 attending one session rated perceived counselor warmth lower ($M = 5.64$, $SD = 2.90$, $n = 14$) than any other subgroup except females 23 and older attending two sessions ($M = 5.00$, $SD = 1.73$, $n = 3$). Again, the standard deviation was larger and the n smaller for the females 23 and older attending two sessions, than was the case for females 18 to 22 years old attending one session. Females 18 to 22 attending two or more sessions tended to rate perceived warmth much more similarly to the clients in the other subgroups.

Item 15 (the counselor appearing skilled) came very close to manifesting a significant response effect, $F(20, 57) = 1.71$, $p. < .0592$ with the full model of univariate factors accounting for 37.47 percent of the variance in ratings. The only univariate factor found to have a significant effect for item 15 was the gender x age x number of sessions attended interaction, $F(1, 77) = 4.65$, $p. < .0352$. The ratings indicated again that the three age x gender x number of sessions attended subgroups with the lowest ratings were females 18 to 22 years old attending only one session ($M = 5.69$, $SD = 2.53$, $n = 13$, as 1 of the 14 did not respond to this item), females 23 and older attending two sessions ($M = 5.33$, $SD = 2.31$, $n = 3$), and the one male who responded of the two 18 to 22-year-old males attending three sessions ($M = 3.00$, $n = 1$). Given the n of 1 male and n of 3 for females 23 and older attending 2 sessions and the large standard deviation, it appears that the largest percentage of lower ratings of perceived counselor skill was given by 18 to 22-year-old females attending one session.

Despite significant differences found on these CSI items discussed, no significant response effect was found for item 16 (satisfaction), $F(20, 57) = 1.27$, $p. < .2343$. Table 3.3 presents mean ratings and standard deviations for CSI items 1, 4, 9, 15, and 16 by the gender/age groups and number of sessions attended. These same subgroups (females 18 to 22 years of age attending one session, males 18 to 22 years of age attending three sessions, and females 23 years of age and older attending two sessions), and additionally, males 23 and older attending two sessions ($n = 3$), gave the lower overall satisfaction ratings (see Table 3.3) although they were not significantly lower ($p. < .05$) than ratings from the other subgroups. The 2 males 18 to 22 attending three sessions who gave lower satisfaction ratings ($M = 3.00$, $SD = 1.41$) represented 9.09 percent of all clients responding in that gender/age group and the 3 males 23 and older attending two sessions who gave lower ratings ($M = 4.33$, $SD = 3.06$) represented 20 percent of that gender age group. The 3 females 23 and older attending two sessions who gave lower satisfaction ratings ($M = 3.67$, $SD = 1.53$) represented 16.67 percent of that gender/age group while the females 18 to 22 years old attending one session and giving lower satisfaction ratings ($M = 4.64$, $SD = 3.27$) represented 37.84 percent of that gender/age group.

TABLE 3.3

MEANS AND STANDARD DEVIATIONS OF ALL CLIENTS
RATING THE ITEM BY GENDER/AGE GROUP AND NUMBER
OF SESSIONS ATTENDED FOR CLIENT SATISFACTION INDEX
ITEMS MANIFESTING SIGNIFICANT DIFFERENCES AND ITEM 16

	Females 18 to 22 Years of Age							Males 18 to 22 Years of Age						
Session Number	1	2	3	4	5	6	7	1	2	3	4	5	6	7
Item 1	3.21	5.3	5.86	6.5	6	.	9	4.11	5.83	2.5	6	9	8	7
	(2.36)	(2.54)	(2.85)	(3.27)	.	.	.	(2.62)	(3.06)	(2.12)	(1.41)	.	(0.00)	.
	n=14	n=10	n=7	n=6	n=1	.	n=1	n=9	n=6	n=2	n=2	n=1	n=2	n=1
Item 4	3.86	6.5	8	7	10	.	10	7.67	7.17	2.5	7.5	9	10	8
	(3.25)	(2.84)	(2.24)	(2.97)	.	.	.	(2.87)	(2.23)	(.71)	(2.12)	.	(0.00)	.
	n=14	n=10	n=7	n=6	n=1	.	n=1	n=9	n=6	n=2	n=2	n=1	n=2	n=1
Item 9	5.64	7.8	7.71	8.67	10	.	9	7.78	8.83	6	9	10	9	8
	(2.90)	(2.04)	(3.30)	(2.07)	.	.	.	(2.73)	(1.60)	(4.24)	(0.00)	.	(1.41)	.
	n=14	n=10	n=7	n=6	n=1	.	n=1	n=9	n=6	n=2	n=2	n=1	n=2	n=1
Item 15	5.69	8.6	7	8.2	10	.	10	7.78	8.33	3	8.5	10	8.5	10
	(2.53)	(1.26)	(2.52)	(1.64)	.	.	.	(2.39)	(1.37)	.	(.71)	.	(.71)	.
	n=13	n=10	n=7	n=5	n=1	.	n=1	n=9	n=6	n=1	n=2	n=1	n=2	n=1
Item 16	4.64	6.78	7.29	7	10	.	9	7.75	7.16	3	8.5	9	7.5	9
	(3.27)	(1.64)	(2.29)	(2.12)	.	.	.	(2.60)	(3.31)	(1.41)	(.71)	.	(2.12)	.
	n=14	n=9	n=7	n=5	n=1	.	n=1	n=8	n=6	n=2	n=2	n=1	n=2	n=1

	Females 23 Years of Age and Older							Males 23 Years of Age and Older						
Session Number	1	2	3	4	5	6	7	1	2	3	4	5	6	7
Item 1	5.8	2	6.5	7	4	9	.	5.67	2	.	.	4	5	.
	(2.74)	(1.00)	(4.95)	.	.	.	.	(3.74)	(1.73)	.	.	.	(1.41)	.
	n=10	n=3	n=2	n=1	n=1	n=1	.	n=9	n=3	.	.	n=1	n=2	.
Item 4	7.7	7	6	7	7	9	.	7.22	8.67	.	.	7	8.5	.
	(2.21)	(2.00)	(5.66)	.	.	.	.	(2.59)	(1.53)	.	.	.	(2.12)	.
	n=10	n=3	n=2	n=1	n=1	n=1	.	n=9	n=3	.	.	n=1	n=2	.
Item 9	8.9	5	8	9	8	10	.	6.56	7.33	.	.	7	6.5	.
	(1.20)	(1.73)	(2.83)	.	.	.	.	(3.47)	(2.31)	.	.	.	(4.95)	.
	n=10	n=3	n=2	n=1	n=1	n=1	.	n=9	n=3	.	.	n=1	n=2	.
Item 15	9	5.33	6.5	9	9	9	.	7.22	6.67	.	.	4	6.5	.
	(1.70)	(2.31)	(4.95)	.	.	.	.	(2.64)	(2.52)	.	.	.	(4.95)	.
	n=10	n=3	n=2	n=1	n=1	n=1	.	n=9	n=3	.	.	n=1	n=2	.
Item 16	7.7	3.67	6.5	7	10	9	.	7.11	4.33	.	.	7	8	.
	(2.75)	(1.53)	(4.95)	.	.	.	.	(3.33)	(3.06)	.	.	.	(2.83)	.
	n=10	n=3	n=2	n=1	n=1	n=1	.	n=9	n=3	.	.	n=1	n=2	.

A common element among all of these subgroups is the attending of less than four sessions; and therefore, the client, therapist, and client x therapist interaction variables that determine attending four or more sessions appear critical to predicting satisfaction with services received. Nevertheless, the only two subgroups with mean satisfaction ratings less than 4 (somewhat satisfied) included a total of only 5 clients. Further, while very brief psychotherapy was on the whole well received, females 18 to 22 years old who attended only one session felt significantly less comfortable with the counselor, felt the counselor to be significantly less warm and significantly less skilled, and felt somewhat, but not significantly, less satisfied. Other gender x age x number of sessions attended subgroups with significantly lower ratings represented a smaller percentage of the given gender/age group in the sample.

All other univariate effects significant at the $p. < .05$ level found for individual CSI items with significant response effects with the exception of the CSI item 1, age x number of sessions attended, significant interaction were due to age x gender x number of sessions attended interaction as was the significant ($p. < .05$) multivariate effect. Since the MANOVA revealed significant differences by gender x age x number of sessions attended interaction, reporting the subsequent correlational analyses and comparisons with the clients divided into four groups by gender and age appeared warranted to further clarify gender x age x number of sessions attended differences. The groups were as follows: females 18 to 22 years of age, males 18 to 22 years of age, females 23 years of age and older, and males 23 and older. The mean ratings and standard deviations for each item on the Client Satisfaction Index are presented in Table 3.4 by these gender/age groups.

Table 3.5 summarizes the correlations of all of the hypothesized components of counseling (CSI items 1–15) with satisfaction by gender/age group. The results further confirmed the utility of the Client Satisfaction Index (CSI). All of the CSI items correlated significantly in the positive direction with satisfaction for all four groups with the exception of item 14 ("The counselor encouraged me to discuss any feelings I might have about him/her during the sessions") which did not reach significance at the $p. < .05$ level for any group but the females 18 to 22 years old. Further, as presented in Table 3.5, item 14 approached statistical significance for males of both age groups. Thus, for the most part the components of counseling that were hypothesized to be associated with satisfaction were correlated significantly in the positive direction with satisfaction for all gender/age groups with the exception of item 14.

TABLE 3.4

MEAN RATINGS, STANDARD DEVIATIONS,
AND NUMBER OF RESPONDENTS BY GENDER/AGE GROUP
FOR CLIENT SATISFACTION INDEX ITEMS 1-16

	Females 18 to 22 Years		Males 18 to 22 Years		Females 23 Years and Older		Males 23 Years and Older	
	n=39		n=23		n=18		n=15	
1	M=4.95 SD=2.87		M=5.26 SD=2.78		M=5.39 SD=2.97		M=4.73 SD=3.28	
2	M=5.08 SD=2.52		M=6.17 SD=2.72		M=5.44 SD=3.65		M=5.47 SD=2.88	
3	M=5.56 SD=2.74		M=7.04 SD=2.38		M=7.00 SD=2.59		M=6.07 SD=3.26	
4	M=6.08 SD=3.31		M=7.35 SD=2.71		M=7.39 SD=2.33		M=7.67 SD=2.23	
5	M=6.55 SD=3.15	a	M=7.83 SD=2.15		M=7.78 SD=2.10		M=6.67 SD=3.04	
6	M=5.95 SD=2.73	a	M=6.14 SD=2.96	d	M=5.29 SD=3.08	f	M=5.73 SD=2.94	
7	M=5.63 SD=2.96	a	M=5.65 SD=3.07		M=5.56 SD=3.60		M=5.47 SD=3.25	
8	M=5.33 SD=3.16		M=5.71 SD=2.63	e	M=6.24 SD=3.49	f	M=5.07 SD=3.28	
9	M=7.23 SD=2.80		M=8.22 SD=2.26		M=8.17 SD=1.98		M=6.73 SD=3.08	
10	M=6.49 SD=2.90		M=7.35 SD=2.64		M=7.11 SD=2.74		M=5.93 SD=3.17	
11	M=4.69 SD=2.65		M=5.52 SD=3.12		M=5.56 SD=2.96		M=4.53 SD=3.56	
12	M=4.51 SD=2.71	b	M=5.05 SD=2.50	d	M=5.56 SD=3.18		M=4.07 SD=3.32	h
13	M=5.08 SD=2.96	b	M=5.52 SD=2.50	e	M=6.11 SD=3.03		M=5.20 SD=3.32	
14	M=4.42 SD=3.18	c	M=5.14 SD=3.18	d	M=5.00 SD=3.35	g	M=4.29 SD=3.69	h
15	M=7.30 SD=2.41	b	M=8.05 SD=2.08	d	M=8.11 SD=2.42		M=6.80 SD=2.70	
16	M=6.24 SD=2.79	b	M=7.32 SD=2.73	d	M=7.06 SD=2.96		M=6.67 SD=3.13	

*The number of respondents per item is as indicated at the head of the column unless otherwise noted (i.e. a, b, c, etc.) by the item.
a (n=38), b (n=37), c (n=36), d (n=22), e (n=21), f (n=17),
g (n=16), h (n=14)

The relationship of the ratings on items 1 through 16 with the number of times a person was seen for very brief psychotherapy was examined by the gender/age groups. Table 3.6 presents these correlations. It is noteworthy that for females 18 to 22 years of age the ratings on most items including satisfaction were significantly related to the number of sessions attended. The exceptions to this were items 8 (counselor assisted breaking of the problem into smaller parts), and 14 (counselor encouraged discussion of feelings about the counselor). This is particularly noteworthy by comparison to the other groups for which no items were correlated significantly at the $p. < .05$ level with number

TABLE 3.5

CORRELATIONS OF CLIENT SATISFACTION INDEX
ITEMS 1-15 WITH SATISFACTION BY GENDER/AGE GROUP

ITEM	Females 18 to 22 n=37	Males 18 to 22 n=22	Females 23 and Older n=18	Males 23 and Older n=15
1	r=.62025	r=.73215	r=.68586	r=.82423
	p=.0001	p=.0001	p=.0017	p=.0002
2	r=.59970	r=.68064	r=.60199	r=.78791
	p=.0001	p=.0005	p=.0082	p=.0005
3	r=.72807	r=.80762	r=.61394	r=.86937
	p=.0001	p=.0001	p=.0067	p=.0001
4	r=.87768	r=.78710	r=.58524	r=.65929
	p=.0001	p=.0001	p=.0107	p=.0075
5	r=.71517	r=.74065	r=.66391	r=.76785
	p=.0001	p=.0001	p=.0027	p=.0008
6	r=.68209	r=.66453	r=.74617	r=.85873
	p=.0001	p=.0007	p=.0006 c	p=.0001
7	r=.87565	r=.77568	r=.87993	r=.88693
	p=.0001	p=.0051	p=.0001	p=.0001
8	r=.69918	r=.69547	r=.85075	r=.64132
	p=.0001	p=.0001	p=.0001 c	p=.0100
9	r=.79630	r=.57554	r=.71173	r=.56742
	p=.0001	p=.0051	p=.0009	p=.0274
10	r=.82797	r=.93661	r=.62258	r=.87453
	p=.0001	p=.0001	p=.0058	p=.0001
11	r=.57487	r=.85172	r=.76294	r=.63154
	p=.0002	p=.0001	p=.0002	p=.0116
12	r=.66583	r=.65382	r=.65794	r=.69309
	p=.0001	p=.0010	p=.0030	p=.0060 e
13	r=.75794	r=.71323	r=.79364	r=.80348
	p=.0001	p=.0004 b	p=.0001	p=.0003
14	r=.46905	r=.41636	r=.37297	r=.47191
	p=.0045 a	p=.0605	p=.1548 d	p=.0884 e
15	r=.68899	r=.74499	r=.81118	r=.75050
	p=.0001	p=.0001	p=.0001	p=.0013

* The number of respondents is as indicated at the head of the
  column unless otherwise noted (i.e. a, b, c, d, etc.).
  a (n=36), b (n=21), c (n=17), d (n=16), e (n=14)

of sessions attended with the exception of items 1 (increased understanding as a result of counseling) and 14 (counselor encouraged discussion of feelings about the counselor) for males 18 to 22 years old.

TABLE 3.6

CORRELATIONS OF CLIENT SATISFACTION INDEX ITEMS
WITH NUMBER OF SESSIONS ATTENDED
BY GENDER/AGE GROUP

ITEM	Females 18 To 22 Years	Males 18 To 22 Years	Females 23 Years And Older	Males 23 Years And Older
1	r=.47465 p=.0023	r=.43122 p=.0399	r=.14802 p=.5578	r=-.09772 p=.7290
2	r=.42512 p=.0070	r=.29073 p=.1784	r=-.01500 p=.9529	r=-.05185 p=.8544
3	r=.47708 p=.0021	r=-.01589 p=.9426	r=.08782 p=.7290	r=.05655 p=.8414
4	r=.49318 p=.0014	r=.15621 p=.4766	r=-.02260 p=.9291	r=.14759 p=.5996
5	r=.52457 p=.0007	r=.17206 p=.4324	r=-.01403 p=.9560	r=-.04156 p=.8831
6	r=.40221 p=.0123	r=.15366 p=.4948	r=.05683 p=.8285	r=-.07049 p=.8029
7	r=.35695 p=.0278	r=-.04319 p=.8449	r=.09941 p=.6947	r=-.23255 p=.4043
8	r=.26564 p=.1022	r=.13288 p=.5658	r=-.05754 p=.8264	r=.11388 p=.6861
9	r=.40296 p=.0110	r=.14132 p=.5201	r=.01597 p=.9499	r=.00656 p=.9815
10	r=.39263 p=.0134	r=.02272 p=.9180	r=.09524 p=.7070	r=.07326 p=.7953
11	r=.40631 p=.0103	r=-.07593 p=.7306	r=.05701 p=.8222	r=-.18153 p=.5173
12	r=.37028 p=.0241	r=.31628 p=.1516	r=-.03041 p=.9046	r=-.08678 p=.7680
13	r=.49160 p=.0020	r=.29578 p=.1930	r=.04869 p=.8478	r=-.09586 p=.7340
14	r=.14347 p=.4039	r=.45186 p=.0348	r=.05548 p=.8383	r=-.04171 p=.8874
15	r=.40766 p=.0123	r=.21987 p=.3255	r=-.06432 p=.7998	r=-.20459 p=.4645
16	r=.43914 p=.0065	r=.06954 p=.7584	r=.11454 p=.6509	r=.09277 p=.7423
Mean # of Sessions Attended	2.33 (SD=1.40)	2.57 (SD=1.88)	2.06 (SD=1.55)	2.13 (SD=1.88)

The Effects of Therapist Gender and Experience on Client Satisfaction

A multivariate analysis of variance (MANOVA) indicated that there was no significant multivariate main effect due to differences with regard to ratings on CSI items 1 through 16, by individual therapists of the 12 therapists with clients responding, $F(208, 525.23) = .91, p. < .7842$. Thus, it was acceptable to group therapists by experience level and gender to test for differences by therapist gender, therapist experience level, and therapist experience level x gender interaction on the CSI items. Therapists were divided into an experience level category such that "more experienced" therapists were defined as those with seven or more years of full-time post-Ph.D., post-MSW, or postpsychiatric residency experience practicing psychotherapy. "Less experienced" therapists were those with less than seven years of full-time postgraduate experience. Seven years was chosen in order to be consistent with the findings of Orlinsky and Howard (1980) who found male therapists with less than seven years of experience to be less successful than males with seven or more years of experience who were found to be as effective as the female therapists in that study. The mean satisfaction rating by all responding clients combined for less experienced therapists was 6.56 $(SD = 3.14, n = 34)$ and for more experienced therapists it was 6.83 $(SD = 2.70, n = 58)$. The mean satisfaction rating for all female therapists combined regardless of level of experience with all clients taken together was 6.86 $(SD = 2.75, n = 44)$ and for male therapists the mean satisfaction rating was 6.60 $(SD = 2.97, n = 48)$. Looking at mean satisfaction ratings by therapist experience and gender groups showed mean ratings as follows: less experienced female therapists $M = 6.73$ $(SD = 3.12, n = 26)$; more experienced female therapists $M = 7.05$ $(SD = 2.12, n = 18)$; less experienced male therapists $M = 6.00$ $(SD = 3.38, n = 8)$; more experienced male therapists $M = 6.74$ $(SD = 2.85, n = 40)$.

The MANOVA testing for therapist experience, therapist gender, and therapist gender x experience interaction effects on CSI items 1–16 indicated that there were no significant effects due to therapist experience level; $F(16, 59) = 1.23, p. < .2724$; therapist gender, $F(16, 59) = .94, p. < .5280$, or therapist experience x gender interaction, $F(16, 59) = .56, p. < .9019$, on CSI item ratings at the multivariate level.

A 4×4 analysis of variance with four therapist gender/experience categories by four client gender/age groups in this case was not used given the small n's in many cells. Although it might first appear (see Table 3.7) that the client gender/age x therapist gender/experience level satisfaction rating means suggest differences that would be useful clinically. An examination of the standard deviations in the cells shows that there was for the most part too large a degree of variability in the satisfaction ratings to warrant any conclusions from gender/age of client by gender/experience of therapist effects on satisfaction ratings. However, it appears that trends from these data might suggest hypotheses for future studies done with even larger samples.

TABLE 3.7

MEAN SATISFACTION RATINGS BY GENDER/AGE OF CLIENT
BY GENDER/EXPERIENCE LEVEL OF THERAPIST

	Female Clients 18 to 22 Years	Male Clients 18 to 22 Years	Female Clients 23 Years and Older	Male Clients 23 Years and Older	Totals
Less Experienced Female Therapists	M=5.73 SD=2.97 n=6	M=5.33 SD=4.16 n=11	M=8 SD=2.96 n=3	M=8 SD=2.65 n=9	M=6.73 SD=3.12 n=26
More Experienced Female Therapists	M=6.50 SD=2.43 n=3	M=8.33 SD=1.15 n=12	M=8.5 SD=.71 n=3	M=7 . n=2	M=7.05 SD=2.12 n=1
Less Experienced Male Therapists	M=5.50 SD=3.11 n=1	M=6.67 SD=4.93 n=4	. . n=3	M=6 . .	M=6.0 SD=3.38 n=1
More Experienced Male Therapists	M=6.8 SD=3.16 n=3	M=7.69 SD=2.10 n=10	M=5.43 SD=2.82 n=13	M=6.30 SD=3.59 n=7	M=6.74 SD=2.85 n=10
Totals	M=6.24 SD=2.79 n=37	M=7.32 SD=2.73 n=22	M=7.06 SD=2.96 n=18	M=6.67 SD=3.13 n=15	M=6.73 SD=2.86 n=92

The means suggest that both male and female clients 23 years of age and older were somewhat more satisfied with less experienced female therapists than were the younger clients. However, these older clients were about equally satisfied with experienced female therapists as they were with less experienced female therapists and the older clients were less satisfied with male therapists regardless of experience level. Both male and female clients 18 to 22 years of age tended to be more satisfied with services received when the provider regardless of gender was more experienced.

The male client group 18 to 22 years of age, which gave the highest satisfaction ratings overall, did rate services provided by less experienced female therapists lower than services provided by any other therapist gender/experience group. Likewise, satisfaction ratings differed very little by client age or client gender alone. Male clients 18 to 22 receiving services from less experienced female therapists gave the lowest satisfaction ratings, and the ratings by females 23 and older receiving services from more experienced male therapists gave the next lowest satisfaction ratings followed closely by female clients 18 to 22 years of age receiving services from less experienced male and then from less experienced female therapists.

Male clients 23 and older reported greater satisfaction with less experienced female therapists and female clients 23 and older were more satisfied with either more or less experienced female therapists than with experienced male therapists. However, taking into consideration both the MANOVA examining the effects of therapist gender and experience and the MANOVA examining the effects of client gender, age, and number of sessions attended, the greater portion of the variance in satisfaction ratings appears to be due to client gender, age, number of sessions attended, and related interaction factors, than to therapist experience, therapist gender, or therapist experience x gender interaction effects.

Treatment Process Factors Predicting Client Satisfaction

A stepwise multiple regression analysis was done with each gender/age group and with all clients combined to determine the treatment process factors as measured by CSI items 2, 3, 4, 5, 6, 8, 9, 10, 11, 13, 14, and 15 that best predicted client satisfaction (item 16). Item 1, "I understand myself better as a result of counseling," item 7, "I accomplished what I had hoped to . . . ," and item 12, "I have become more certain of my ability to make good decisions" were seen as reflecting self-report with regard to the final outcome of the intervention, and thus, were not included as potential predictors in the analysis. Including these other outcome related items would in all probability mask the portion of the variance in satisfaction ratings accounted for by the process related factors.

For all clients combined a model emerged that accounted for 85.28 percent of the variance. The model included item 10, counselor encouragement that the client could improve the situation, accounting for 67.91 percent of the variance; item 4, feeling comfortable with the counselor, accounting for 12.29 percent of the variance; item 6, counselor-assisted clarification of means of dealing with frustration, accounting for 3.54 percent of the variance; and item 15, the counselor appearing skilled, accounting for 1.55 percent of the variance.

The model that emerged for females 18 to 22 years of age accounted for 90.48 percent of the variance in satisfaction ratings, consisted of item 10, counselor encouragement that the client could improve the situation, accounting for 81.12 percent of the variance; item 4, feeling comfortable with the counselor, accounting for 7.53 percent of the variance; and, item 6, counselor-assisted clarification of means of dealing with frustration, accounting for 1.83 percent of the variance.

The model for males 18 to 22 years of age that emerged accounted for 93.18 percent of the variance, and included item 10, counselor encouragement that the client could improve the situation, accounting for 83.35 percent of the variance and item 15, the counselor appearing skilled, accounting for 9.83 percent of the variance.

The model for females age 23 and older that emerged accounted for 84.72 percent of the variance and included item 8, counselor assisted breaking of the problem into smaller parts, accounting for 70.32 percent of the variance, and item 15, the counselor appearing skilled accounting for 14.40 percent of the variance.

The model for males age 23 and older that emerged accounted for 87.38 percent of the variance. This model also included item 10, counselor encouragement that the client could improve the situation, accounting for 74.28 percent of the variance, and item 3, feeling understood by the counselor, accounting 13.11 percent of the variance. Table 3.8 lists the *F* and *p.* values and *Beta* weights for these five models.

Thus, item 10, encouragement by the counselor/therapist that the client could improve the situation was found to be a significant predictor of satisfaction for all groups except for females 23 and older. This encouragement accounted for between 74 and 83 percent of the variance in satisfaction ratings itself for the gender/age groups and close to 68 percent when looking at all clients combined. Item 4, feeling comfortable with the counselor, which accounted for 7.53 percent of the variance for females 18 to 22, did not emerge as a significant predictor for any other gender/age group. However, it did emerge as significant for all clients combined and accounted for over twelve percent of the variance in satisfaction ratings for all clients combined.

Item 6, "The counselor helped me to clarify how I had been coping with frustration" also emerged as a significant predictor of satisfaction for females 18 to 22 years of age and accounted for 1.83 percent of the variance. For all clients combined item 6 accounted for approximately 16.5 percent of the variance. Item 15, "The counselor seemed to be a

TABLE 3.8

STEPWISE REGRESSION ANALYSES RESULTS OF SIGNIFICANT
CLIENT SATISFACTION INDEX PROCESS VARIABLES
AS PREDICTORS OF SATISFACTION BY GENDER/AGE
GROUP AND BY ALL CLIENTS COMBINED

All Clients Combined			
Variable	Beta Weight	F	p.
(10) The counselor encouraged me to believe that I could improve my situation	0.35737695	165.058	0.0001
(4) I felt comfortable with the counselor	0.2549114	47.7912	0.0001
(6) The counselor helped me clarify how I had been dealing with frustration	0.28474906	16.5197	0.0001
(15) The counselor seemed skilled	0.21776085	7.8898	0.0063
Model		108.058(4,67)	0.0001

Females 18 to 22 Years of Age			
Variable	Beta Weight	F	p.
(10) The counselor encouraged me to believe that I could improve my situation	0.40992313	128.8618	0.0001
(4) I felt comfortable with the counselor	0.32280569	19.248	0.0001
(6) The counselor helped me clarify how I had been dealing with frustration	0.22267792	5.373	0.028
Model		88.67(3,28)	0.0001

Males 18 to 22 Years of Age			
Variable	Beta Weight	F	p.
(10) The counselor encouraged me to believe that I could improve my situation	0.80237924	80.0977	0.0001
(15) The counselor seemed skilled	0.43815884	21.6139	0.0003
Model		102.45(2,15)	0.0001

Females 23 Years of Age and Older			
Variable	Beta Weight	F	p.
(8) The counselor helped me to break the problem down into smaller parts	0.46707266	33.172	0.0001
(15) The counselor seemed skilled	0.55603697	12.2443	0.0039
Model		36.03(2, 13)	0.0001

Males 23 Years of Age and Older			
Variable	Beta Weight	F	p.
(10) The counselor encouraged me to believe that I could improve my situation	0.52278557	34.6554	0.0001
(3) The counselor understood me	0.48594224	11.427	0.0061
Model		38.10(2,11)	0.0001

skilled counselor," accounted for 9.83 percent of the variance in satisfaction ratings for males 18 to 22 years of age and 14.40 percent of the variance in ratings for females 23 and older. For all clients combined, perceived counselor skill accounted for 1.55 percent of the variance in satisfaction ratings. Item 8, "The counselor helped me break the problem down into smaller parts", accounted for 70.32 percent of the variance in satisfaction ratings for females 23 and older. This item was not a significant predictor for any other group. "The counselor understood me," item 3, accounted for 13.11 percent of the variance in satisfaction ratings for males 23 and older and likewise was not a predictor for any other gender/age group.

To summarize, particular ingredients predictive of client satisfaction included: the counselor appearing skilled, the counselor assisting in breaking the problem into smaller parts, clarification of the client's means and methods of dealing with frustration, the client feeling understood by the counselor, and the client feeling comfortable with the counselor, all of which appear to be no surprise. However, by far the single greatest predictor of satisfaction was counselor encouragement that the client could improve his or her situation. It was not expected that this factor would account for so much of the variance in satisfaction ratings as it is not a salient part of insight-oriented psychodynamic theories of brief psychotherapy although it certainly is seen as integral to supportive treatment. Apparently this population is seeking a treatment that is highly supportive and insight-oriented work must occur in that context. Nevertheless, increased self-understanding (CSI item 1) was strongly and significantly correlated with satisfaction for all gender/age groups too.

Thus, it appears that these clients wanted increased self-understanding, but they apparently wanted encouragement more as it was even more strongly correlated with satisfaction than was increased self-understanding for all gender/age groups except females 23 and older and the difference for this group was small. Cognitive therapy does, of course, emphasize the importance of helping the client/patient acquire hope. These findings are consistent too with the framework of Alfred Adler (1925) who conceptualized most patients as being discouraged and needing encouragement. Encouraging a client may seem from one perspective to be relying on unfounded suggestion to produce a "transference cure" at the expense of "working through" the problems via an analysis of transferential feelings resulting in insight and a corrective emotional experience. However, there appears to be no data reported in the literature demonstrating that the supportive techniques such as encouragement reduce the potential for insight despite "clinical lore" to the contrary, and these data suggest that supportive and insight-oriented aspects of treatment can complement each other in producing greater client satisfaction.

The Relation of Symptoms of Depression
And Anxiety to Client Satisfaction

A multivariate analysis of variance was done with BDI, SDS, and SAS scores grouped by the severity levels as independent variables and ratings on CSI items 1 through 16 as dependent variables to determine if there were significant differences in the CSI ratings by inventory severity level. Clients were distributed by inventory severity level as follows: BDI, none ($n = 23$), mild ($n = 20$), moderate ($n = 16$), severe ($n = 16$), no BDI ($n = 18$); SDS, none ($n = 29$), mild ($n = 24$), moderate ($n = 20$), severe ($n = 5$), no SDS ($n = 17$); SAS, none ($n = 31$), mild ($n = 36$), moderate ($n = 10$), severe ($n = 1$), no SDS ($n = 17$). No multivariate overall main effect was found by BDI severity level, $F(48, 119,76) = 1.22$, $p. < .1894$. No multivariate overall main effect by SAS level was found, $F(48, 119.76) = 1.04$, $p. < .4265$. However, a multivariate overall main effect by SDS level was found, $F(48, 119.76) = 1.66$, $p. < .0144$.

With regard to univariate response effects on the CSI individual items, only item 4 (feeling comfortable with the counselor), $F(9, 55) = 3.13$, $p. < .0041$, univariate SDS severity level factor, $F = 5.32$, $p. < .0027$; item 5 (counselor authenticity), $F(9, 55) = 3.14$, $p. < .0040$, univariate SDS severity level factor, $F(3, 55) = 6.60$, $p. < .0007$; and item 14 (encouragement for the client to share feelings about the counselor), $F(9, 55) = 2.10$, $p. < .0453$, reached the $p. < .05$ level of significance. However, the SDS severity level univariate factor did not reach the $p. < .05$ level of significance for item 14. Item 16 (satisfaction) showed no significant difference in rating by inventory severity level, $F(9, 55) = 1.49$, $p. < .1730$, although the univariate SDS severity factor level was significant, $F(3, 55) = 2.91$, $p. < .0427$. The SAS severity level univariate factor for item 5 was also significant, $F(3, 55) = 2.78$, $p. < .0498$, but was considered uninterpretable given the lack of a multivariate SAS severity level main effect.

Concerning the effects of SDS severity level on item 4 (feeling comfortable with the counselor), the mean for clients in the severe range ($M = 7.40$, $SD = 3.78$) was significantly higher than the mean for clients in the mild ($M = 5.38$, $SD = 3.24$) and moderate ($M = 6.10$, $SD = 3.14$) ranges.

The difference between clients' in the severe SDS range and the none range ratings on item 4 ($M = 8.21$, $SD = 1.80$) did not reach the $p. < .05$ level of statistical significance. Ratings on item 4 by clients in the none range were significantly higher than the ratings of clients in the mild range. With regard to feeling comfortable with the counselor, clients in the none range perceived more comfort than did clients scoring in the SDS mild range, and clients in the severe SDS range perceived more comfort with the counselor than those in the mild and the moderate SDS severity ranges.

For item 5 (counselor authenticity), the mean ratings by clients in the mild ($M = 5.39$, $SD = 3.04$) range was significantly lower than the mean ratings by clients in the none ($M = 8.21$, $SD = 1.80$) range. Clients in the severe ($M = 6.80$, $SD = 3.49$) and moderate ($M = 6.95$, $SD = 2.91$) ranges had comparable mean ratings. However, the clients in the none range gave the highest mean rating. Thus, clients in the none range of depressive symptoms as measured by the SDS perceived the counselor to be more authentic than did clients in the mild, moderate and severe SDS ranges of depressive symptoms. Counselors may have, in fact, been different with these different groups of clients as they may have felt more comfortable and more authentic, with the least symptomatic clients. Further, counselors may have concluded that they should make a concerted effort to present in a warm and empathic manner to the most SDS symptomatic clients.

For item 14 (counselor encouraged sharing of feelings about the counselor) the mean for clients in the none range ($M = 6.21$, $SD = 3.04$) was significantly higher than the mean for clients in the mild range ($M = 3.45$, $SD = 2.96$) and while the mean for clients in the none range was also higher than the mean for clients in the moderate range ($M = 4.18$, $SD = 2.85$) and the severe range ($M = 2.80$, $SD = 4.02$), these differences were not significant at the $p. < .05$ level. Apparently, clients with the least severe depressive symptoms perceived the most counselor encouragement to share feelings about the counselor with the counselor. Counselors may have actually solicited such material more with clients who were less depressed having assessed that less depressed clients could tolerate it more easily.

Item 16 (satisfaction) ratings showed that clients in the none SDS range had the highest mean ($M = 7.57$, $SD = 2.50$) closely followed by the mean rating by those in the severe range ($M = 6.80$, $SD = 3.49$). Clients in the mild range ($M = 5.65$, $SD = 2.87$) and in the moderate range (M = 5.95, SD = 3.08) had the lower mean ratings. Thus, for all clients taken together, regardless of gender or age group, those in the none and those in the severe SDS range of depressive symptoms were somewhat, albeit not significantly, and perhaps due to chance, more satisfied with services received than were clients in the mild and moderate ranges of depressive symptoms as measured by the SDS.

Concerning the SAS and satisfaction, the one client in the severe range gave a rating of 1 indicating that the client was not at all satisfied. Differences were unremarkable among clients in the none (M = 6.77, SD = 2.94), mild (M = 6.46, SD = 2.78), and moderate (M = 6.56, SD = 3.13) ranges. Satisfaction by BDI ranges showed that clients in the severe range (M = 6.13, SD = 3.50) gave lower ratings than did clients in the none (M = 7.26, SD = 2.82) and mild (M = 6.50, SD = 2.61) ranges. Clients in the moderate range (M = 6.00, SD = 2.83), however, gave the lowest satisfaction ratings of all. These differences were not significant at the $p.$ < .05 level nor do they appear remarkable.

Given that there was a significant multivariate main effect by SDS severity level on CSI ratings, exploratory stepwise regression analyses were done to determine whether the Client Satisfaction Index process variables predicting client satisfaction differed by severity on the SDS. Clients were divided into two groups. Those in the none and mild ranges were combined as were clients in the moderate and severe ranges of the SDS. A stepwise regression analysis was done with each group to determine which CSI process variable items were significantly predictive of client satisfaction. The regression analysis done to predict satisfaction for those clients with SDS scores in the none and mild ranges at intake resulted in a model, $F(4, 42)$ = 72.70, $p.$ < .0001, with counselor encouragement (item 10) accounting for 70.04 percent of the variance, F = 102.85, $p.$ < .0001, (*Beta* weight = .42987988); perceived counselor skill (item 15) accounting for 11.22 percent of the variance, F = 25.74, $p.$ < .0001, (*Beta* weight = .40275742); counselor assisted clarification of means of coping with frustration (item 6) accounting for 2.60 percent of the variance, F = 6.75, $p.$ < .0129, (*Beta* weight = .23083985), for a total of 83.85 percent of the variance in satisfaction ratings accounted for by these factors in the group with SDS scores in the none and mild ranges.

The regression analysis for clients with SDS scores in the moderate and severe ranges resulted in a model, $F(2, 19)$ = 62.91, $p.$ < .0001, including feeling understood by the counselor (item 3) accounting for 78.66 percent of the variance in satisfaction ratings, F = 73.71, $p.$ < .0001

(*Beta* weight = .62488574) and counselor encouragement (item 10) accounting for 8.22 percent of the variance $F = 11.91$, $p. < .0001$ (*Beta* weight = .43958425). The model of both variables together accounted for 86.88 percent of the variance in satisfaction ratings for clients with initial SDS scores in the moderate and severe ranges.

Thus, encouragement appears slightly more important in predicting satisfaction for clients in the SDS none and mild ranges than to clients in the SDS moderate and severe ranges. The other components differed such that the counselor appearing skilled and counselor assisted clarification of means of dealing with frustration was predictive of satisfaction for clients in the none and mild SDS ranges of depressive symptoms while the client's feeling understood by the counselor was most predictive of satisfaction for clients in the SDS moderate and severe ranges of depressive symptoms.

A correlation matrix showed that for female clients 18 to 22 years of age the total scores at intake time on the BDI, SDS, and SAS correlated with subsequent satisfaction rating as follows: BDI ($n = 32$), $r = -.44816$, $p. < .0101$; SDS ($n = 33$), $r = .42435$, $p. < .0138$; SAS ($n = 33$), $r = -.38661$, $p. < .0262$. Inventory items having significant correlations with satisfaction for this group of clients were BDI item 1 (feeling sad or unhappy), $r = -.44601$, $p. < .0105$; BDI item 9 (ideas of self harm/suicidal ideation), $r = -.38712$, $p. < .0286$; and BDI item 17 (tiredness) $r = -.44833$, $p. < .0101$; SDS item 10 (tiredness), $r = -.52972$, $p. < .0018$; SDS item 11 (confusion/"clear" mind), $r = -.38636$, $p. < .0289$; SDS item 15 (irritability), $r = -.42448$, $p. < .0138$; SAS item 3 (panic), $r = -.40260$, $p. < .0202$; SAS item 4 (subjective mental disintegration), $r = -.51728$, $p. < .0021$; SAS item 18 (facial flushing), $r = -.40721$, $p. < .0187$; and, SAS item 10 (heart palpitations), $r = -.40935$, $p. < .0180$.

For male clients 18 to 22 BDI, SDS, and SAS total score at intake time correlations with subsequent satisfaction ratings were as follows: BDI ($n = 16$), $r = -.03039$, $p. < .9111$; SDS ($n = 16$), $r = .26869$, $p. < .3134$; SAS ($n = 16$), $r = .36503$, $p. < .1645$. Thus, no inventory scores were significantly correlated with satisfaction for this group. Further, no BDI items were significantly correlated with satisfaction ratings for males 18 to 22 although SDS item 5 (appetite) was, $r = .51557$, $p. < .0409$; as was SAS item 12 (faintness), $r = -.60928$, $p. < .0122$.

For female clients 23 and older ($n = 15$) the full inventory correlations with satisfaction were as follows: BDI ($n = 15$), $r = -.10862$, $p. < .7000$; SDS ($n = 15$), $r = -.10334$, $p. < .7140$; SAS ($n = 15$), $r = -.15169$,

$p. < .5894$. The inventory items correlating significantly with satisfaction ratings were: SDS item 7 (weight loss), $r = .52021, p. < .0468$; SDS item 19 (passive suicidal ideation), $r = -.51577, p. < .0491$; and, SAS item 18 (facial flushing), $r = -.54490, p. < .0357$.

For male clients 23 and older ($n = 11$) the full inventory correlations with satisfaction were: BDI ($n = 10$), $r = .53215, p. < .1130$; SDS ($n = 11$), $r = .08433, p. < .8053$; SAS ($n = 11$), $r = .25521, p. < .4488$. The only significant individual item correlates of satisfaction were: BDI item 1 (feeling sad or unhappy), $r = .63298, p. < .0495$; BDI item 5 (guilt or worthlessness), $r = .81780, p. < .0038$; and, SDS item 5 (appetite), $r = .73819, p. < .0095$. Thus, only for females 18 to 22 years of age did total BDI, SDS, and SAS scores correlate with satisfaction such that higher scores on the measures of depression and anxiety were associated with lower satisfaction ratings.

For all clients combined inventory total scores correlated with satisfaction ratings as follows: BDI, $r. = -.13855, p. < .2358$: SDS, $r. = -.16987, p. < .1451$; and SAS, $r. = -.13061, p. < .2640$. Thus, taking all clients together the total score at the time of intake on these measures was not significantly related to satisfaction ratings. Total scores on these inventories were related to satisfaction ratings at the $p. < .05$ level for females 18 to 22 years of age and for no other gender/age group.

A series of stepwise regression analyses using the items from one inventory at a time was done to identify BDI, SDS, and SAS items that were significant predictors of satisfaction ratings. For all subjects combined the only BDI item reaching the $p. < .05$ level of significance was item 17 (tiredness) which accounted for 9.97 percent of the variance in satisfaction ratings, $F(1, 71) = 7.86, p. < .0065$ (*Beta* weight $= -1.12657143$). The only SDS item emerging as a significant predictor of satisfaction was item 2 (diurnal variation) accounting for 5.35 percent of the variance, $F(1, 72) = 4.07, p. < .0474$ (*Beta* weight $= -.67308052$) and the only SAS item emerging was item 12 (faintness) accounting for 6.98 percent of the variance, $F(1, 73) = 5.48, p. < .0220$ (*Beta* weight $= -2.62184874$).

For females 18 to 22 years of age a model accounting for 33.38 percent of the variance emerged, $F(1, 29) = 7.27, p. < .0028$, that included BDI item 15 (work inhibition) accounting for 21.11 percent of the variance, $F = 8.03, p. < .0082$ (*Beta* weight $= -1.42546702$), and BDI item 1 (feeling sad or unhappy) accounting for 12.27 percent of the variance, $F = 5.34, p. < .0281$ (*Beta* weight $= -1.31566908$). Higher scores were predictive of less satisfaction. Using the SDS for females in this age group only item 10 (tiredness) emerged as a significant predictor, $F(1, 30) = 11.70$, $p. < .0018$ (*Beta* weight $= -1.41176471$), and accounted for 28.06 percent of the variance in satisfaction ratings for this group. A higher score was predictive of less satisfaction. Using the SAS, a model, $F(3, 29) = 8.69$, $p. < .0003$, emerged accounting for 47.33 percent of the variance. The model included item 4 (subjective mental disintegration), $F = 11.32$, $p. < .0021$ (*Beta* weight $= -1.62188773$), accounting for 26.76 percent of the variance, item 18 (facial flushing), $F = 4.59$, $p. < .0403$ (*Beta* weight $= -1.42842922$), accounting for 9.73 percent of the variance, and item 16 (urinary frequency) $F = 5.97$, $p. < .0208$ (*Beta* weight $= .99617930$), accounting for 10.85 percent of the variance. Higher scores on items 4 and 18 in conjunction with a lower score on item 16 was predictive of less satisfaction.

For males 18 to 22 years of age no BDI items emerged as significant predictors of satisfaction and only item 5 (appetite) of the SDS emerged, $F(1, 14) = 5.07$, $p. < .0409$ (*Beta* weight $= .99029126$), and accounted for 26.58 percent of the variance. A higher score was predictive of greater satisfaction. However, a model emerged with the SAS, $F(1, 12) = 12.86$, $p. < .0005$, that accounted for 76.28 percent of the variance in satisfaction ratings. The model included SAS item 12 (fainting spells) which accounted for 37.12 percent of the variance, $F = 8.27$, $p. < .0122$ (*Beta* weight $= -7.27240143$), item 17 (sweating) which accounted for 21.38 percent of the variance, $F = 6.70$, $p. < .0225$ (*Beta* weight $= 1.26164875$), and item 7 (body aches and pains), $F = 8.99$, $p. < .0111$ (*Beta* weight $= .94086022$), which accounted for 17.78 percent of the variance in satisfaction ratings. A higher rating on item 12 in conjunction with lower ratings on items 7 and 17 was predictive of less satisfaction.

For females 23 and older no BDI items emerged as significant predictors at the $p. < .05$ level. With the SDS, item 7 (weight loss) accounted for 27.06 percent of the variance, $F = 4.82$, $p. < .0468$ (*Beta* weight $= 2.71000000$), and item 15 (irritability) accounted for 23.87 percent of the variance, $F = 5.84$, $p. < .0326$ (*Beta* weight $= -1.47000000$). They emerged as significant predictors in a model and accounted for 50.93 percent of the variance, $F(2, 12) = 6.23$, $p. < .0140$. A higher score on item 16 with a lower score on item 7 was predictive of less satisfaction. Using the SAS with this group of females a model accounting for 50.26 percent of the variance, $F(2, 12) = 6.06$, $p. < .0151$, emerged and included item 8 (fatigability) which accounted for 29.69 percent of the variance, $F = 5.49$, $p. < .0357$ (*Beta* weight $= -2.00458716$), and item 16 (urinary frequency) which accounted for 20.57 percent of the variance, $F = 4.9633$,

$p. < .0458$ (*Beta* weight $= -1.33486239$). A higher score on item 8 with a lower score on item 16 was predictive of less satisfaction.

For males 23 and older BDI item 5 (guilt or worthlessness) accounted for 66.88 percent of the variance, $F(1, 8) = 16.15, p. < .0038$ (*Beta* weight $= 2.81578947$). A lower score was predictive of less satisfaction. SDS item 5 (appetite) accounted for 54.49 percent of the variance, $F(1, 9) = 10.78, p. < .0095$ (*Beta* weight $= 1.93023256$). A lower score was predictive of less satisfaction. No SAS items met the $p. < .05$ level of significance. Thus, anxiety related items appear more able to predict subsequent satisfaction with services for all the gender age groups except males 23 and older. For the older males greater feelings of guilt and appetite loss were more predictive of greater satisfaction.

Discriminant Function and
Validation/Cross Validation
Analyses

The 95 clients were randomly divided into two groups by computer program. Group one, consisting of 55 clients, was used to derive a model to discriminate among CSI satisfaction ratings from 1 to 10. The variables of therapist experience, therapist/client gender match, client age, client gender/age group, and CSI treatment process variable measures (items 2, 3, 4, 5, 6, 8, 9, 10, 11, 13, 14, and 15) were entered as potential discriminators. A model, $F(36, 117.9087) = 4.398, p. < .0001$, with four discriminators emerged consisting of item 13, "I felt that I was working together with the counselor," $F = 17.813, p. < .0001$, partial $r^2 = .4379$; item 10, "The counselor encouraged me to believe that I could improve my situation," $F = 2.871, p. < .0128$, partial $r^2 = .3916$; item 14, "The counselor encouraged me to discuss any feelings I might have about him/her during the sessions," $F = 2.025, p. < .0689$, partial $r^2 = .3453$; and, item 6 "The counselor helped me clarify how I had been dealing with frustration," $F = 1.788, p. < .1108$, partial $r^2 = .3418$. When this discriminant function was applied to group two (the forty clients not included in the sample on which the discriminant function was derived), only 6 of 40 client's satisfaction ratings would have been in error by more than two points on the scale of 1 to 10 and only 2 of the 40 would have erred by more than 3 rating points on the satisfaction scale.

For exploratory and comparison purposes a discriminant function analysis was done on the entire sample. This resulted in a model, $F(10,$

146) $= 14.365$, $p. < .0001$, including item 10, "The counselor encouraged me to believe that I could improve my situation," $F = 55.203$, $p. < .0001$, partial $r^2 = .5890$; item 4, "I felt comfortable with the counselor," $F = 9.639$, $p. < .0002$, partial $r^2 = .2023$; item 8, "The counselor helped me to break the problem down into smaller parts," $F = 5.374$, $p. < .0066$, partial $r^2 = .1253$; item 6, "The counselor helped me clarify how I had been dealing with frustration," $F = 2.032$, $p. < .1072$, partial $r^2 = .5860$; and, item 14, "The counselor encouraged me to discuss feelings I might have toward him/her during the sessions," $F = 2.269$, $p. < .1107$, partial $r^2 = .5850$.

In the validation group on which the first discriminant function was derived, all variables but item 14 had varying degrees of a linear relationship with satisfaction. The relationship of item 14 scores with satisfaction scores was more variable than was the relationship of other CSI items with satisfaction as indicated by the correlations of all items with item 16. The mean item 14 rating by satisfaction ratings 1 through 10 for the entire sample is presented in Table 3.9. Thus, it appears that for some clients perceiving the counselor to be somewhat (a rating of approximately 4) encouraging of the discussion of feelings the client might have toward the counselor was associated with satisfaction while for other clients it was associated with an extreme lack of satisfaction. Yet the highest satisfaction ratings (9 and 10) were associated with the highest ratings (8 and 7 respectively) on counselor encouraged discussion of feelings the client might have toward the counselor (item 14). As indicated by the large standard deviations for item 14 mean ratings at the extremes of the satisfaction rating continuum, item 14 ratings were quite variable even for clients giving the same satisfaction ratings. In a *post hoc* attempt to understand this pattern it was hypothesized that clients giving higher item 14 ratings and lower satisfaction ratings would have attended fewer sessions and thus the "relationship with the therapist," "transference," or "immediacy" aspects of treatment had been introduced prematurely that is, prior to the establishment of a relationship with the therapist adequate to tolerate such an examination.

A review of the correlations of item 14 with satisfaction ratings by number of sessions attended showed a strong, significant correlation for clients attending one session ($r = .47758$, $p. < .0028$, $n = 37$) and for clients attending three sessions ($r = .68132$, $p. < .0370$, $n = 11$). Correlations for clients attending two sessions ($r = .17862$, $p. < .4385$, $n = 21$), four sessions ($r = .09461$, $p. < .8237$, $n = 8$), five sessions ($r = .94491$,

TABLE 3.9

MEANS AND STANDARD DEVIATIONS
FOR ITEM 14 BY SATISFACTION RATING
FOR ALL CLIENTS COMBINED

Satisfaction Rating (Item 16)	Item 14 Mean	Item 14 SD	n
1	3.25	3.24	8
2	2.67	1.53	3
3	2.25	1.5	4
4	2.6	2.61	5
5	3.11	2.71	9
6	6.5	3.02	6
7	3.07	2.25	15
8	4.1	2.88	10
9	8	1.5	9
10	7	3.46	17

*3 clients did not respond to item 16,
 6 did not respond to item 14, and
 1 did not respond to item 14 and item 16.

$p. < .2123, n = 3$) and six sessions ($r = .68584, p. < .2011, n = 5$), however, were not statistically significant. Thus, there was no apparent trend showing a stronger positive correlation of item 14 with satisfaction as the number of sessions attended increased. It appears likely, therefore, that the number of sessions attended is by itself inadequate to determine the likelihood of client satisfaction being increased or decreased by the counselor encouraging the client to discuss feelings about the counselor. However, a review of the correlations of item 14 with satisfaction by number of sessions attended by the gender/age groupings was more revealing.

For female clients 18 to 22 years of age coming to only one session the ratings of satisfaction correlated with item 14 ratings ($r = .54414, p. < .0546, n = 13$) more strongly than for males of that age group ($r = .21902, p. < .6370, n = 7$) attending one session. Yet, females in this age group attending one session had a mean satisfaction rating of 4.64 ($SD = 3.27$) and a mean item 14 rating of 3.46 ($SD = 3.04$) whereas the males in that age group attending one session had a mean satisfaction rating of 7.75 (SD = 2.69) and a mean item 14 rating of 4.63 (SD = 3.25).

For females 23 and older attending one session the relationship between item 14 and satisfaction was slightly negative (r = $-.02843$, $p.$ < .9421, n = 9). Nevertheless, their mean satisfaction rating was 7.70 (SD = 2.75) while the mean item 14 rating was 5.50 (SD = 3.50). In contrast, for the males in the 23 years and older age group attending one session the correlation was the strongest and most significant of all groups (r = .87106, $p.$ < .0049, n = 8). The mean satisfaction rating was 7.11 (SD = 3.33) and mean item 14 rating 4.63 (SDS = 3.66).

Thus, for males 23 and older attending one session, client reported counselor encouragement to discuss feelings the client might have about the counselor was highly related to satisfaction such that more perceived encouragement to do so was related to more satisfaction. This was also true, but less so, for females 18 to 22 years old attending one session while for males 18 to 22 and females 23 and older there was no significant relationship between satisfaction and counselor encouragement for the client to discuss feelings about the counselor.

None of the correlations between item 14 and satisfaction by gender/age group for clients attending two sessions were statistically significant at the $p.$ < .05 level. They were as follows: females 18 to 22 (r = .57696, $p.$ < .2306, n = 6), females 23 and older (r = $-.94491$, $p.$ < .2123, n = 3) and males 23 and older (r = $-.94491$, $p.$ < .2123, and n = 3). For females 18 to 22 attending three sessions the correlation was strong but did not reach the $p.$ < .05 level (r = .67102, $p.$ < .0989, n = 7). Yet for this same gender/age group attending four sessions the correlation was negative (r = $-.31009$, $p.$ < .6116, n = 5). Since only 2 males in the 18 to 22 age group attended three sessions, and 2 attended four sessions while another 2 attended six sessions, correlations were not calculated, but the mean ratings for satisfaction and item 14 indicated that higher ratings on satisfaction were associated with higher ratings on item 14. Means were as follows for males 18 to 22 years of age: three sessions, satisfaction M = 3.00 (SD = 1.41); item 14 M = 4.24 (SD = 0); four sessions, satisfaction M = 8.5 (SD = .71); item 14 M = 7.5 (SD = .71); and six sessions, satisfaction M = 7.5 (SD = 2.12); item 14 M = 8.5 (SD = 2.12).

For the 2 females 23 and older attending three sessions the mean satisfaction rating was also 6.5 (SD = 4.95) and the mean item 14 rating was 6.5 (SD = 4.95). These standard deviations were notably large. For the 2 males 23 and older attending six sessions the satisfaction mean of

8.00 (*SD* = 2.83) exceeded the item 14 mean of 5.00 (*SD* = 5.66). Again, the standard deviation indicates high intersubject variability. Thus, taking into account gender, age, and number of sessions attended, it appears that an early (even in the first session) introduction by the counselor of the counselor's openness to hearing whatever the client would like to discuss with regard to feelings the client might have about the counselor (and presumably the counselors' intervention) may assist client satisfaction especially with males 23 and older and females 18 to 22, but it may have a negative effect with females 23 and older.

Gender of the therapist may be another interacting variable. For example, it was found that females 23 years of age and older were less satisfied with male (vs. female) therapists. It is possible that client gender and age may interact with therapist gender and/or experience level with regard to the counselor encouraging the client to share feelings about the counselor. However, taking together the variable correlations of satisfaction with item 14 for all clients combined across number of sessions attended, the correlations of satisfaction with item 14 by the gender/age groups regardless of the number of sessions attended and the small *n*'s when the data is viewed by gender/age x number of sessions attended, it appears that it would be erroneous to form conclusions about the relationship of counselor encouraged discussion of the client's feelings about the counselor with satisfaction by gender, age, or number of sessions attended. It can be said that this variable is less consistently related to satisfaction and that it seems likely that it may in certain contexts negatively influence satisfaction.

Given these variable findings it seems likely that other factors or interactions not accounted for here influenced the relationship of item 14 and satisfaction. Such factors might include the manner in which the client thought the counselor would respond to a remark that could be taken as critical, for example, the client expressing a wish that the counselor be either more or less verbally active. Further, the client's assessment of the counselor's intention in encouraging a discussion of feelings about the counselor might be a moderating variable. It is understandable that a female 23 or older might be more uncomfortable with such a discussion with a male counselor/therapist who is older than she but not old enough to be easily seen in a fatherly role. Yet, a female 18 to 22 may be more likely to see the same older male counselor/therapist as a benign fatherly type and feel comfortable with the therapist asking her to share feelings about him should any occur. In this case it is obviously important whether the father-aged male is in general felt by the client to be benign.

The findings with regard to item 14 are reminiscent of findings in an earlier study (Talley, Roy, and Moorman, 1986) that found a highly significant and strongly positive correlation between satisfaction with services received and the counselor/therapist encouraging the client to relate current concerns to past experiences with the family of origin for males 18 to 22 years of age. The correlation between these same two variables for males 23 and older was extremely weak and far from statistical significance. Further, there was a positive correlation between these two variables that approached statistical significance for females 23 and older that was not found for females 18 to 22 years of age. A strong, significant and positive correlation was found for males between the ages of 18 and 22 between their rating on an item worded, "at times talking about my situation was uncomfortable" and the satisfaction rating. Again, no such relationship between the two items was found for males 23 and older. There was a negative correlation between this item and satisfaction for females between the ages of 18 and 22 although it did not reach statistical significance at the *p.* < .05 level and a positive but nonsignificant relationship between these two variables was found for females 23 and older (Talley, Roy, and Moorman, 1986).

The variables of counselor encouragement to relate current concerns to past experiences with the family of origin and at times feeling that talking about the situation was uncomfortable for the client might be considered aspects of an insight-oriented, anxiety-provoking, more psychodynamically-oriented treatment as might the item in the present study referring to the counselor encouraging the client to express feelings about the counselor to the counselor. The variable correlation for these items with satisfaction that seemed to be in part a function of gender and age group suggest a hypothesis that might be tested in future studies. Specifically, it appears that some psychodynamically-oriented, anxiety-provoking techniques aiming toward insight may not be as associated with satisfaction for very brief psychotherapy as the more supportive aspects of the treatment such as encouragement that the situation can improve. Gender/age group may be a moderating variable as encouragement was highly correlated with satisfaction for all gender/age groups. However, in this investigation, counselor solicited expression of feelings the client had about the counselor to the counselor was significantly correlated with satisfaction only for females 18 to 22 years of age. Yet in our earlier study (Talley, Roy, and Moorman, 1986) females 18 to 22 years of age were found to associate feeling uncomfortable at times and relating current concerns to past experiences in the family of origin less with satisfaction than the other gender/age groups. Still, encouragement by the counselor that the client can improve the situation seems by far more predictive of satisfaction for all gender/age groups than do other variables.

Correlations of Client Satisfaction Index Items with Dysphoria Percent Change Scores by Gender/Age Group

Correlation matrices of the CSI items 1 through 16 and BDI, SAS, SDS, VAS–A, and VAS–D percent change scores by each of the four gender/age groups showed that for females 18 to 22 years of age CSI item 14, "The counselor encouraged me to discuss any feelings I might have about him/her during the session," correlated significantly and negatively with SAS percent change scores ($r = -.37499$, $p. < .0345$, $n = 32$). A correlation approaching but falling short of significance at the $p. < .05$ level was also obtained for item 14 and the VAS–D percent change score ($r = -.36846$, $p. < .0586$, $n = 27$).

For males in the 18 to 22-year-old age group CSI item 7, "I accomplished what I had hoped to by coming to CAPS," correlated significantly in the positive direction with SDS percent change score ($r = .49031$, $p. < .0457$, $n = 17$), and the correlation of CSI item 7 with percent change score on the SAS approached significance at the $p. < .05$ level ($r = .47339$, $p. < .0549$, $n = 17$). Significant correlations were found between CSI item 11, "My methods of dealing with the problems I face have changed as a result of coming," and percent change score on the SDS ($r = .66759$, $p. < .0034$, $n = 17$), and the SAS ($r = .68056$, $p. < .0026$, $n = 17$).

For females 23 and older significant correlations were found between CSI item 16, "In summary, I am satisfied with the services I received," and VAS–A percent change score ($r = .64894$, $p. < .0423$, $n = 10$) and between CSI item 16 and VAS–D percent change score ($r = .72007$, $p. < .0125$, $n = 11$).

For males 23 and older no correlations of CSI items and percent change scores reached significance at the $p. < .05$ level.

Client Satisfaction Index Process Variables
Predictive of Symptom Improvement

Three stepwise regression analyses were done to determine which Client Satisfaction Index (CSI) process variables were significant predictors of the BDI, SAS, and SDS percent change scores. Process variables included all CSI variables with the exception of those reflective of outcome such as item 1 (increased self-understanding), item 7 (accomplishing what was hoped for), item 12 (having become more certain of making good decisions), and item 16 (satisfaction with services received).

With regard to the BDI percent change score no CSI item emerged as a significant ($p. < .05$) predictor of BDI percent change score. Concerning the SAS a model emerged consisting of five predictors that resulted in a significant F value, $F(5, 61) = 3.76, p. < .0050$. These five items accounted for 23.56 percent of the variance in percent change scores on the Zung Self-rating Anxiety Scale. The five items included item 14 (counselor encouragement to discuss feelings the client might have about the counselor), item 15 (the counselor appearing skilled), item 9 (the counselor seeming to be a warm person), item 10 (counselor encouragement that the client could improve the situation), and item 4 (feeling comfortable with the counselor). Table 3.10 summarizes the *Beta* weight values, partial r^2's, F values, and probability values for these five variables.

The stepwise regression analysis to predict percent change score for the SDS resulted in a model consisting of two items. The model was significant, $F(2, 64) = 5.15, p. < .0084$, and the two significant predictors were item 14 (counselor encouragement to discuss feelings about the counselor), $F(1, 65) = 5.82, p. < .0186$, partial $r^2 = .0822$, *Beta* weight $= -.03271584$, and item 8 (counselor assisted breaking up the problem into smaller parts), $F(2, 64) = 4.19, p. < .0449$, partial $r^2 = .0564$, *Beta* weight $= .02250411$.

It is interesting to note that counselor encouragement to discuss feelings about the counselor was weighted negatively in the equation predicting percent change score for both the SDS and the SAS and that, oddly, feeling comfortable with the counselor was negatively weighted in the equation for percent change on the SAS as was perceiving the counselor to be a warm person. The weighting of these latter two items negatively seems at variance with both theory and with their relation to client satisfaction as reported in this chapter. However, counselor encouragement to discuss feelings about the counselor has been associated with

TABLE 3.10

CLIENT SATISFACTION INDEX PROCESS VARIABLE
PREDICTORS OF ZUNG SELF-RATING ANXIETY
SCALE PERCENT CHANGE SCORE FOR
ALL CLIENTS COMBINED

	Beta Weight	F	p	partial r^2
Item 4	-0.0212792	2.64	0.1095	0.0331
Item 9	-0.03328452	3.64	0.0611	0.0368
Item 10	0.02796719	5.5	0.0223	0.0549
Item 14	0.02411797	6.22	0.0154	0.0329
Item 15	0.05514381	9.1	0.0037	0.078

negative satisfaction ratings at least with some clients as also reported in this study. Further, differences in response to treatment do not appear to be consistent entirely with what might be expected from theory. Perhaps those with more anxiety felt less comfortable with the counselor and that the counselor was less warm because of their greater anxiety. This same greater measured anxiety at the time of initial testing would allow for a greater percent change score in pre- vs. posttreatment measures. Moreover, the individual F, p. and partial r^2 scores for these two variables were the smallest in the model and did not reach the $p. < .05$ level themselves. Perceived counselor skill and counselor encouragement that the client could improve the current situation were positively associated with measured anxiety reduction while perceived counselor warmth and feeling comfortable with the counselor were negatively weighted as predictors of anxiety reduction. Counselor encouragement to discuss feelings the client might have about the counselor was positively weighted with regard to predicted anxiety reduction as measured by the SAS but negatively weighted with regard to predicted reduction of depressive symptoms as measured by the SDS. Counselor assisted breaking of the problem into smaller parts was positively weighted with regard to predicted reduction of depressive symptoms.

Reported Improvement in Academic and Social Functioning and Percentages Seeking Further Treatment Elsewhere

Concerning self-rated change, or lack of change, following counseling with regard to academic performance, males reported a greater net gain percentage (percent "better" minus percent "worse") than did females. Reported net gains by gender/age group were as follows: females 18 to 22 ($n = 32$), 25 percent net gain; males 18 to 22 ($n = 21$), 34 percent net gain; females 23 and older ($n = 16$), 13 percent net gain; males 23 and older ($n = 13$), net gain 38 percent. A Chi Square test comparing males of all ages to females of all ages by grouping those who responded to the item as "same" with those responding "worse" such that there were two categories ("better" and "not better") indicated that 28.30 percent of the females and 44.44 percent of the males reported a "better" academic performance. The difference between the males and the females appears noteworthy, but did not reach statistical significance, X^2 (1, 81) = 2.461, $p. < .117$.

With regard to self-ratings comparing the quality of the client's relationships with others prior to the intervention and afterward, net gains (percent "better" minus percent "worse") were as follows: females 18 to 22 ($n = 33$), 55 percent net gain; males 18 to 22 ($n = 21$), 52 percent net gain; females 23 and older ($n = 17$), 23 percent net gain; and males 23 and older ($n = 14$), 50 percent net gain. A Chi Square, X^2 (1, 84) = .518, $p. < .472$ comparing the two genders revealed no statistically significant differences by gender. Nevertheless, males 23 and older reported more than twice the net gain percentage as did females in that age group.

With regard to seeking further treatment elsewhere (item 17); 29 percent of the males 23 and older did so at the recommendation of the counselor as did 27 percent of the males 18 to 22 years old while only 18 percent of the females in each age group did so. Further, 14 percent of the older males and 5 percent of the younger males reported seeking additional treatment on their own in contrast to none of the females in the older age group and only 3 percent of the younger age females doing so. Thus, males of both age groups, although on the whole giving higher satisfaction ratings than females, nevertheless, were more likely to seek further services. Moreover, of clients attending four, five, or six sessions, a greater percentage (56.96 percent, $n = 16$) accepted a referral for further treatment than did those who attended one, two, or three sessions

(12 percent, n = 74). One of the two clients attending seven sessions acknowledged accepting a recommendation for further treatment.

SUMMARY AND CONCLUSIONS

From the present data it appears that very brief psychotherapy as defined by lasting from between one to seven (inclusive) sessions was received by its consumers as on the whole "quite satisfactory." This finding is in accord with the conclusions of Howard et al. (1986) with regard to the first seven sessions of psychotherapy. Further, the more sessions within the one to seven session range the client attended the more likely it was for the client to give a higher rating for satisfaction with the treatment. All of the components of counseling listed on the present Client Satisfaction Index were highly correlated with satisfaction with the exception of the counselor encouraging the client to share feelings the client might have about the counselor with the counselor. This variable appeared to be associated with satisfaction for some clients but not for others. Females between the ages of 18 and 22 attending only one session felt somewhat less satisfied with services received than did clients in the other gender/age groups.

Satisfaction ratings were significantly and inversely related to the severity level on the Beck Depression Inventory completed prior to the first session for females 18 to 22 years of age. This is consistent with the findings of Steinmetz et al. (1983) that BDI score at intake is a good predictor of outcome and the findings of Rounsaville et al. (1981). Further, the findings of Luborsky et al. (1979), Kernberg et al. (1972) concerning ego strength, Barron (1953), and Kirtner and Cartwright (1958) concerning initial level of disturbance appear consistent with our finding regarding BDI score at intake. However, no significant correlation between satisfaction and the BDI, the Zung SAS or the Zung SDS was found for any of the other gender/age groups. Other individual items from the BDI, SDS, and SAS that were predictive of subsequent satisfaction with services were identified by gender/age group. The Client Satisfaction Index when factor analyzed showed two principal factors both relating to client satisfaction in general that accounted for over 73 percent of the variance in scores thus suggesting that this is a viable instrument to measure satisfaction with very brief psychotherapy.

Differences by age and gender were also found on the variables of perceived counselor authenticity, feeling comfortable with the counselor, the counselor seeming to be warm and the counselor seeming to be skilled. However, no significant differences in satisfaction were attributed to the effects of age or gender. The conclusions of Balch et al. (1977), Denner and Halprin (1974), Feifel and Eells (1963), Larsen (1978), and Larsen et al. (1979) are in agreement with this finding of no significant differences by age. The present finding of no significant satisfaction differences by gender is consistent with the conclusions of Hibbs (1976), Larsen (1978), Balch et al. (1977), Denner and Halprin (1974), Frank, Salzman, and Fergus (1977), Heubush and Horan (1977) and Scher (1975) and in contrast to the finding of Bugge, Hendel and Moen (1985) who found that females were more satisfied than males with psychotherapeutic services. For the most part females between the ages of 18 and 22 who attended only one session gave lower ratings on these variables, and further, a higher percentage of females in this age group attended only one session than was the case for any other gender/age group.

No statistically significant differences in client satisfaction were found to be due to therapist gender, therapist experience, or therapist gender x experience interaction. However, some trends appeared that might suggest hypotheses for future investigations. This finding with regard to therapist experience level is consistent with conclusions of earlier studies (Feifel and Eells, 1963; Frank et al., 1977). The present finding of no significant satisfaction differences by gender of therapist is contrary to the finding of Jones et al. (1987) who found that patients who had female therapists reported more symptom improvement as well as more satisfaction with treatment. However, as noted in Chapter II, the preponderance of the data concerning the effects of therapist gender on outcome suggest that therapist gender does not significantly affect outcome although all of the studies assessing outcome reported have not measured client/patient satisfaction with treatment.

With regard to length of treatment, although the MANOVA testing for a main effect due to length of treatment revealed that the overall effects due to length of treatment were not significant at the $p. < .05$ level (i.e., $p. = . 08$). An examination of the means shows that clients attending four to seven sessions gave higher satisfaction ratings than those attending one to three sessions and that for females 18 to 22 years of age there was a strong positive and significant correlation between satisfaction rating and number of sessions attended. Thus, our findings suggest the possibility that differences between earlier studies with regard to satisfaction and length of treatment may be due to the span of time or duration of treatment under study (weeks *vs.* months *vs.* years) and the gender and age groups under investigation. Our findings showed a positive but not statistically significant relationship between length of treatment and client satisfaction for all clients combined. Again, a significant relationship for females 18 to 22 years of age was found between length of treatment and client satisfaction.

Thus, our results differ from Luborsky et al. (1971) and Orlinsky and Howard (1976) who found a significant positive relationship between length of therapy and outcome. The present findings are perhaps more in agreement with the findings of Denner and Halprin (1974), Larsen et al. (1979), Talley, Roy, and Moorman (1986), and Dyck and Azim (1983) who concluded that length of treatment does not have a significant effect on client satisfaction. Of course, another source of differences may be the types of measures employed such that some, but not all, other outcome measures may correlate strongly and significantly with some but not all client satisfaction measures.

The treatment process factors as measured by the Client Satisfaction Index items that predicted satisfaction with treatment and dysphoria percent change scores were reported, and most notably the factor of counselor encouragement that the client could improve the situation accounted for the bulk of the variance. There was some variability with regard to other factors predicting satisfaction rating by gender/age group. Other factors included the counselor appearing warm, skilled and understanding and the counselor helping the client understand prior means of dealing with frustration, feeling comfortable with the counselor and counselor assisted breaking the problem into smaller parts. Discriminant function analyses yielded for the most part the same conclusions as did the stepwise regression analyses. Most notably the salience of counselor encouragement that the client could improve the situation was again apparent. Client satisfaction with services was not consistently related to percent change scores on the psychometric instruments utilized.

Chapter IV

THE EFFECTS OF SAMPLE GROUP AND GENDER ON THE ZUNG SELF-RATING DEPRESSION AND ANXIETY SCALES AND THE BECK DEPRESSION INVENTORY ITEM AND TOTAL SCORES

Joseph E. Talley, Lisa D. Hinz, Melinda A. Maguire,
and John C. Barrow

REVIEWS OF THE LITERATURE

The Zung Self-rating Depression Scale

The Zung Self-rating Depression Scale (SDS) was developed from research interest in sleep disturbances associated with depression (Zung, 1965). It is a twenty-item self-report inventory that reliably measures the psychological and physical symptoms of depression (McKegney, Aronson, and Ooi, 1988; Zung, 1965; 1967). Factor analysis studies have demonstrated the construct validity of the SDS. Factors identified repeatedly have confirmed its sensitivity to the affective, cognitive, and somatic symptoms of depression (Bolon and Barling, 1980; Giambra, 1977; Kivela and Pahkala, 1987; Steuler, Rank, Olsen, and Jarvik, 1980). The inventory is a paper and pencil test that also has been demonstrated to be valid when administered verbally (Griffin and Kogut, 1988).

Respondents to the SDS rate the frequency of depressive features on a four-point scale indicating the presence or absence of symptoms from: 1 (none or a little of the time), to 4 (most or all of the time). Total scores are related to symptom severity, with a score of fifty serving as the cutoff score for clinically significant depression. Norms are available for converting SDS raw scores into categories representing different levels of symptom severity. The SDS has been used as the criterion measure for indicating the presence of Major Depressive Disorder when studying the presence of biological markers associated with the disorder (Friedman, Stolk, Harris, and Cooper, 1984; Maes, DeRuyter, Claes, and Suy, 1988; Ward, Bloom, Dworkin, Fawcett, Narsimhachari, and Friedel, 1982).

In addition, the SDS has demonstrated adequate sensitivity and excellent specificity in distinguishing clinically depressed from nondepressed individuals (McNair, 1974; Turner and Romano, 1984; Zung, 1973a), patients with endogenous from nonendogenous patterns of depressive symptomatology (White, White, and Razani, 1984), and patients with depression from those with other psychiatric diagnoses (Turner and Romano, 1984).

Age and gender differences in severity of depression and presence of specific depressive symptoms have been demonstrated in SDS scores. These score differences seem to represent real life differences in depression in the elderly, and differences between males and females. Females have consistently received higher total SDS scores than males, and elderly females have been shown to be more likely to suffer from somatic symptoms of depression (Berry, Storandt, and Coyne, 1984; Byrne, Doyle, and Pritchard, 1977; Knight, Waal-Manning, and Spears, 1983; Merz and Ballmer, 1984; Zetin, Sklansky, and Cramer, 1984).

The SDS has been demonstrated to have good predictive validity as a screening measure of depression (Agrell and Dehlin, 1989; Biggs, Wylie, and Ziegler, 1978; Schaefer, et al., 1985; Zung, 1967). Using the SDS, the incidence of depression in the general population has been estimated to be between 15 and 20 percent and is believed to be vastly under diagnosed without the application of some sort of diagnostic aid, especially in the elderly (Bradshaw and Parker, 1983; Kukull, Koepgell, Inui, Borson, Okimoto, Rasking, and Gale, 1986; Zung, Magill, Moore, and George, 1983). The SDS is recommended for use as a screening measure in general medical populations as an adjunct to clinical judgment in making diagnoses. The presence of the screening instrument as a diagnostic aid helps general practitioners or family practitioners better care for their patients by discovering and/or confirming in patients a psychiatric diagnosis. Thus, primary care providers are better prepared to refer for psychiatric/psychological treatment (Bradshaw and Parker, 1983; Ihezue and Kumaraswamy, 1986; Rosenthal, Goldfarb, Carlson, Sagi, and Balaban, 1987; Zung, Magill, Moore, and George, 1983).

The validity of the SDS has been tested and proven in many different languages and countries (Auslander, Levav, and Nachmani, 1988; Bennett, 1986; Byrne, 1980; Chang, 1985; Fukuda and Kobayashi, 1975; Ihezue and Kumaraswamy, 1986; Jegede, 1976; Master and Zung, 1977; Matsubara, 1985; Rhee and Shin, 1978; Schnurr, Hoaken, and Jarrett, 1976; Zung,

1969). Indeed, over the years, the SDS seems to have become a standard in psychiatric research against which new instruments are validated (DeForge and Sobel, 1988; Dunn and Sacco, 1989; Hickie and Snowdon, 1987).

The instrument is probably most often used in psychiatric research as an outcome measure in medication or psychotherapy trials. That is, it is used to determine the presence or absence of depression before and after some sort of psychotherapeutic intervention. The SDS has been used to determine the efficacy of self-help programs (Neumann, 1981), electro-convulsive shock therapy (Cohen, Penick, and Tarter, 1974), various psychological therapies (Hodgson, 1981; Lambert, Hatch, Kingston, and Edwards, 1986; Riedel, Fenwick, and Jillings, 1986), and to determine the effectiveness of therapeutic dosages of various pharmacological treatments for depression (Burrows, Foenander, Davies, and Scoggins, 1976; DeMaio and Levi-Minzi, 1979; Ehrensing and Kastin, 1978; Gardner, 1983; Lapierre and Butter, 1978; Mukherjee and Davey, 1986; Pishkin et al., 1978; White, Pistole, and Boyd, 1980; Ziegler, Clayton, Taylor, Tee, and Biggs, 1976).

It has been used with diverse treatment populations including hospitalized depressed patients (White, Pistole, and Boyd, 1980), depressed outpatients (Burrows, Foenender, Davies, and Scoggins, 1976), alcoholics (Equi and Jabara, 1976), the elderly (McKegney, Aronson, and Ooi, 1988; Zung and Zung, 1986), the general population (Cooke, 1980; Zung, 1972b), the physically injured (Crosby, 1969), and medical populations (O'Leary, Shoor, Lorig, and Holman, 1988; Shaw and Ehrlich, 1987). It has been used to determine the psychiatric status of patients following various medical procedures such as coronary bypass surgery (Sokol, Folks, Herrick, and Freeman, 1987). The SDS has also been used to explore and explain depressive symptomatology experienced in college student populations (Hodgson, 1981; Ivanoff, Layman, and von Singer, 1973).

In summary, The Zung Self-rating Depression Scale is an easily administered, readily scored self-report inventory of depressive symptomatology that has shown an impressive range of application largely in psychiatric research. It is reported to be a highly reliable and valid measure that for some is the standard by which new instruments are currently validated.

The Zung Self-rating Anxiety Scale

Like the SDS, the Zung Self-rating Anxiety Scale (SAS) is a twenty-item, self-report screening measure. It was designed to assess the psychological and physical manifestations of anxiety (Zung, 1971a). However, unlike the Zung Self-Rating Depression Scale which has been the subject of a vast amount of research, investigations of the SAS are limited. Depression and anxiety often have been investigated together and some would say that there is not sufficient evidence to demonstrate that the two are distinct syndromes (Zung, 1971b; 1973b). However, other studies have clearly shown that although depression and anxiety often coexist, they can be reliably discriminated with the SDS and SAS (Knight, Waal-Manning, and Godfrey, 1983).

The SAS uses the same four-point format for assessing the frequency of anxiety symptoms and it has demonstrated excellent internal consistency and good reliability in assessing anxiety disorders (Zung, 1971a). Norms are provided that categorize the different levels of anxiety (Zung, 1971a; 1971b). The construct validity of the SAS has been confirmed by correlating scores obtained on it with scores from other established measures of anxiety (Zung, 1971a; 1974).

In addition, the SAS has demonstrated significant specificity in differentiating anxiety patients from those with other diagnoses (Zung, 1971b). The SAS has been used as an outcome measure in psychiatric research designed to determine the most effective psychological (McFarlain, Mielke, and Gallant, 1976; Woodward and Jones, 1980) or pharmacological treatment(s) for anxiety disorders (deJonghe, Swinkels, Tuynman-Qua, and Jonkers, 1989; Fabre, McLendon, and Mallette, 1979; Lapierre and Lee, 1976; Mukherjee and Davey, 1986; Zung, 1973b). In addition, the SAS has been used in studies examining the presence of biological markers for anxiety (Edlund and Swann, 1989; Friedman, Stolk, Harris, and Cooper, 1984).

The construct validity of the SAS has been studied in different countries (Jegede, 1977), and with various patient populations. For example, out-patients with anxiety disorders (Fabre, McLendon, and Mallette, 1979; Woodward and Jones, 1980; Zung, 1973b), inpatients with anxiety disorders (Zung, 1971a), alcoholics (McFarlain, Mielke, and Gallant, 1976), medical patients (Garcia-Oyola and Curioso, 1989), and family practice patients (Zung, 1986) have been studied. It also has been adapted for use with mentally retarded persons (Lindsay and Michie, 1988).

Thus, the Zung Self-rating Anxiety Scale is a simply administered, simply scored, self-report inventory that reliably distinguishes anxious from nonanxious subjects. It has been used as an outcome measure in psychiatric research and is available for more widespread use.

The Beck Depression Inventory

The Beck Depression Inventory (BDI) is a twenty-one item self-report instrument designed to measure depth or intensity of depression as a symptom. It was neither conceptualized nor designed to be a tool for diagnosing subtypes of mood disorder (Beck, Ward, Mendelson, Mock, and Erbaugh, 1961; Kendall, Hollon, Beck, Hammen, and Ingram, 1987). Subjects are asked to rate each of twenty-one inventory items from zero to three in terms of level of depressive symptomatology. Norms are provided for categorizing depth of depression by the total score (i.e., none, mild, moderate, or severe). The BDI originally was designed as a clinician-administered technique but evolved into a self-administered inventory (Beck et al., 1961; Beck and Steer, 1984).

The BDI is probably the most widely used depression screening device. Its psychometric properties have been widely studied and are well proven (Beck and Beamesderfer, 1974; Beck and Steer, 1984; Beck et al., 1961). As a measure of intensity of depressive symptoms, the BDI has been found to correlate highly with both clinician ratings and patient self-ratings of depth of depression (Beck et al., 1961; Hammen, 1980). The BDI has proven extremely reliable in both test-retest situations and tests of internal consistency (Beck and Steer, 1984; Hatzenbuehler, Parpal, and Matthews, 1983). In addition, it has proven to be very sensitive to changes in depressive symptomatology over time (Beck et al., 1961).

A short form of the BDI containing thirteen of the original twenty-one items has been devised and validated with both clinical and nonclinical populations (Beck and Beck, 1972; Gould, 1982). The BDI short form has been found to be a reliable and sensitive screening device (Beck and Beck, 1972). However, Kendall et al. (1987) cautioned against the use of the BDI short form. They reported that the short form might yield less accurate scores than the original version.

The BDI was originally intended for use in general medical practice and family medical practice. Physicians in general practice were said to need a reliable, valid, and relatively simple screening device upon which to base referrals for psychiatric treatment (Beck and Beck, 1972).

The BDI is still used in many medical settings, but its use has burgeoned far beyond the waiting rooms of medical practitioners.

As noted earlier, the BDI is the most widely used self-administered depression scale in use today. It is used not only for screening in various clinical settings, but it is also used as a research criterion measure. As of 1984 there were over five-hundred published studies using the BDI as a measure of level of depression, and it has consistently demonstrated high levels of reliability and construct validity (Steer, Beck, and Garrison, 1986). Aside from the absolute number of studies employing the BDI, other evidence for its widespread use comes from the fact that BDI scores were used to calculate effect sizes in a meta-analytic study of the clinical significance of psychotherapy for unipolar depression (Nietzel, Russell, Hemmings, and Gretter, 1987). Therefore, it would seem to be sound research practice to include the BDI as a criterion or outcome measure in studies of the effectiveness of psychotherapy.

The BDI has often been used in studies of university student depression, either alone (Hammen and Padesky, 1977; Hatzenbuehler et al., 1983), or in combination with other assessment techniques (Beckham, 1989; Doerfler and Richards, 1983; Gotlib, 1984; Hammen, 1980; Oliver and Burkham, 1979; Vredenburg, O'Brien, and Krames, 1988). The BDI often has been used to describe the depth and other characteristics of the depressive experience of university students (Gotlib, 1984; Hammen, 1980; Hatzenbuehler, et al., 1983; Oliver and Burkham, 1979; Vredenburg, O'Brien, and Krames, 1988). There is some controversy about whether the depressive experience of university students is equivalent to that of adult populations. This concern is especially salient when students have been randomly selected for study participation from introductory psychology classes and have not presented themselves for psychological services (Gotlib, 1984; Hammen, 1980). Some researchers suggest that mild depression is "normal" in university students (Oliver and Burkham, 1979) and thus recommend using higher BDI scores as indicators of depression. Other investigators suggest that lower (Kendall, et al., 1987) or the usual (Bumberry, Oliver, and McClure, 1978) BDI norms should be used with university students.

Bumberry et al. (1978) attempted a validation of the BDI in a university population using psychiatric estimate of depth of depression as the criterion. Using only fifty-six subjects they found psychiatric estimate of depth of depression to correlate .77 with the BDI score (standard error = .14, $p. < .001$). It was found that distinguishing between the moderate and severe levels was problematic regarding agreement between psychiatric rating and BDI score but that using a cut-off score of ten on the BDI did distinguish between normal and depressed scores. Nevertheless, nine of the fifty-six students were still categorized differently by psychiatric ratings than the BDI. "Normals" were found to have a mean BDI score of 3.94 with a standard deviation of 4.46. This study used as subjects students presenting with a psychiatric referral from the student health service and other students who were randomly sampled. The sampling procedures and small *n* leave the results of this study questionable.

O'Neil and Marziali (1976) hypothesized that depressive symptoms are normative in the eighteen to twenty-two age group when people are faced with the difficult developmental tasks of (1) separation-individuation, (2) career choice, and (3) establishment of sexual and couple identity. The authors concluded that depressed mood is frequently experienced by both male and female postadolescents in the process of growing toward maturation. They added that it is important to differentiate students with depression accompanying developmental issues from those with mood disorders. The BDI will not accomplish this differential diagnosis. This is not a fault of the instrument as it was not designed to diagnose.

Gotlib (1984) administered the BDI and other psychological assessment instruments to a nonclinical sample of university students. In a very controversial statement, he suggested that in general, university students do not experience distinct psychiatric disorders, but rather they experience something that he stated "might best be labeled dysphoria, malaise, or general psychological distress" (p. 26). He added that *all* self-report instruments used in nonclinical samples, including the BDI measured general psychological distress rather than distinct psychiatric syndromes.

Because a majority of psychological research is carried out with university student subjects, researchers have questioned the generalizability of this data to other populations. Various levels of intensity of depression, from mild to severe, have been found using the BDI as the criterion measure in university student populations (Hammen, 1980; Hatzenbuehler et al., 1983). However, it has also been found that elevated BDI scores in university samples (and community samples) are not always associated with mood disorders, nor are they always stable over time (e.g., two to three weeks). It has been hypothesized that this lack of consistency is due to the BDI's inability to distinguish stable from unstable depressive subtypes with most of the change in scores coming from the unstable depressed subjects (Hammen, 1980). It also seems likely that changes in scores, especially decreases in high scores, may be due to regression toward the mean that always must be accounted for in test/retest situations due to the diminishing of transient depressed states.

Hatzenbuehler et al. (1983) proposed that the revised BDI and BDI instructions (Beck and Steer, 1984) that require subjects to rate their depressive symptoms over the previous week would reduce some instability of scores. Hatzenbuehler et al. (1983) suggested that investigators might use two different assessment techniques, one pre and one post, in order to reduce retesting effects. In a review of three depression inventories, Lambert and his colleagues (1986) found that contrary to previous reports, the BDI showed significantly less change in depression scores following treatment than did other measures. Nonetheless, investigators are cautioned about instability of BDI scores when using them as an outcome measure in research on the effects of psychotherapy.

Hammen and Padesky (1977) used a large, nonclinical sample of university student BDI scores in a discriminant function analysis in order to determine whether or not gender differences in depression existed between the two groups. The investigators found that *depth* of depression did not show gender differences, but that the *pattern* of depressive symptoms did show significant differences. They explained that the pattern of depressive symptoms was not simply a function of larger male/female differences in the total population. Hammen and Padesky (1977) found that depressed males (a BDI score of 15 or greater) were less likely than females to cry, more likely to demonstrate social withdrawal, to manifest a sense of failure, and to demonstrate somatic symptoms. Depressed females were more likely than males to demonstrate indecisiveness, and self dislike. The authors concluded that the patterns in the depressed males and females appeared not to be an extension of gender stereotyped responding but rather reflected real gender differences in the expression of depressive symptomatology.

Hammen and Padesky's (1977) results are in contrast to those of Berry, Storandt, and Coyne (1984) who found greater depth of depression in females than in males, and no differences in pattern of depression between younger males and females in a volunteer community sample. Pattern differences found were among elderly, but not younger depressed persons. In addition, Kashani and Priesmeyer (1983) found that one-third of a clinical sample of college students requesting psychological services was diagnosed as depressed by DSM–III criteria. These authors also found no significant gender differences in type or pattern of symptoms reported by male and female university-age students. Other researchers also using the BDI with nonclinical university samples have not found significant gender differences in either depth of depression or pattern of depressive symptoms (Oliver and Burkham, 1979; Robbins and Tanck, 1984).

In comparison, some studies of clinical samples of university students have found females more likely to demonstrate depression or deeper levels of depression than males (O'Neil and Marziali, 1976). The evidence of gender differences in depth and pattern of depressive symptoms is mixed. There seems to be a trend for differences to be expressed only in clinical samples and not in nonclinical samples, although it is not entirely a clear trend. More research is necessary in order to clarify possible gender differences in depressive symptomatology among persons of university age.

The BDI has frequently been used as a criterion measure of change in studies examining the effectiveness of various psychotherapeutic interventions (Persons, Burns, and Perloff, 1988; Schmidt and Miller, 1983; Schneider and Agras, 1985). Usually the BDI is used in combination with other outcome measures that corroborate its effectiveness as a sensitive measure of change. For example, Schneider and Agras (1985) investigated the effectiveness of cognitive-behavioral group psychotherapy with bulimic clients. They used frequency of binge-purge episodes as the primary dependent variable indicating therapeutic change, but also used BDI scores as one secondary criterion measure of change. The investigators found that binge/purge frequency was dramatically reduced over the sixteen-week course of therapy, and that depth of depression also was significantly reduced.

In general, BDI total scores are compared pre- and post-treatment in order to assess the effectiveness of psychotherapeutic interventions or the amount of change in depressive symptomatology (Persons et al., 1988; Schmidt and Miller, 1983; Schneider and Agras, 1985). At times, total BDI scores for individual items (e.g., weight loss) have been correlated with treatment outcome (Hoberman, Lewinsohn, and Tilson, 1988; Parker, 1985; Persons et al., 1988). For example, Persons and her colleagues found that people with higher total BDI pretreatment scores were more likely to benefit from "homework assignments" given in the course of psychotherapy than were lower initial scorers. Hoberman et al. (1988) also found that, while controlling for regression effects, higher pretreatment level of depression (as indicated by higher total BDI score) was a significant predictor of positive treatment outcome.

The BDI has also been employed as a dependent variable in order to assess the differential effectiveness of various types of psychotherapy for depression (McLean and Hakstian, 1979; Shapiro, Sank, Shaffer, and Donovan, 1982). For example, Shapiro and colleagues (1982) compared the effectiveness of individual and group cognitive-behavioral therapy for depression in a community sample. They found both treatments to be equally effective and concluded that the group treatment would be more cost-effective in their particular setting. Other studies comparing different types of psychotherapies for the treatment of depression show no clear superiority of one treatment over another (McLean and Hakstian, 1979; Nietzel, Russell, Hemmings, and Gretter, 1987), although there is some evidence for the superiority of cognitive therapy (Dobson, 1989).

The BDI frequently has been used as an outcome measure in order to assess the effectiveness of psychotherapy with university students suffering from depressive symptoms (Beckham, 1989; Claiborn, Crawford, and Hackman, 1983; Doerfler and Richards, 1983; Gold, Jarvinen, and Teague, 1982; Propst, 1980). Many of these treatments or parameters of treatment have been found to be successful in reducing depressive symptoms as measured by the BDI. For instance, Gold, Jarvinen, and Teague (1982) investigated the usefulness of a guided imagery treatment in modifying college students' depression. The authors found that vividness of image (rated on a scale of one to ten) was significantly related to depression reduction. Other types of psychological treatment approaches also have been demonstrated effective using the BDI as a criterion measure of change (Beckham, 1989; Claiborn, Crawford, and Hackman, 1983; Doerfler, and Richards, 1983).

In summary, there exists a vast amount of clinical and research support for using the Beck Depression Inventory. The BDI has sound psychometric properties and a long history of use. The concept of depression in postadolescent populations has sometimes been controversial, but the BDI seems to be a sound instrument for assessing changes resulting from psychotherapeutic interventions.

The purpose of this portion of the study was to explore the effects of sample group and gender on the SDS, SAS, and BDI with samples of young adults. Previous studies with the Zung scales have more often been done with older age groups, inpatients, or with persons from other cultures. Previous studies with the BDI using young adult subjects have yielded mixed findings, utilized smaller samples, or used what might be seen as less fitting techniques of statistical analysis. The data utilized in this portion consisted of the first administration SDS, SAS, and BDI scores by all subjects who completed at least one of these measures as described in Chapter II of this volume.

RESULTS AND DISCUSSION

Gender and Sample Group Effects on the
Zung Self-rating Depression Scale

Repeated measures multivariate analyses of variance were done with the SDS, the SAS, and the BDI separately with individual item scores treated as multiple dependent variables in order to ascertain whether there were effects for scale (SDS items), scale × group interaction, scale × gender interaction, scale × group × gender interaction, and effects for group, gender, and group × gender interaction. The repeated measures model was chosen as there is an assumption within each scale that each item relates to every other item since they all measure some aspect of the underlying trait of either depression or anxiety; therefore, each item on the scale represents a repeated measure of the underlying trait. Because there were no BDI scores for the vocational group, only the clinical, random and medical samples were included in the analyses.

There was a significant multivariate overall main scale effect due to the SDS inventory items, $F(19, 511) = 89.44$, $p. < .0001$, such that there were significant differences among the individual items across all subjects regardless of gender or group indicating that each item of the SDS did not measure depression to the same degree. There was a significant multivariate scale × group interaction effect, $F(38, 1022) = 3.98$, $p. < .0001$, indicating that the magnitude of response on the individual SDS items varied by group membership such that the pattern of responses across the items differed by group. Thus, even if the total scores were the same, total scores by subjects from the different groups were to a significant degree accrued on different items. There was a significant multivariate scale × gender interaction effect, $F(19, 511) = 4.50$. $p. < .0001$, indicating that the magnitude of reponse on the individual SDS items varied by gender. (See Table 4.1 for specific items on which differences by group and/or gender occurred.) However, the overall multivariate effect due to scale × group × gender interaction was not statistically significant, $F(38, 1022) = .78$, $p. < .8228$. Therefore, these response differences on items that were affected by group membership showed no significant different effects by gender. The multivariate effects across all items combined for gender and gender × group interaction were not significant at the $p. < .05$ level; however, the effect for group membership was significant, $F(2, 532) = 53.52, p. < .0001$. Thus, across all items combined, males and females did not differ significantly, whereas the significant scale × gender interaction effect indicates that males and females did differ significantly with regard to the magnitude of elevation on individual items.

The dependent variables (i.e., the Zung Self-rating Depression Scale items) on which significant effects were found are summarized in Table 4.1. The clinical group had significantly higher scores than the random and medical groups on all items with the exceptions of diurnal variation (item 2), weight loss (item 7), constipation (item 8), and suicidal rumination (item 19). The clinical group had in addition the highest mean, although not significantly ($p. < .05$) higher, on these four items with the exception of weight loss. The medical group had a mean that was approximately equal to the mean of the clinical group on weight loss (item 7) and constipation (item 8).

Males and females responded differently with regard to diurnal variation, crying spells, decreased libido, constipation, and tiredness/fatigue such that the scores for diurnal variation indicated that males felt better than females in the morning and that females acknowledged more "crying spells or feeling like it" and more decreased libido as well as more trouble with constipation and more tiredness than did the males. Thus, it must be noted that particularly with a young population, differences on these items may be due to gender differences rather than due to a dysphoria characteristic of a group presenting for clinical services.

With regard to the effects of group and gender on the Zung Self-rating Depression Scale total score alone, an analysis of variance (ANOVA), $F(5, 530) = 24.57$, $p. < .0001$, showed a significant main effect due to group only, $F(2, 533) = 52.63$, $p. < .0001$. The mean score for the clinical group, ($M = 42.77, SD = 9.40$) was significantly higher than the mean score for the random group ($M = 34.59$, $SD = 8.65$) and significantly higher than the mean score for the medical group ($M = 33.61$, $SD = 6.62$). Although there were no significant differences in the total scores on the SDS by gender, the item analysis differences indicate that the total scores may be the result of accumulating points on different items by gender.

TABLE 4.1

SIGNIFICANT (p.<.05) FINDINGS FROM THE
REPEATED MEASURES MULTIVARIATE ANALYSIS OF VARIANCE OF
THE ZUNG SELF-RATING DEPRESSION SCALE ITEMS BY GROUP AND GENDER

	Univariate Overall F		Univariate Factor F			
			Gender		Group	
	df=5, 529		df=1, 533		df=2, 532	
	F	p	F	p	F	p
Item 1 Depressed Affect	23.6	0.0001	.	.	51.68	0.0001
Item 2 Diurnal Variation	2.6	0.0243	4.04	0.045	.	.
Item 3 Crying Spells	28.95	0.0001	23.59	0.0001	37.03	0.0001
Item 4 Sleep Disturbance	9.99	0.0001	.	.	20.00	0.0001
Item 5 Decreased Appetite	4.02	0.0014	.	.	9.39	0.0001
Item 6 Decreased Libido	6.29	0.0001	5.05	0.0251	9.79	0.0001
Item 8 Constipation	4.36	0.0007	4.59	0.0325	.	.
Item 9 Tachycardia	7.34	0.0001	.	.	14.21	0.0001
Item 10 Tiredness/Fatigue	6.29	0.0001	6.82	0.0093	10.78	0.0001
Item 11 Confusion	13.07	0.0001	.	.	28.59	0.0001
Item 12 Psychomotor Retardation	11.24	0.0001	.	.	26.69	0.0001
Item 13 Psychomotor Agitation	6.26	0.0001	.	.	10.02	0.0001
Item 14 Hopelessness	13.13	0.0001	.	.	28.86	0.0001
Item 15 Irritability	11.77	0.0001	.	.	24.57	0.0001
Item 16 Indecisiveness	12.32	0.0001	.	.	25.14	0.0001
Item 17 Personal Devaluation	7.71	0.0001	.	.	13.51	0.0001
Item 18 Emptiness	6.45	0.0001	.	.	12.56	0.0001
Item 20 Dissatisfaction	12.39	0.0001	.	.	26.52	0.0001

*No significant differences were found on
weight loss (item 7) and suicidal ideation (item 19).
Thus, they were omitted from the table.

Gender and Sample Group Effects on the
Zung Self-rating Anxiety Scale

A repeated measures multivariate analysis of variance indicated that there was a significant multivariate effect due to the scale, $F(19, 515)$ = 68.84, $p. < .0001$. Thus, like the SDS, individual items on the SAS did not measure anxiety to the same degree or were not sensitive at the same magnitude across all subjects. There was a significant scale × group interaction at the multivariate level, $F(38, 1030) = 3.27$, $p. < .0001$, showing again, as with the SDS, the pattern of items on which higher scores were manifested revealed a significant difference by group. There was a significant multivariate scale × gender interaction, $F(19, 515) = 1.93$, $p. < .0105$, suggesting that the pattern of responses by males differed from the pattern of responses by females in terms of the magnitude of response made on the individual items such that males tended to accrue their points on different items than did females. The overall pattern of items with higher scores was significantly different for males than for females. The multivariate scale × group × gender interaction effect was not significant, $F(38, 1030) = 1.04$, $p. < .4094$. The lack of a significant multivariate scale × gender × group interaction effect suggests that while the pattern of items with higher scores may differ by gender and by group, the differences by group were not significantly affected in a different way for females than for males. Therefore, the significant differences found between males and females were not significantly affected by whether they were in the clinical, random, or medical group although there were significant differences among these groups. There was a significant multivariate effect due to group, $F(2, 536) = 50.85$, $p. < .0001$. The effects for gender and group × gender interaction were not significant. As with the SDS, males and females did not differ significantly across all items combined on the SAS while the significant scale × gender interaction effect indicated that males and females did tend to accrue their points on different items.

On both items 7 and 8, "I am bothered by headaches, neck and back pains," and "I feel weak and get tired easily," females had significantly higher mean scores than did males. All items showing significant differences in scores by group showed the clinical group to have significantly higher scores than the other two groups. The random and medical groups were not significantly different from each other on any item.

Although items 12 and 16, had significant F scores for the overall item as a dependent variable, there were no univariate factors that showed significant effects at the $p. < .05$ level.

The clinical sample had the highest mean on each item of the SAS and for the items indicated (see Table 4.2) these effects were significant. On item 7, "I am bothered by headaches, neck and back pains," and item 8, "I feel weak and I get tired easily," the means were significantly higher for females than for males. Thus, given the overall significant multivariate effect due to group as well as the univariate item by item comparisons, it appears that the items indicated show the clinical population seeking services to differ significantly from those not seeking services and those seeking medical services. The pattern of responses between males and females differed especially on items 7 and 8 and elevated scores on these two items by females may be taken as gender effects.

With regard to the total score alone of the Zung Self-rating Anxiety Scale and the effects of group and gender and group × gender interaction, an analysis of variance, $F(5, 533) = 26.62$, $p. < .0001$, indicated a significant effect only for the group factor, $F(2, 536) = 50.85$, $p. < .0001$, such that the mean of the clinical group ($M = 38.42$, $SD = 8.80$) was significantly higher than the mean of the random group ($M = 30.94$, $SD = 7.07$) and significantly higher than the mean of the medical group ($M = 30.62$, $SD = 5.83$). Thus, although males and females as a group showed elevations on different SAS items, the total scores of males and females did not differ significantly as was also the case with the SDS. Further, as with the SDS, significant differences were found among the clinical, random, and medical groups with regard to the patterns of individual items on which elevations occurred in addition to significant differences among groups with regard to the total SAS score.

Gender and Sample Group Effects on the
Beck Depression Inventory

A repeated measures multivariate analysis of variance revealed a significant multivariate scale effect for the BDI across items, $F(20, 511) = 18.9122$, $p. < .0001$. Thus, all items on this inventory were not equally sensitive to the underlying variable of depression across all subjects. Said another way, each item did not measure the underlying variable to the same degree or with sensitivity at the same magnitude. A significant

TABLE 4.2

SIGNIFICANT (p.<.05) FINDINGS FROM THE
REPEATED MEASURES MULTIVARIATE ANALYSIS OF VARIANCE OF
THE ZUNG SELF-RATING ANXIETY SCALE ITEMS BY
SAMPLE GROUP AND GENDER

	Univariate Overall F		Univariate Factor F			
			Gender		Group	
	df=5, 533		df=1, 537		df=2, 536	
	F	p	F	p	F	p
Item 1 Anxiousness	16.35	0.0001	.	.	32.14	0.0001
Item 2 Fear	5.25	0.0001	.	.	12.53	0.0001
Item 3 Panic	25.74	0.0001	.	.	43.34	0.0001
Item 4 Mental Disintegration	21.98	0.0001	.	.	46.94	0.0001
Item 5 Apprehension	13.5	0.0001	.	.	29.84	0.0001
Item 6 Tremors	6.4	0.0001	.	.	14.16	0.0001
Item 7 Body Aches and Pains	8.67	0.0001	18.33	0.0001	7.5	0.0006
Item 8 Easy Fatigability	6.97	0.0001	4.79	0.0291	13.95	0.0001
Item 9 Restlessness	9.67	0.0001	.	.	21.99	0.0001
Item 10 Palpitation	6.1	0.0001	.	.	10.53	0.0001
Item 12 Faintness	3.1	0.0091	.	.	.	.
Item 13 Dyspnea	3.64	0.003	.	.	4.99	0.0071
Item 15 Nausea and Vomiting	5.28	0.0001	.	.	4.27	0.0145
Item 16 Urinary Frequency	3.21	0.0073	.	.	.	.
Item 17 Sweating	4.51	0.0005	.	.	9.03	0.0001
Item 18 Facial Flushing	3.1	0.009	.	.	5.97	0.0027
Item 19 Insomnia	11.82	0.0001	.	.	25.46	0.0001
Item 20 Nightmares	4.65	0.0004	.	.	6.89	0.0011

*No significant differences were found on the items measuring confusion (item 11) and hopelessness (item 14).
Thus, they were omitted from the table.

multivariate scale × group interaction, $F(40, 1022) = 4.1797$, $p. < .0001$, was found but no significant multivariate effect due to the scale × gender interaction was found, $F(20, 511) = 1.2317$, $p. < .2221$. These findings suggest that there was a significant difference among the groups with regard to the pattern of items on which the elevations occurred and points were accrued and that no such difference was found between males and females on the BDI. The multivariate scale × group × gender interaction effect was also not significant, $F(40, 1020) = 1.0158$, $p. < .4447$. The effects due to differences by group were not significantly and differently affected by the differences due to gender with regard to the pattern of elevations manifested on individual BDI items. Thus, the effect of group was not significantly affected by whether the subject was a female or a male with regard to the pattern of elevations manifested on the individual BDI items.

The multivariate effect across all items combined for group was significant, $F(2, 533) = 54.74$, $p. < .0001$, while the multivariate effect for gender, $F(1, 530) = 1.42$, $p. < .2345$, and the group × gender interaction effect, $F(2, 533) = .76$, $p. < .4671$, were not significant. These findings suggest that individual subjects vary in the magnitude of response given to different items such that each item may not actually measure the phenomena (in this case depression) to the same degree. Further, these intrasubject differences interacted with group membership such that the individual items appearing sensitive in measuring depression differed by group membership.

As was indicated by the multivariate effect due to scale × group, individual items on the BDI showed significant differences by group. The clinical group showed the higher mean for each item with the exceptions of feeling old or unattractive (item 14), and weight loss (item 19). There were no significant differences among the groups on these two items indicating that elevations on these items may not show differences by groups as did the other items with regard to persons seeking psycho-therapeutic services *vs.* those seeking medical services *vs.* a random sample of such young adults in a university setting. (The relevant statistics for the BDI items on which there were differences among the clinical, the medical, and the random groups significant at the $p. < .05$ level are presented in Table 4.3). Since the multivariate analysis showed no significant differences by gender the univariate statistics are not reported for the gender effect on the BDI items.

These findings are consistent with the results found using the BDI

TABLE 4.3

SIGNIFICANT (p.<.05) FINDINGS FROM THE
REPEATED MEASURES MULTIVARIATE ANALYSIS OF VARIANCE
OF THE BECK DEPRESSION INVENTORY ITEMS BY
SAMPLE GROUP

	Univariate Overall F		Univariate Factor F	
			Group	
	df=5, 530		df=2,532	
	F	p	F	p
1-Sadness	26.04	0.0001	51.86	0.0001
2-Pessimism/ Hopelessness	15.97	0.0001	37.25	0.0001
3-Failure	6.37	0.0001	11.64	0.0001
4-Dissatisfaction	11.09	0.0001	22.19	0.0001
5-Guilt	13.82	0.0001	29.97	0.0001
6-Punishment	2.51	0.029	3.74	0.0243
7-Self- disappointment	20.83	0.0001	40.84	0.0001
8-Self-criticism	7.59	0.0001	17.01	0.0001
9-Suicide, thoughts of self-harm	4.98	0.0002	11.88	0.0001
10-Crying	8.54	0.0001	16.12	0.0001
11-Irritability	3.81	0.0021	7.16	0.0009
12-Loss of interest in others	5.62	0.0001	10.63	0.0001
13-Indecisiveness	16.47	0.0001	39.67	0.0001
15-Difficulty working	15.43	0.0001	36.36	0.0001
16-Sleep disturbances	9.99	0.0001	15.34	0.0001
17-Tiredness	7.23	0.0001	14.05	0.0001
18-Appetite disturbances	5.19	0.0001	10.31	0.0001
20-Somatic preoccupation	5.97	0.0001	8.61	0.0002
21-Libido	3.07	0.0095	6.49	0.0016

*No significant differences were found for weight loss
 (item 19) and feeling old or unattractive (item 14).
 Thus, they were omitted from the table.
**Given that the multivariate effect for gender was not
 significant, univariate analyses for gender effects
 were not reported.

total score alone. An analysis of variance with the BDI total score at the initial testing as the dependent variable and group, gender, and group × gender interaction as independent variables was significant, $F(5, 530)$ = 26.64, $p. < .0001$. A significant main effect appeared only for the group effect, $F(2, 533)$ = 54.74, $p. < .0001$, indicating that there was a significant difference among the means on the total BDI scores produced by the different groups and no significant difference on the mean BDI total score between males and females. The mean BDI total score for the clinical group was 14.88 (SD = 8.68) whereas the mean for the random group was 7.78 (SD = 7.25) and the mean for the medical group was 6.03 (SD = 4.71). The mean BDI total score for all females regardless of group membership was 12.50 (SD = 8.94) and the mean for all males regardless of group membership was 10.42 (SD = 8.63). The mean for females in the clinical group was 15.76 (SD = 8.60) while the mean for males in the clinical group was 13.85 (SD = 9.23). The mean total BDI score for females in the random sample was 8.70 (SD = 7.87) and the mean for males in the random sample was 6.78 (SD = 6.46). The mean total BDI score for females in the medical sample was 5.77 (SD = 4.73) and the mean for males in the medical sample was 6.59 (SD = 4.77).

To summarize, there was a significant difference on the BDI for the scale × group interaction effect such that a significant difference was found in how the points were accrued across the individual items by group as is reflected in Table 4.3. This finding was also true of the SDS and SAS. With regard to the BDI and the scale × gender interaction effect, no significant difference between males and females was found concerning the pattern of items on which elevations occurred. It might be said that the magnitude of affective disturbance as measured by the individual BDI items did not significantly differ by gender as it did by group membership on the BDI and by group membership and gender on the SDS and the SAS. Thus, the findings of this study with regard to differences by gender and BDI score are in agreement with the findings of Hammen and Padesky (1977) in that no significant differences were found in the degree of depression by gender. Nevertheless, the present findings differ with Hammen and Padesky's (1977) finding of a "significant and interpretable sex difference in the pattern of symptom expression" (p. 609).

The lack of support for the latter finding in the present study may have been due to sample differences as the Hammen and Padesky (1977) sample was comprised of volunteers from introductory psychology classes while the present study utilized clinic populations and a stratified random sample contacted by mail. The earlier study noted that the majority of the sample were 18 and 19 years of age whereas the present sample previously described in this volume included a majority of subjects who were older than 19 years of age. Finally, the statistical analyses used by Hammen and Padesky (1977) were stepwise discriminant function analyses whereas the present study utilized a repeated measures multivariate analysis of variance, which appeared to be the better choice of techniques to address the question of whether there was a gender effect on individual items concerning response magnitude.

However, to explore this question further, a stepwise discriminant function analysis was done with subjects in the random sample and another was done with subjects in the clinical sample who scored over 15 on the BDI in the present study. This cut-off score was employed in the second data analysis by Hammen and Padesky (1977) to, in a sense, force the question of whether any items would differentiate by gender at the $p. < .05$ level. Of four BDI items emerging to differentiate the present random sample by gender, only weight loss (item 19), $F(1, 163) = 4.464$, $p. < .0361$, also appeared on the list of 9 items differentiating males from females in the total sample analysis reported by Hammen and Padesky (1977). Females reported more weight loss than males. Other items in the model emerging for the present study included feelings of self-reproach and disappointment (item 7), $F = 5.239$, $p. < .0233$, feeling like a failure (item 3), $F = 4.939$, $p. < .0276$, and somatic concerns (item 20), $F = 4.380$, $p. < .0379$. This entire model accounted for less than 12 percent of the variance in the scores of males vs. females. Looking at the means for these items, the mean for males with regard to feelings of failure and self-disappointment/self-reproach were higher than the means for females on these items, whereas the mean score for females was higher on weight loss and somatic concerns in the random sample. Again, the repeated measures multivariate analysis of variance did not detect any differences that were significant concerning these or any other individual item means on the BDI.

With regard to items differentiating males from females of those subjects in the subset of their sample with a total BDI score of 15 or greater, Hammen and Padesky (1977) reported a model including 8 items whereas the present sample yielded a model including 3 items when utilizing the stepwise discrininant function analysis with subjects who had a BDI total score of 15 or greater. Only one of these three items, loss of interest in others (item 12), was also in the eight item model reported in the earlier investigation. The model generated in this study included feeling old or unattractive (item 14); $F(1, 132) = 10.194$, $p. < .0018$; pessimism (item 2), $F = 7.779$, $p. < .0061$; and, the common item, loss of interest in others (item 12) $F = 4.602$, $p. < .0338$.

The total variance accounted for by this model was less than 16 percent. The means revealed that males had a higher mean score on the pessimism item while females had the higher means on loss of interest in others and feeling old and unattractive. Nevertheless, as reported, significant differences were not detected by the repeated measures multivariate analysis of variance.

Differences in findings between the present study and the Hammen and Padesky (1977) study may be artifacts of the particular samples, of course, or may be due to the difference in sample size. The earlier study's sample was much larger. Further, the studies actually address two different age groups as noted and the present study utilized a sample with greater age variability. The use of a stratified random sample contacted by mail and samples taken from clinic populations further differentiate the populations studied and also may account for the differences in findings, particularly with regard to the differences yielded by the stepwise discriminant function analyses. The choice of statistical analysis technique actually suggests that the earlier study examined the question, "What BDI items will differentiate by gender?" A question answerable by a stepwise discriminant function analysis. The present analysis, by contrast, asked the question, "Do significant response differences by gender exist in terms of the magnitude of response on the individual BDI items?" The latter question appeared to be the more meaningful as the answer might inform the interpretation of elevated BDI item scores. That is, the results of our analysis might lead one to conclude that elevations on the items identified are more indicative of gender differences than of psychopathology.

The Beck Depression Inventory
and Scoring Method

Two methods of scoring the BDI have been endorsed by Beck's Center for Cognitive Therapy as equally valid (D. Tannenbaum, personal communication, April, 1987). Both methods deem any inventory with more than three items omitted to be invalid. One scoring method counts missing items as a zero while the other method assigns a prorated score to missing items such that the missing items receive the mean score of the other items. Thus, with the prorating method of scoring the total score would be higher unless the total score were a zero.

Post hoc comparisons with the BDI data were done to examine the nature of the omitted items and the magnitude of their effect on the total score by comparing the total scores of inventories with 1 to 3 missing items using the different scoring methods. Of 536 BDI's completed by all subjects combined at the time of first assessment, a total of 71 inventories had at least one missing item. Four subjects, all female and all in the clinical group, omitted more than 3 items and thus, their scores were invalid by either method of scoring. Of the 67 still valid but incomplete inventories 4 were from the medical sample ($n = 66$), and each was missing one item. Nine were from the random sample ($n = 168$), and again each was missing 1 item. Fifty-four were from the clinical group ($n = 302$) with 39 omitting 1 item, 12 omitting 2 items, and 3 omitting 3 items.

To determine whether inventories with 1 to 3 omitted items were significantly different from inventories without omitted items, t tests were done using each scoring method to compare the groups. In order to control for possible differences by group and given the small number of inventories with missing items in the random and medical groups, the tests were done with those in the clinical group omitting 1 to 3 items ($n = 54$) and those omitting none ($n = 248$). Clients with 1 to 3 items omitted on the BDI completed just prior to their first session had a mean score of 16.22 (SD = 8.93) when scored using zeros for missing items and 17.36 (SD = 9.63) when using the prorating method of assigning missing items a score. There was a mean difference of 1.14 on these 54 inventories depending on the scoring method used. This was a statistically significant difference ($t = 8.58$, $p. = .0001$). Using the prorating scoring method, the mean score ($M = 17.36$, $SD = 9.63$) of the 54 inventories missing 1 to 3 items was significantly higher than the mean score ($M = 14.59$, $SD = 8.61$) of the 248 inventories in the clinical group with no items missing ($t = -2.19$, $p. < .0368$). Even when missing items were scored as a zero the 54 inventories with 1 to 3 items missing had a mean of 16.53 ($SD = 9.13$) which was approximately two points higher than the mean of the other 248 inventories. This difference was not statistically significant at the $p. < .05$ level.

Looking case by case at how the 54 inventories with 1 to 3 missing items were affected by the method of scoring, 12 of the 54 would have had a score more than one point greater if the mean score of completed items had been used, 5 inventories would have increased by more than two points with this method, and one of these inventories would have been increased by 6 points. Thus, from these data it appears that persons omitting items on the BDI have on the whole higher scores than persons who do not omit items and that using a zero for omitted items may underestimate the total score at least for those seeking psychotherapeutic services.

Of the 329 females from all groups who returned a BDI (valid or invalid), 9 subjects (2.74 percent) omitted rating feelings of dissatisfaction (item 4), 13 subjects (3.95 percent) omitted rating thoughts of self-harm (item 9), and 19 subjects (5.78 percent) omitted rating interest in sex (item 21). Of the 207 males who completed a BDI, 6 subjects (2.90 percent) omitted rating self-disappointment (item 7), 13 subjects (6.28 percent) omitted rating self-criticism (item 8), and 14 subjects (6.76 percent) omitted rating thoughts of self-harm (item 9). It appears that in the self-report of depressive symptoms on the BDI that males may not wish to comment on self-criticism, and self-disappointment while females may not wish to comment on feelings of dissatisfaction and sexual interest. Both males and females, but especially males, may not wish to comment on suicidal ideation. Thus, these symptoms might be inquired about during the initial interview if omitted on the BDI in a manner showing sensitivity to the difficulty felt in responding to questions regarding these matters. In clinical practice the omission of the suicidal ideation item must lead to an inquiry if adequate care is to be delivered.

Since inventories with omitted items appear to be at least somewhat higher on average than inventories without omitted items, it is possible that scoring missing items as a zero on the BDI gives a misrepresentative lower score. Subsequent studies with larger samples need to test again the hypothesis that there is no difference in the scoring method. This question appears to be completely ignored in the literature. Unfortunately, investigations utilizing the BDI have very rarely reported the scoring method employed in the study.

SUMMARY AND CONCLUSIONS

In conclusion, the SDS, the SAS, and the BDI, all showed significant differences by group on the majority of items. Thus, most all of the items in addition to the total scores served to identify differences in the clinical sample as compared to the other samples. Further, the pattern of responses differed by gender on the SDS and SAS but not on the BDI. Thus, on the two Zung inventories (the SDS and the SAS) males and females tended to accrue points toward their total score on different items, whereas this was not the case on the BDI. No group × gender interaction effect was found on any of the inventories. A scale effect was found for SDS, the SAS, and the BDI, such that individual items apparently did not measure affective disturbance to the same degree or magnitude. Thus, items may be differentially sensitive to affective phenomena. Finally, on the BDI pro-rating the score for missing items appears preferable to scoring missing items as a zero.

Chapter V

ANXIETY AND DEPRESSION VISUAL ANALOGUE SCALES AS PREDICTORS OF ZUNG SELF-RATING DEPRESSION SCALE, ZUNG SELF-RATING ANXIETY SCALE AND BECK DEPRESSION INVENTORY SCORES

W.J. Kenneth Rockwell, Joseph E. Talley,
and Lisa D. Hinz

REVIEW OF THE VISUAL ANALOGUE SCALE LITERATURE

Visual Analogue Scales (VAS) have been used as psychological assessment tools since the beginning of this century (Freyd, 1923; Hayes and Patterson, 1921), but were greatly popularized and propagated by Aitken (e.g., Aitken, 1969). Use of a Visual Analogue Scale most often requires that a person be presented with a ten centimeter horizontal line, although sometimes vertical lines have been used (Aun, Lam, and Collett, 1986; Dixon and Bird, 1981; Sriwatanakul, Kelvie, Lasagna, Calemlim, Weis, and Mehta, 1983). The line is anchored at the polar extremes to represent opposite ends of a subjective feeling state continuum. For example, the line might be anchored by the statements, "I am not depressed at all," vs. "I am as depressed as I have ever been." The subject is asked to mark the line once with a perpendicular slash mark, at the place best representing his or her current experience in terms of the feeling state being measured. In certain circumstances, Visual Analogue Scales are completed by someone reporting about the experience of another person (Jakobsen, Blom, Brondbjerg, and Lenler, 1990).

The advantages of the Visual Analogue Scale method are ease of graphic presentation, increased compliance, and simplicity and speed of both administration and scoring (Feinberg, Carroll, Smouse, and Rawson, 1981; Rubinow, Roy-Byrne, Hoban, Gold, and Post, 1984). Scoring is performed by taking a measurement from the side of the line representing the low end of the feeling to the mark made by the subject. Scores can be computed on any sort of scale, though they most often range from zero to ten centimeters (McCormack, Horne, and Sheather, 1988). Higher scores indicate greater intensity of the feeling being measured. One disadvantage of the VAS is that if a subject rates his/her mood at the extreme high or low end of the scale and is asked to repeat the measure, there is no room for change if in fact the mood worsens or improves further in the extreme direction (Little and McPhail, 1973). Thus, there is a "ceiling effect" (Gift, 1989). One suggestion for dealing with potential ceiling effects is to open the ends of the scale in order to allow for more extreme ratings (Borg, 1982; Gift, 1989). Another disadvantage of the Visual Analogue Scale is that it only measures intensity of feeling and one can give no indication of the heterogeneity of experiences within a feeling state (Gift, 1989; Peet, Ellis, and Yates, 1981). Investigators have solved this problem by employing several visual analogue scales in order to tap different dimensions of experience (Beaumont, Gringras, and Ankier, 1984; Bond and Lader, 1974; Little, 1989).

The VAS has been discussed as appropriate for use with diverse populations because it uses few words (Gift, 1989). Since it requires little vocabulary for explanation and use, the VAS can be used successfully with uneducated patients (Aun, Lam, and Collett, 1986; Sriwatanakul et al., 1983), illiterate persons (Faravelli, Albanesi, and Poli, 1986), elderly and possibly demented patients (Rozenbilds, Goldney, Gilchrist, and Martin, 1986), and subjects with severe head injuries (Kinsella, Moran, Ford, and Ponsford, 1988). In addition, the use of few words has been hailed as a great virtue of the VAS because it thus avoids individual interpretations of the descriptors (Gift, 1989; Sriwatanakul et al., 1983).

The psychometric properties and clinical uses of the Visual Analogue Scale have been widely studied and well proven with the VAS as a dependent measure of various feeling states. The VAS has demonstrated excellent validity, good reliability, and excellent sensitivity as a measure of mood in a variety of patient populations (Aitken, 1969; Folstein and Luria, 1973; Lundenburg, 1980; Luria, 1975; 1979; Knight and Thirkettle, 1986). However, it has been suggested in at least one study that the VAS lacks the sensitivity to differentiate between levels of nonclinical depression (Peet et al., 1981).

Demonstrations of validity usually have been those of construct and concurrent validity; both have been proven by comparing VAS scores with scores from established psychological assessment devices (Folstein and Luria, 1973; Little and Penman, 1989; Luria, 1975; Mehta, Spear, and Whittington, 1980). Validity of both horizontal and vertical scales has been demonstrated. The horizontal VAS used as a measure of mood or depression has been demonstrated to have construct validity when correlated with the Beck Depression Inventory (Davies, Burrows, and Poynton, 1975; Doerfler and Richards, 1983; Little and McPhail, 1973; Miller and Naylor, 1989), the Hamilton Rating Scale (Davies, Burrows, and Poynton, 1975; Feinberg et al., 1981; Mehta, Spear, and Whittington, 1980), and the Zung Self-Rating Depression Scale (Davies et al., 1975; Folstein and Luria, 1973). The VAS has become so widely used that it has at least once been used as the standard against which a new instrument was measured (Dratcu, de Costa, and Calil, 1987). Some have deemed the VAS to be superior to other assessment tools because of its speed and simplicity (Little and McPhail, 1973) while others disagree stating that the simplicity sacrifices a portion of its validity (Feinberg et al., 1981; Little and Penman, 1989).

The use of the Visual Analogue Scale as a measure of anxious mood has been widely validated with groups of patients anticipating or experiencing dental anxiety or surgical procedures (Bassi, Albizzati, Ferrarese, Frattola, Cesana, Piolti, and Farolfi, 1989; Ray and Fitzgibbon, 1981; Tabor and Jinsson, 1987). The VAS is probably preferred in medical/surgical situations because it is very fast and easy to use in difficult situations. In addition, the VAS as a measure of anxiety has been shown to be highly correlated with standard assessment procedures such as the State Trait Anxiety Scale (Folstein and Luria, 1973; Davies et al., 1975).

Discriminant validity has been demonstrated with the VAS as a measure of the subjective experience of airway obstruction (Aitken, 1969), chronic and experimentally produced pain (Price, McGrath, Rafii, and Buckingham, 1983), and depressed and manic mood variations (Luria, 1975; McClelland, Kerr, Stephens, and Howell, 1979; Zealley and Aitken, 1969). Luria (1975) discussed what he called "diagnostic validity" (seemingly the equivalent of discriminant validity). He found that various levels of depression and mania could be reliably distinguished from other mental disorders and from no mental disorder.

Test-retest reliability in immediate as well as delayed administrations has consistently been superior (Cella and Perry, 1986; Luria, 1975). In general, reliability coefficients have been larger with shorter time delays and with stronger sensations (McCormack, Horne, and Sheather, 1988).

In addition, it seems that subjects are better able to reproduce their ratings of extreme experiences than those toward the middle of the scale (Dixon and Bird, 1981). Reliability coefficients have been demonstrated to be highest when subjects are rating current experiences rather than trying to recall previous feelings or sensations (Carlsson, 1983).

Bond and Lader (1974) provided reliability coefficients by correlating similar items (e.g., alert-drowsy and attentive-dreamy, $r = .66$). Thus, they provided an estimate of a kind of internal consistency of the visual analogue scale as a measure of mood. High interrater reliability of the VAS has been found when two or more raters use the VAS to rate their perceptions of the feeling state of another person (Little and McPhail, 1973; Remington, Tryer, Newson-Smith, and Cicchetti, 1979).

Faravelli, Albanesi, and Poli (1986) demonstrated that the VAS as a measure of depression did not have a skewed distribution of scores like the left-skewed distributions of physician rating instruments. Thus, they concluded that the VAS has a potential for gathering more sensitive data on subjective feeling states. Visual Analogue Scale ratings of subjective feeling states with clinical populations have been demonstrated to be very sensitive measures of change (Knight and Thirkettle, 1986; Lundenburg, 1980).

The nature of the scores obtained from VAS ratings (i.e., ratings of intensity of subjective feeling) might prove too simplistic for some statistical analyses. Researchers might be led to believe that the VAS lacks sensitivity and thus use other criterion measures. As mentioned, some investigators have solved this problem by using more than one Visual Analogue Scale in order to assess different dimensions of participants' feeling states (Beaumont, Gringras, and Ankier, 1984; Bond and Lader, 1974; Little, 1989).

Visual Analogue Scales have been widely used as assessment and outcome measures of various physical and psychological conditions. The psychological and psychiatric literature contains hundreds of studies in which VAS's have been used to assess the status of diverse dependent variables. Dependent variables have included physical pain in adults and children (Choini'ere, Melzack, Rondeau, Girard, and Paquin, 1989; Schechter, 1985), dyspnea (Renfroe, 1988), tension headache (Mathew, Mishra, and Kumaraiah, 1987), physiological symptom severity (Berrios, Ryley, Garvey, and Moffat, 1988), premenstrual symptoms (Rubinow, Roy-Byrne, Hoban, Gold, and Post, 1984), physical and psychological symptoms associated with pregnancy and childbirth (Ballinger, Kay,

Naylor, and Smith, 1982; Kendell, McGuire, Connor, and Cox, 1981; Twining, 1983; Knight and Thirkettle, 1986), psychotropic medication effects (Matussek and Hoehe, 1989), frequency of hallucinations (Junginger and Frame, 1985), fatigue (Krupp, Alvarez, Larocca, and Scheinberg, 1988), appetite (Cookson and Silverston, 1986; Robinson, McHugh and Folstein, 1975), ability to cope with surgery (Ray and Fitzgibbon, 1981), effectiveness of computer assisted relaxation (Baer and Surman, 1985), and level of self-esteem (Greer and Burgess, 1987).

The most common medical use of the VAS has been in the assessment of the experience of pain (Carlsson, 1983; Price et al., 1983; Sriwatanakul et al., 1983). The prevailing use of the Visual Analogue Scale in psychological assessment has been in the measurement of mood states, especially anxiety and depression (Cella and Perry, 1986; Folstein and Luria, 1973; Luria, 1979; Monk, 1989). In fact, it has often been called the Visual Analogue mood Scale (Knudsen, Bjorndal, Johnsen, and Pfeiffer-Petersen, 1984), and much of the research into the psychometric properties of the Visual Analogue Scale has been performed with it as a measure of mood (Folstein and Luria, 1973; Luria, 1975; 1979).

The VAS has been an effective outcome measure in studies of mood states. Researchers claim that it is very sensitive to feeling state changes over time (Gift, 1989; Little and McPhail, 1973; Remington et al., 1979). It has been used extensively as a measure of change in mood or depressive symptomatology with pregnant and postpartum females (Ballinger, Kay, Naylor, and Smith, 1982; Hapgood, Elkind, and Wright, 1988; Kendell, McGuire, Connor, and Cox, 1981; Twining, 1983; Knight and Thirkettle, 1986). Often, subjects are given a number of Visual Analogue Scales printed on separate pieces of small paper and asked to rate their mood daily or several times daily. These studies have shown that depressed mood can be effectively tracked across time using a Visual Analogue Scale.

The Visual Analogue Scale has been used extensively in psychiatric research as an outcome measure in investigations of various psychotropic medications. The VAS has been demonstrated to be a reliable, valid, and sensitive measure of the effects of psychotropic medications. It has been used to track the effects of different medications given to similar groups, as well as effects of similar medications given to different groups (Beaumont, Gringras and Ankier, 1984; Knudsen et al., 1984; Lapierre and Butter, 1978; Lundenburg, 1980; Mehta, Spear, and Whittington, 1980). For example, Lapierre and Butter (1978) found the VAS to be as sensitive or more sensitive than the Hamilton Depression Rating Scale (an interviewer administered depression rating scale), or the Zung Self-rating Depression Scale in detecting the clinical effects of two antidepressant medications in agitated and retarded depression. Beaumont, Gringras, and Ankier (1984) used several Visual Analogue Scales to track therapeutic antidepressant medication effects as well as drug side effects over a period of time. Measurements with the VAS were correlated with both the Zung Self-rating Depression Scale and the Hamilton Depression Rating Scale administered by a physician.

In addition, the VAS has also been used as an outcome measure in studies of the effectiveness of psychotherapy. The VAS has been demonstrated to be as effective an assessment device as the Beck Depression Inventory in measuring the changes in depressed mood resulting from participation in psychotherapy (Beckham, 1989; Doerfler and Richards, 1983; Little and McPhail, 1973). Beckham (1989) used a Visual Analogue Scale as a treatment effect measure in investigating the efficacy of cognitive-behavioral treatment for depression. He found that mood improvement as measured by the VAS in the first therapy session was an excellent predictor of successful treatment outcome. Doerfler and Richards (1983) also used the VAS as a pretreatment depression screening device with a sample of depressed university undergraduate females. Thus, there is a precedent for using the VAS to assess mood (i.e., depression and anxiety) and for using it as an outcome measure in studies of the effectiveness of psychotherapy.

The purpose of this portion of our study was to examine the utility of Visual Analogue Scales for depression and anxiety as screening instruments through a series of exploratory statistical analyses. Specifically, we investigated the potential of Visual Analogue Scales to identify dysphoric persons by discerning the ability of the VAS–D to predict Zung SDS and Beck Depression Inventory scores, and the VAS–A to predict Zung SAS scores.

The subjects have been described in the method section found in Chapter II. All subjects with an available score on at least one measure were included in the data analyses.

RESULTS AND DISCUSSION

In order to explore the possibility that the relationship of Visual Analogue Scale scores to other scale scores varied by age group, the correlations of the VAS–D with the SDS and the BDI, and the VAS–A with the SAS for subjects in the clinical group 18 to 22 years of age were compared to the correlations for subjects 23 years of age and older. For subjects 18 to 22 years old the VAS–D and the SDS correlated strongly and significantly in the positive direction (see Table 5.1) as did the VAS–A and SAS and the VAS–D and the BDI. The same was true for subjects 23 and older with regard to the VAS–D and the SDS, the VAS–A and the SAS, and the VAS–D and the BDI. Correlations between measures of different affects (VAS–A with VAS–D, SDS with SAS, and BDI with VAS–A) by age group were also strong, positive and highly significant for both age groups. Thus, the scale with scale correlations were not remarkably different regardless of age group. Correlations by age group are presented in Table 5.1. Correlations at the initial and at follow-up testing by sample group between same and different affect measures for all subjects regardless of age are presented in Table 5.2A and Table 5.2B respectively.

TABLE 5.1

SCALE WITH SCALE CORRELATIONS BY AGE GROUP
FOR THE CLINICAL SAMPLE AT INITIAL TESTING

	18 to 22 Years of Age	23 Years of Age and Older
VAS-D with SDS	r=.59207 p=.0001 (n=185)	r=.58514 p=.0001 (n=53)
VAS-D with BDI	r=.59795 p=.0001 (n=179)	r=.48566 p=.0003 (n=52)
VAS-A with SAS	r=.59625 p=.0001 (n=190)	r=.66324 p=.0001 (n=52)
SDS with BDI	r=.79834 p=.0001 (n=221)	r=.79982 p=.0001 (n=65)
VAS-D with VAS-A	r=.54943 p=.0001 (n=186)	r=.43538 p=.0008 (n=51)
SDS with SAS	r=.78366 p=.0001 (n=228)	r=.79155 p=.0001 (n=66)
BDI with VAS-A	r=.44665 p=.0001 (n=183)	r=.45583 p=.0008 (n=51)

Since the Visual Analogue Scales might predict Zung and Beck scale scores differently for the different sample groups, regression equations to determine the amount of variance accounted for by a visual analogue scale were done for each sample group (Random, Clinical, Vocational, and Medical) separately using scores from the time of initial testing. The VAS–D was found to predict Zung Self-rating Depression Scale scores by group as follows: Clinical sample, 34.35 percent of the variance, $F(1, 243)$ = 127.138, $p. < .0001$; Random sample, 43.25 percent of the variance,

TABLE 5.2A

CORRELATIONS FOR SAME AFFECT MEASURES BY
CLINICAL, RANDOM, MEDICAL, AND VOCATIONAL SAMPLES
AT INITIAL AND FOLLOW-UP ASSESSMENTS

Initial Assessment	VAS-A and SAS	VAS-D and SDS	VAS-D and BDI	BDI and SDS
Clinical	r=.60222 p=.0001 n=250	r=.58608 p=.0001 n=245	r=.58189 p=.0001 n=237	r=.79768 p=.0001 n=293
Random	r=.61627 p=.0001 n=159	r=.65765 p=.0001 n=160	r=.61683 p=.0001 n=159	r=.82477 p=.0001 n=166
Medical	r=.59386 p=.0001 n=58	r=.57117 p=.0001 n=58	r=.60442 p=.0001 n=58	r=.65429 p=.0001 n=66
Vocational	r=.46672 p=.0002 n=60	r=.68779 p=.0001 n=61	. . .	. . .
Follow-up Assessment				
Clinical	r=.68170 p=.0001 n=83	r=.74894 p=.0001 n=83	r=.82785 p=.0001 n=81	r=.78421 p=.0001 n=91
Random	r=.50892 p=.0001 n=117	r=.64596 p=.0001 n=118	r=.57865 p=.0001 n=122	r=.80762 p=.0001 n=122
Medical	r=.67604 p=.0001 n=35	r=.45046 p=.0061 n=35	r=.84497 p=.0001 n=35	r=.27969 p=.0936 n=37
Vocational	r=.72291 p=.0023 n=15	r=.58292 p=.0226 n=15	. . .	. . .

$F(1, 158) = 120.413$, *p.* $< .0001$; Medical sample, 32.62 percent of the variance, $F(1, 56) = 27.115$, *p.* $< .001$; Vocational sample, 47.38 percent of the variance, $F(1, 60) = 54.027$, *p.* $< .0001$. Thus, a larger percent of the variance in SDS scores is predicted by the VAS–D scores for the vocational sample which had the least variability of scores and fewer elevated

TABLE 5.2B
CORRELATIONS FOR DIFFERENT AFFECT MEASURES
BY CLINICAL, RANDOM, MEDICAL AND VOCATIONAL SAMPLES
AT INITIAL AND FOLLOW-UP ASSESSMENTS

Initial Assessment	VAS-A and VAS-D	VAS-A and BDI	VAS-A and SDS	VAS-D and SAS	BDI and SAS	SAS and SDS
Clinical	r=.52941 p=.0001 n=243	r=.44781 p=.0001 n=241	r=.53328 p=.0001 n=249	r=.47087 p=.0001 n=245	r=.65990 p=.0001 n=296	r=.78470 p=.0001 n=302
Random	r=.64829 p=.0001 n=159	r=.50659 p=.0001 n=158	r=.56974 p=.0001 n=159	r=.52489 p=.0001 n=160	r=.77365 p=.0001 n=166	r=.79469 p=.0001 n=167
Medical	r=.66501 p=.0001 n=58	r=.62352 p=.0001 n=58	r=.43908 p=.0006 n=58	r=.54962 p=.0001 n=58	r=.58865 p=.0001 n=66	r=.71420 p=.0001 n=66
Vocational	r=.69043 p=.0001 n=61	. . .	r=.50734 p=.0001 n=61	r=.50741 p=.0001 n=60	. . .	r=.78942 p=.0001 n=67
Follow-up Assessment						
Clinical	r=.66878 p=.0001 n=81	r=.66878 p=.0001 n=81	r=.62464 p=.0001 n=83	r=.66469 p=.0001 n=83	r=.72531 p=.0001 n=91	r=.80464 p=.0001 n=94
Random	r=.59267 p=.0001 n=117	r=.49282 p=.0001 n=116	r=.46674 p=.0001 n=117	r=.51892 p=.0001 n=118	r=.72997 p=.0001 n=122	r=.78904 p=.0001 n=124
Medical	r=.57937 p=.0003 n=35	r=.57937 p=.0003 n=35	r=.06466 p=.7121 n=35	r=.49869 p=.0023 n=35	r=.66232 p=.0001 n=37	r=.19506 p=.2473 n=37
Vocational	r=.66755 p=.0065 n=15	. . .	r=.39686 p=.1430 n=15	r=.50555 p=.0545 n=15	. . .	r=.48172 p=.0588 n=16

scores on both instruments. By comparison, Beck Depression Inventory scores were predicted by SDS scores as follows: Clinical sample, 63.63 percent of the variance, $F(1, 291) = 509.098$, $p. < .0001$; Random sample, 68.02 percent of the variance, $F(1, 164) = 348.887$, $p. < .0001$; and Medical sample, 42.81 percent of the variance, $F(1, 64) = 47.907$, $p. < .0001$.

With regard to the VAS–A as a predictor of the Zung Self-rating Anxiety Scale, results were as follows: Clinical sample, 36.27 percent of the variance, $F(1, 248) = 141.122$, $p. < .0001$; Random sample, 37.98

percent of the variance, $F(1, 157) = 96.140$, $p. < .0001$; Medical sample, 35.27 percent of the variance, $F(1, 56) = 30.509$, $p. < .0001$; and Vocational sample, 21.79 percent of the variance, $F(1, 59) = 16.441$, $p. < .0001$. Thus, for the vocational group the VAS–A was less predictive of SAS scores than for the other groups.

The BDI was a better predictor of SDS scores than was the VAS–D. However, it must be noted that the SAS was also a better predictor of SDS scores than was the VAS–D. SAS scores predicted the variance in SDS scores by sample group as follows: Clinical sample, 61.57 percent of the variance, $F(1, 300) = 480.739$, $p. < .0001$; Random sample, 63.15 percent of the variance, $F(1, 165) = 282.794$, $p. < .0001$; Medical sample, 51.01 percent of the variance, $F(1, 64) = 66.634$, $p. < .0001$; and Vocational sample, 62.16 percent of the variance, $F(1, 66) = 108.409$, $p. < .0001$. This in part may be simply due to the greater likelihood that a score derived from a group of related items can predict another score derived from a second group of related items better than an individual item can predict a score derived from a group of items. This would be especially likely if some of the items added into a composite score were not necessarily related to the individual item serving as the predictor such as in the present case in which the Visual Analogue Scales contain no somatic referents while the SDS, the SAS, and the BDI all have items relating to somatic phenomena. For all subjects combined the VAS–A predicted less of the variance of the VAS–D, 41.75 percent, $F(1, 520) = 372.723$, $p. < .0001$) than the SDS predicted of the SAS, 67.50 percent, $F(1, 601) = 1247.995$, $p. < .0001$). This appears favorable for the Visual Analogue Scales and suggests that they may have more specificity value than the Zung scales. Given the high correlation between the SDS and SAS it seems quite likely that some items (perhaps those with somatic referents) on the Zung scales are not affect specific and thus do not enhance the validity of the scales but rather may detract from their validity.

Correlations of the VAS–D with the Zung Self-rating Depression Scale items are presented in Table 5.3A. Diurnal variation (item 2) did not reach statistical significance for the clinical, vocational, or medical groups and was very weak for all groups. Decreased appetite (item 5) did not reach significance for the clinical group, the vocational group, or the medical group and was a relatively weak correlation by comparison for all groups. Decreased libido (item 6) was not significantly correlated with the VAS–D for the vocational group. Decreased weight (item 7) was not significantly correlated with the VAS–D for any group and the same was true of constipation (item 8). Tachycardia (item 9) was not significantly correlated with the VAS–D for the medical group.

Concerning the correlations of the Visual Analogue Scale for anxiety with the items of the Zung Self-rating Anxiety Scale (see Table 5.3B), all items correlated significantly with the VAS–A for the clinical group and all items for the random group correlated significantly except faintness (item 12), dyspnea (item 13), urinary frequency (item 16), sweating (item 17), and facial flushing (item 18). For the medical group all items excepting tremors (item 6), dizziness (item 11), faintness (item 12), dyspnea (item 13), paresthesis (item 14), sweating (item 17), and nightmares (item 20) correlated significantly with the VAS–A. The vocational group was unusual in that 13 of the 20 items did not correlate significantly with the VAS–A. These items included fear (item 2), tremors (item 6), body aches and pains (item 7), palpitation (item 10), dizziness (item 11), faintness (item 12), dyspnea (item 13), paresthesis (item 14), nausea and vomiting (item 15), urinary frequency (item 16), sweating (item 17), facial flushing (item 18), and nightmares (item 20). It is possible that those in the vocational group felt some inclination to deny symptoms of anxiety, and thus, the correlations did not reach significance.

However, faintness (item 12) did not reach significance for any group but the clinical group and the correlation was weak for the clinical group. Dyspnea (item 13) did not reach significance for any of the three comparison groups and barely did for the clinical group and the correlation was quite weak. Paresthesis (item 14) showed a weak correlation for the clinical and the random groups with the VAS–A and significance was not reached for the medical or the vocational groups and the correlation was weak for the random group although it did reach significance. Likewise, urinary frequency (item 16) showed a very weak correlation for the clinical group and it did not reach significance for the vocational group or the random sample. Sweating (item 17) did not reach significance for any group but the clinical group and the correlation was not as strong as it was for the majority of the other items. The correlations for facial flushing (item 18) were not notably strong and did not reach significance for the random or the vocational group. Finally, the correlations for nightmares (item 20) with the VAS–A were not significant for the vocational group or the medical group and the correlation for the clinical group was weaker than most.

As is presented in Table 5.3C the VAS–D correlated significantly with

TABLE 5.3A

CORRELATIONS OF THE VISUAL ANALOGUE SCALE-DEPRESSION
WITH THE ZUNG SELF-RATING DEPRESSION SCALE ITEM AND TOTAL SCORES

Zung Item	Group			
	Clinical (n=246)	Random (n=173)	Medical (n=65)	Vocational (n=62)
1-Depressed Mood	r=.6103 p=.0001	r=.7080 p=.0001	r=.6129 p=.0001	r=.6944 p=.0001
2-Diurnal Variation	r=.1229 p=.0543	r=.1545 p=.0424	r=.0502 p=.6912	r=-.0817 p=.5278
3-Crying Spells	r=.4113 p=.0001	r=.4106 p=.0001	r=.3222 p=.0089	r=.2849 p=.0248
4-Sleep Disturbance	r=.3307 p=.0001	r=.2881 p=.0005	r=.4179 p=.0005	r=.2943 p=.0202
5-Decreased Appetite	r=.0656 p=.3057	r=.1600 p=.0355	r=.0750 p=.5226	r=.2392 p=.0611
6-Decreased Libido	r=.2084 p=.0010 a	r=.2897 p=.0001	r=.2524 p=.0425	r=-.0331 p=.7982
7-Decreased Weight	r=.1063 p=.0968 a	r=.1279 p=.0935	r=.0839 p=.5063	r=.1402 p=.2772
8-Constipation	r=.1068 p=.0952 a	r=.0156 p=.8383	r=.1392 p=.2689	r=-.0432 p=.7387
9-Tachycardia	r=.1987 p=.0018 a	r=.3511 p=.0001	r=.2233 p=.0738	r=.2927 p=.0209
10-Fatigue	r=.2024 p=.0015 a	r=.4243 p=.0001	r=.2909 p=.0187	r=.2637 p=.0400 b
11-Decreased Concentration	r=.3998 p=.0001 a	r=.4484 p=.0001	r=.4990 p=.0001	r=.4941 p=.0001 b
12-Psychomotor Retardation	r=.4359 p=.0001	r=.4062 p=.0001	r=.4779 p=.0001	r=.5397 p=.0001
13-Agitation	r=.1476 p=.0206	r=.3109 p=.0001	r=.3039 p=.0138	r=.0228 p=.8607
14-Hopelessness	r=.4759 p=.0001	r=.4431 p=.0001	r=.3351 p=.0064	r=.5808 p=.0001
15-Irritability	r=.3261 p=.0001	r=.4324 p=.0001	r=.4891 p=.0001	r=.5252 p=.0001
16-Indecisiveness	r=.3813 p=.0001	r=.3839 p=.0001	r=.2805 p=.0236	r=.2756 p=.0301
17-Personal Devaluation	r=.4389 p=.0001	r=.4380 p=.0001	r=.3958 p=.0011	r=.5559 p=.0001
18-Emptiness	r=.3591 p=.0001	r=.4589 p=.0001	r=.3514 p=.0041	r=.5331 p=.0001
19-Suicidal Rumination	r=.2823 p=.0001	r=.1577 p=.0383	r=.2337 p=.0610	r=-.0296 p=.8195
20-Dissatisfaction	r=.4848 p=.0001	r=.5385 p=.0001	r=.4758 p=.0001	r=.6681 p=.0001
Total	r=.5861 p=.0001	r=.6579 p=.0001	r=.6489 p=.0001	r=.6883 p=.0001

* The number of respondents is as indicated
  at the head of the column unless otherwise
  noted.
  a (n=245)
  b (n=61)

TABLE 5.3B

CORRELATIONS OF THE VISUAL ANALOGUE SCALE-ANXIETY
WITH THE ZUNG SELF-RATING ANXIETY SCALE ITEM AND TOTAL SCORES

Zung Item	Group			
	Clinical (n=251)	Random (n=172)	Medical (n=65)	Vocational (n=62)
1-Anxiousness	r=.7040	r=.7304	r=.6690	r=.6133
	p=.0001	p=.0001	p=.0001	p=.0001
2-Fear	r=.2886	r=.3884	r=.2832	r=.2080
	p=.0001	p=.0001	p=.0223	p=.1078 b
3-Panic	r=.4723	r=.5519	r=.5313	r=.3772
	p=.0001	p=.0001	p=.0001	p=.0027 b
4-Mental Disintegration	r=.4225	r=.4331	r=.4610	r=.5482
	p=.0001	p=.0001	p=.0001	p=.0001
5-Apprehension	r=.3851	r=.3962	r=.4161	r=.4908
	p=.0001 a	p=.0001	p=.0006	p=.0001
6-Tremors	r=.2939	r=.1550	r=.0333	r=.2083
	p=.0001 a	p=.0423	p=.7920	p=.1042
7-Body Aches and Pains	r=.2786	r=.2326	r=.2449	r=-.0171
	p=.0001 a	p=.0021	p=.0493	p=.8959 b
8-Easy Fatigability	r=.3082	r=.4078	r=.3968	r=.2627
	p=.0001	p=.0001	p=.0011	p=.0391
9-Restlessness	r=.4645	r=.4820	r=.2947	r=.3693
	p=.0001	p=.0001	p=.0172	p=.0031
10-Palpitation	r=.3017	r=.2779	r=.2918	r=.1575
	p=.0001	p=.0002	p=.0184	p=.2216
11-Dizziness	r=.1895	r=.1825	r=-.0399	r=.1872
	p=.0026	p=.0166	p=.7523	p=.1451
12-Faintness	r=.1411	r=.0552	r=.0674	r=.1462
	p=.0253	p=.4717	p=.5939	p=.2567
13-Dyspnea	r=.1267	r=.1202	r=.0689	r=.1743
	p=.0448	p=.1162	p=.5854	p=.1756
14-Paresthesis	r=.1713	r=.1630	r=.0428	r=-.0955
	p=.0066 a	p=.0327	p=.7348	p=.4640
15-Nausea and Vomiting	r=.3404	r=.3005	r=.3225	r=.1232
	p=.0001	p=.0001	p=.0088	p=.3402
16-Urinary Frequency	r=.1509	r=.1329	r=.2640	r=.0259
	p=.0167	p=.0822	p=.0336	p=.8418
17-Sweating	r=.2245	r=.0980	r=.1445	r=-.0193
	p=.0003	p=.2011	p=.2508	p=.8824 b
18-Facial Flushing	r=.2033	r=.0706	r=.2807	r=.2055
	p=.0012	p=.3572	p=.0235	p=.1122 b
19-Insomnia Rumination	r=.3295	r=.4673	r=.4542	r=.3288
	p=.0001	p=.0001	p=.0001	p=.0091
20-Nightmares	r=.1918	r=.2939	r=-.0212	r=.1093
	p=.0023	p=.0001	p=.8671	p=.3977
Total	r=.6022	r=.6102	r=.6494	r=.4668
	p=.0001 a	p=.0001	p=.0001	p=.0001 b

* The number of respondents is as indicated
at the head of the column unless otherwise
noted.
a (n=250)
b (n=61)

all items on the Beck Depression Inventory for all groups with the exception of items 17 and 20 for the medical group. Likewise, the total BDI score was strongly and significantly correlated with the VAS–D for all groups. In general, there appears to be some difference in the vocational group's responses. The correlation for the vocational group of the total Zung Self-rating Anxiety Scale score with the VAS–A was not quite as strong as it was for the other three groups, although all three groups did reach significance. It is noteworthy that the vocational group is the smallest group and much smaller than the clinical and random groups.

The Effects Of Affect Severity Level on the Visual Analogue Scales as Predictors of SDS, SAS, and BDI Scores

In order to investigate the possibility that the predictive ability of the Visual Analogue Scales would differ by severity level (none, mild, moderate, severe) of the score on the criterion instrument, regression analyses were done to ascertain the amount of the variance in scores on the criterion measures (SDS, SAS, BDI) predicted or accounted for by the VAS–D and VAS–A scores. The VAS–D accounted for 23.97 percent, $F(1, 301) = 94.893$, $p. < .0001$, of the variance in Zung Self-rating Depression Scale scores for subjects from all samples combined in scoring in the SDS "none" category. At the "mild" level the VAS–D predicted 7.23 percent, $F(1, 116) = 9.044$, $p. < .0032$, of the variance. At the "moderate" level of the SDS the VAS–D scores accounted for 6.56 percent, $F(1, 74) = 5.198$, $p. < .0255$, of the variance and at the SDS "severe" level, the VAS–D predicted 6.83 percent, $F(1, 26) = 1.906$, $p. < .1792$, of the variance. Thus, the amount of the variance in SDS scores the VAS–D predicted decreased as the severity level of the criterion measure increased and at the "severe" level the $p. < .05$ level of statistical significance was not reached.

As a point of comparison the BDI was able to predict SDS scores by Zung severity level as follows: "none," 39.38 percent, $F(1, 282) = 183.216$, $p. < .0001$, of the variance; "mild," 14.02 percent, $F(1, 127) = 20.173$, $p. < .0001$, of the variance; "moderate," 6.71 percent, $F(1, 77) = 5.534$, $p. < .0212$, of the variance; "severe," 5.89 percent, $F(1, 31) = 1.939$, $p. < .1737$, of the variance. Thus, the BDI could not predict SDS scores substantially better than the VAS–D at the moderate and severe levels.

The VAS–D score predicted BDI scores by BDI severity level as

TABLE 5.3C

CORRELATIONS OF THE VISUAL ANALOGUE SCALE-DEPRESSION
WITH THE BECK DEPRESSION INVENTORY

Beck Item	Group		
	Clinical (n=238)	Random (n=170)	Medical (n=65)
1-Sadness	r=.6476	r=.5184	r=.5129
	p=.0001 a	p=.0006	p=.0001
2-Pessimism/	r=.4039	r=.4216	r=.2263
Hopelessness	p=.0001	p=.0001	p=.0699
3-Failure	r=.3845	r=.4577	r=.2567
	p=.0001 b	p=.0001	p=.0390
4-Dissatisfaction	r=.4284	r=.4513	r=.5573
	p=.0001 c	p=.0001	p=.0001
5-Guilt	r=.2147	r=.3478	r=.4695
	p=.0009 d	p=.0001	p=.0001
6-Punishment	r=.2008	r=.1660	r=.2813
	p=.0022 e	p=.0306 j	p=.0232
7-Self-	r=.3469	r=.3816	r=.3419
disappointment	p=.0001	p=.0001 g	p=.0053
8-Self-criticism	r=.3091	r=.4207	r=.4502
	p=.0001	p=.0001 h	p=.0002
9-Suicide/thoughts	r=.3029	r=.3072	r=.3179
of self-harm	p=.0001	p=.0001 h	p=.0099
10-Crying	r=.3488	r=.3034	r=.2803
	p=.0001	p=.0001 g	p=.0237
11-Irritability	r=.2361	r=.2591	r=.2780
	p=.0002	p=.0006	p=.0249
12-Loss of interest	r=.2536	r=.3538	r=.2148
in others	p=.0001	p=.0001 g	p=.0857
13-Indecisiveness	r=.2910	r=.3107	r=.5200
	p=.0001	p=.0001 j	p=.0001
14-Unattractiveness/	r=.2119	r=.2259	r=.1650
old	p=.0010	p=.0031 j	p=.1889
15-Difficulty	r=.2949	r=.4654	r=.2518
working	p=.0001 f	p=.0001 i	p=.0431
16-Sleep	r=.3267	r=.3709	r=.5203
disturbance	p=.0001	p=.0001	p=.0001
17-Tiredness	r=.2454	r=.4253	r=.2130
	p=.0001	p=.0001	p=.0884
18-Appetite	r=.3123	r=.2878	r=.2810
disturbance	p=.0001 a	p=.0001 i	p=.0245
19-Weight loss	r=.2260	r=.1436	r=.2810
	p=.0005 d	p=.0618 j	p=.8664
20-Somatic	r=.2238	r=.2026	r=.1731
preoccupation	p=.0005 a	p=.0079 i	p=.1679
21-Libido	r=.1884	r=.2307	r=.3212
	p=.0044 d	p=.0025 j	p=.0097
Total	r=.5830	r=.6015	r=.6503
	p=.0001	p=.0001 i	p=.0001

* There were no BDI's for the Vocational Group.

** The number of respondents is as indicated
   at the head of the column unless otherwise
   noted.
   a (n=236)   f (n=239)
   b (n=235)   g (n=169)
   c (n=228)   h (n=168)
   d (n=237)   i (n=171)
   e (n=231)   j (n=164)

follows: "none," 26.25 percent, $F(1, 216) = 76.866$, $p. < .0001$, of the variance; "mild," .7 percent, $F(1, 110) = .774$, $p. < .3810$, of the variance; "moderate," .4 percent, $F(1, 71) = .284$, $p. < .5960$, of the variance; "severe," 2.32 percent, $F(1, 49) = 1.164$, $p. < .2859$, of the variance. Thus, it appears that the VAS–D is able to predict the SDS scores better than BDI scores once the score on the criterion measure exceeds the "none" category. Poorer prediction of the BDI by the VAS–D may be due in part to greater variability of the VAS–D scores in the mid-range of the BDI.

The VAS–A accounted for the variance in SAS scores by severity category of the SAS as follows: "none," 21.17 percent, $F(1, 311) = 83.537$, $p. < .0001$, of the variance; "mild," 6.61 percent, $F(1, 170) = 12.026$, $p. < .0007$, of the variance; "moderate," 4.49 percent, $F = 1.738$, $p. < .1955$, of the variance; "severe," 2.79 percent, $F(1, 2) = .057$, $p. < .8331$. From these data it appears that the VAS–D is a better predictor of the SDS than the VAS–A is a predictor of the SAS. This may be due in large part to the smaller number of subjects in the SAS "severe" category.

As is evident in Table 5.4, the Visual Analogue Scales correlate strongly and significantly in the positive direction for subjects in the "none" severity category for all same affect criterion measures. At the "mild" level of these same affect criterion measures the correlations for the VAS–D with the SDS and the VAS–A with the SAS are still significant but weaker while the correlation of the VAS–D with the BDI is no longer significant. At the "moderate" level the VAS–A correlation with the SAS is no longer significant although the correlation of the VAS–D and the SDS is significant but less so. At the "severe" level no correlations of the Visual Analogue Scales with the same affect criterion measure are strong or significant as is also the case for the VAS–D and the BDI at the mild and moderate levels. By comparison the correlation of the BDI and the SDS is very strong and significant at the none level and remains significant at the mild, moderate, and severe levels. Thus the Visual Analogue Scales scores are less related to the criterion measures as the level of affect severity increases. While this is also true of the BDI correlations with the SDS by level of severity, the two measures are significantly correlated at all levels of severity.

Table 5.4 also shows that the VAS–A and VAS–D are themselves significantly correlated at the none, moderate, and severe levels, and thus, a portion of what is measured is, in all likelihood, common phenomena tapped by both the VAS–A and the VAS–D. (These VAS–D levels were demarcated by quartiles as follows: none = 0.0 to 2.5 cm;

TABLE 5.4

CORRELATIONS OF SCALE WITH SCALE
AT INITIAL ASSESSMENT

	VAS-D with SDS			VAS-D with BDI		
None	r=.48959	p=.0001	n=303	r=.51231	p=.0001	n=218
Mild	r=.26893	p=.0032	n=118	r=.08358	p=.3810	n=112
Moderate	r=.25618	p=.0255	n=76	r=.06308	p=.5960	n=73
Severe	r=.26133	p=.1792	n=28	r=.15233	p=.2859	n=51
	VAS-A with SAS			BDI with SDS		
None	r=.46014	p=.0001	n=313	r=.63451	p=.0001	n=246
Mild	r=.25703	p=.0007	n=172	r=.26773	p=.0019	n=132
Moderate	r=.21183	p=.1955	n=39	r=.32976	p=.0021	n=85
Severe	r=.16692	p=.8331	n=4	r=.27431	p=.0310	n=62
	VAS-A with VAS-D			VAS-A with SDS		
None	r=.35461	p=.0001	n=183	r=.46976	p=.0001	n=306
Mild	r=.12283	p=.2075	n=107	r=.19423	p=.0335	n=120
Moderate	r=.24314	p=.0035	n=142	r=.22805	p=.0523	n=73
Severe	r=.24994	p=.0175	n=90	r=.00967	p=.9603	n=29
	VAS-A with BDI			SAS with SDS		
None	r=.48997	p=.0001	n=221	r=.67077	p=.0001	n=341
Mild	r=.05033	p=.5949	n=114	r=.17046	p=.0404	n=145
Moderate	r=.10992	p=.3580	n=72	r=.30769	p=.0042	n=85
Severe	r=-.27663	p=.0518	n=50	r=.24154	p=.1829	n=32
	SAS with BDI					
None	r=.57122	p=.0001	n=249			
Mild	r=.22408	p=.0095	n=133			
Moderate	r=.26888	p=.0128	n=85			
Severe	r=.08811	p=.4995	n=61			

mild = 2.6 to 5.0 cm; moderate = 5.1 to 7.5 cm; and severe = 7.6 to 10.0 cm.) However, the SAS and SDS were also correlated at all levels except the severe SDS level. Therefore the specificity of the affects measured by the VAS–A and VAS–D appears less at the "none" level. However, the specificity of the VAS–A and VAS–D may increase as severity increases as the correlation between the two measures (that would ideally not correlate highly) decreased as severity category increased. Nevertheless, insofar as the validity test is the correlation of Visual Analogue Scale scores with the SAS, SDS, and BDI as criterion measures the validity of the Visual Analogue Scales in measuring a specific affect at the moderate and severe levels appears less than the validity at the none and mild levels of severity. Thus, at the lower half of the VAS–A and VAS–D affect specificity appears more questionable while at the higher end validity appears more questionable. Table 5.5 presents the VAS–A and the VAS–D means, standard deviations, and number of subjects for each sample group by severity level of the criterion measures.

TABLE 5.5

MEANS AND STANDARD DEVIATIONS OF VISUAL ANALOGUE SCALE-DEPRESSION RATINGS
BY BECK DEPRESSION INVENTORY AND ZUNG SELF-RATING DEPRESSION SCALE
AND VISUAL ANALOGUE SCALE-ANXIETY RATINGS BY ZUNG SELF-RATING ANXIETY
SCALE LEVEL OF SEVERITY WITHIN SAMPLE GROUP AT INITIAL TESTING

Clinical Sample

	SDS	SAS	BDI
none	4.17 (SD=2.62) n=91	4.65 (SD=2.69) n=97	3.69 (SD=2.33) n=67
mild	5.83 (SD=2.32) n=74	6.92 (SD=2.29) n=115	5.61 (SD=2.45) n=72
moderate	7.07 (SD=2.18) n=57	8.70 (SD=1.10) n=34	6.60 (SD=2.42) n=52
severe	8.31 (SD=1.97) n=23	9.55 (SD=.71) n=4	8.02 (SD=1.70) n=46

Random Sample

	SDS	SAS	BDI
none	2.46 (SD=2.19) n=117	3.82 (SD=2.59) n=120	2.23 (SD=1.97) n=106
mild	4.24 (SD=2.19) n=26	6.79 (SD=2.32) n=34	4.56 (SD=2.60) n=28
moderate	7.25 (SD=1.98) n=13	7.76 (SD=1.53) n=5	5.63 (SD=2.43) n=20
severe	7.63 (SD=.67) n=4	.	7.82 (SD=1.32) n=5

Medical Sample

	SDS	SAS	BDI
none	2.37 (SD=2.01) n=49	3.07 (SD=2.26) n=47	2.27 (SD=1.94) n=45
mild	5.21 (SD=2.00) n=7	6.39 (SD=1.83) n=11	4.28 (SD=2.48) n=12
moderate	3.55 (SD=3.89) n=2	.	6.30 (SD=0) n=1
severe	.	.	.

Vocational Sample

	SDS	SAS	BDI
none	3.19 (SD=2.32) n=46	3.77 (SD=2.35) n=49	.
mild	6.99 (SD=2.25) n=11	6.01 (SD=2.61) n=12	.
moderate	7.65 (SD=1.14) n=4	.	.
severe	8.40 (SD=0) n=1	.	.

Visual Analogue Scales as Screening Instruments

In order to establish the Visual Analogue Scales as useful screening instruments, particularly with populations not seeking psychological services, it was necessary to determine a score above which there was an acceptable probability that the same subject would score at least in the mildly symptomatic range on a full inventory such as the BDI, the SAS, or the SDS. The fewer scores above this defined VAS score that were not at least mildly symptomatic on a full inventory (false positives) and the fewer scores below the VAS score that were at least mildly symptomatic (false negatives) the more valid the use of that VAS score as a cut-off point to recommend that the individual take a full inventory.

In an attempt to identify useful cut-off scores on the VAS–A and VAS–D both 2.5 centimeters (cm) and 5.0 cm were explored as the upper limit acceptable not to refer the subject for a full inventory. Thus, 2.6 cm and 5.1 cm were explored as the lower limit for inclusion and all VAS scores from the defined lower limit to 10.0 cm were in the included group (VAS positives). The ratio and percent of accurate hits, false negatives and false positives were computed. An accurate hit was defined as those VAS scores within the designated range of 0.0 through 2.5 cm (or 5.0 cm) who also had a criterion measure score in the "none" range and those VAS scores with the 2.6 cm (or 5.1 cm) through 10.0 cm range who also had criterion measure scores in the mild, moderate, or severe range as defined by the inventory. The findings are presented for each sample group separately.

Findings with the Random Sample

Concerning those completing the VAS–D and the SDS, of the Zung SDS negatives in the random group ($n = 160$) there was an accurate hit rate of 76 of 117 (64.96 percent) using 2.6 cm as the lower limit on the VAS–D for inclusion. Of the Zung SDS positives there was a hit rate of 36 of 43 (83.72 percent). There were 41 of 117 (35.04 percent) false positives and 7 of 43 (16.28 percent) false negatives (all of which were in the Zung SDS mild range) using 2.6 cm as the lower inclusion limit.

Using 5.1 cm as the lower inclusion limit there was an accurate hit rate of 101 of 117 (86.32 percent) of the Zung negatives and a hit rate of 26 of 43 (60.47 percent) of Zung SDS positives. This left 16 of 117 (13.68 percent) false positives and 17 of 43 (39.53 percent) false negatives of which 15 were in the Zung SDS mild range and the remaining two were in the moderate range.

For the random sample completing the VAS–A and the SAS (n = 159), an accurate hit rate of 37 of 39 (94.87 percent) of Zung SAS positives (subjects falling in the Zung SAS mild, moderate, or severe categories) was achieved using a VAS–A score of 2.6 cm or greater for inclusion. Of the Zung SAS negatives ("none" range on the Zung SAS) there was an accurate hit rate of 45 of 120 (37.50 percent). Thus, there was a false positive rate of 75 of 120 (62.50 percent) and a false negative rate of 2 of 39 (5.13 percent). A false positive was defined as a subject who met the VAS–A inclusion of a score of 2.6 cm or greater but who did not meet the Zung SAS criteria for mild, moderate, or severe anxiety. A false negative was defined as a subject who met the Zung SAS criteria for mild, moderate, or severe anxiety but did not also have a VAS–A score of 2.6 cm or greater.

Using 5.1 cm as the lowest cut-off score on the VAS–A for inclusion resulted in an accurate hit rate of 32 of 39 (82.05 percent) of the Zung SAS positives and a hit rate of 77 of 120 (64.17 percent) Zung SAS negatives. Thus, there were 42 of 120 (35 percent) false positives and 7 of 39 (17.95 percent) false negatives all of which were in the Zung SAS mild range using a 5.1 lower inclusion limit on the VAS–A.

Comparing the VAS–D to the BDI (n = 159) using a score of 2.6 cm or greater on the VAS–D for inclusion, there was an accurate hit rate of 72 of 106 (67.92 percent) for the BDI negatives and a hit rate of 41 of 53 (77.36 percent) of the BDI positives leaving a false positive rate of 34 of 106 (32.08 percent) and a false negative rate of 11 of 53 (20.75 percent) of which 8 were in the BDI mild range. The remaining 3 false negatives were in the moderate range.

Using 5.1 cm as the lower limit VAS–D score for inclusion there was an accurate hit rate of 95 of 106 (89.62 percent) of BDI negatives and a hit rate of 30 of 53 (56.60 percent) BDI positives. Thus, there were 11 of 106 (10.38 percent) VAS–D false positives and 23 of 53 (43.40 percent) false negatives of which 15 were in the BDI mild range and 8 were in the BDI moderate range.

Findings with the Medical Sample

With regard to the VAS–D and the Zung SDS for the medical group with a total of 58 subjects completing both measures, using the 2.6 cm VAS–D score as the lower limit for inclusion there was an accurate hit rate of 34 of 49 (69.39 percent) Zung SDS negatives and a hit rate of 7 of 9 (77.78 percent) Zung SDS positives leaving a false positive rate of 15 of 49 (30.61 percent) and a false negative rate of 2 of 9 (22.22 percent). Of the false negatives 1 scored in the SDS mild range and 1 in the moderate range.

Using a VAS–D 5.1 cm score as the lower limit for inclusion, 43 of 49 (87.76 percent) SDS negatives were accurately identified and there was an accurate hit rate of 6 of 9 (66.67 percent) SDS positives. Thus, using the 5.1 cm score there was a false positive rate of 6 of 49 (12.24 percent) and a false negative rate of 3 of 9 (33.33 percent). Of these three false negatives 2 scored in the SDS mild range and 1 scored in the moderate range.

Of a total of 58 subjects completing the VAS–A and Zung SAS in this group there was an accurate hit rate of 19 of 47 (40.43 percent) Zung SAS negatives using a 2.6 cm VAS–A score lower limit for inclusion and a hit rate of 11 of 11 (100 percent) Zung SAS positives all in the Zung mild range. Thus, there were 28 of 47 (59.57 percent) VAS–A false positives from this group and no false negatives.

Using a VAS–A score of 5.1 cm as the lower limit for inclusion there was an accurate hit rate of 35 of 47 (74.47 percent) Zung SAS negatives and a hit rate of 10 of 11 (90.91 percent) Zung SAS positives leaving 12 of 47 (25.53 percent) false positives and 1 of 11 (9.09 percent) as a false negative which was in the Zung SAS mild range.

Concerning the VAS–D and BDI score as the criterion measure, using a VAS–D score of 2.6 cm as the lower limit for inclusion there was an accurate hit rate of 31 of 45 (68.89 percent) BDI negatives and of 8 of 13 (61.54 percent) BDI positives. Thus, there was a false positive rate of 14 of 45 (31.11 percent) and a false negative rate of 5 of 13 (38.46 percent). All 5 false negatives scored in the BDI mild range.

Using 5.1 on the VAS–D as the lower limit for inclusion there was an accurate hit rate of 40 of 45 (88.89 percent) BDI negatives and of 7 of 13 (53.85 percent) BDI positives. This left a false positive rate of 5 of 45 (11.11 percent) and a false negative rate of 6 of 13 (46.15 percent) of which 5 were in the BDI mild range and 1 was in the moderate range.

Findings with the Vocational Sample

Concerning the 62 subjects in the vocational group completing both the SDS and the VAS–D, the Zung SDS positives were identified by the VAS–D using a score of 2.6 cm or greater such that there was an accurate hit rate of 22 of 46 (47.83 percent) Zung SDS negatives and a hit rate of 16 of 16 (100 percent) Zung SDS positives. Thus, there was a 24 of 46 (52.17 percent) rate of false positives and no false negatives of the 16 Zung positives.

Using a VAS–D score of 5.1 cm as the lower limit for inclusion, there was an accurate hit rate of 36 of 46 (78.26 percent) Zung SDS negatives and a rate of 13 of 16 (81.25 percent) Zung SDS positives. Thus, there was a false positive rate of 10 of 46 (21.74 percent) and a false negative rate of 3 of 16 (18.75 percent). All 3 false negatives scored in the SDS mild range. There were no BDI's from this group for comparison to VAS–D scores.

There were 61 subjects in the vocational sample completing the SAS and VAS–A. Using a lower limit inclusion score of 2.6 cm on the VAS–A there was an accurate hit rate of 18 of 49 (36.73 percent) Zung SAS negatives and 11 of 12 (91.67 percent) Zung SAS positives. All positives scored in the SAS mild range. There was a false positive rate of 31 of 49 (63.27 percent) and a false negative rate of 1 (scoring in the mild range) of 12 (8.33 percent).

Using a cut-off score of 5.1 cm on the VAS–A for the lower limit of inclusion there was an accurate hit rate of 34 of 49 (69.39 percent) Zung SAS negatives and 8 of 12 (66.67 percent) Zung SAS positives. Thus, there was a false positive rate of 15 of 49 (30.61 percent) and a false negative rate of 4 of 12 (33.33 percent). The false negatives were all in the SAS mild range.

Findings with the Clinical Sample

A total of 245 subjects in the clinical group completed both the VAS–D and the Zung SDS just prior to their first session. Using 2.6 cm as the VAS–D cut-off lower limit score for inclusion to identify Zung SDS positive scores an accurate hit rate of 29 of 91 (31.87 percent) Zung SDS negatives was obtained and a hit rate of 140 of 154 (90.91 percent) Zung SDS positives was obtained. There was a false positive rate of 62 of 91 (68.13 percent) and a false negative rate of 15 of 154 (9.74 percent). Of these false negatives 9 were in the SDS mild range, 4 were in the moderate range, and 2 were in the severe range.

Using 5.1 cm as the VAS–D cut-off lower limit score for inclusion there was an accurate hit rate of 53 of 91 (58.24 percent) Zung SDS negatives and a hit rate of 120 of 154 (77.92 percent) Zung SDS positives resulting also in 38 of 91 (41.76 percent) false positives and 34 of 154 (22.08 percent) false negatives. Of the false negatives 24 were in the mild range, 9 were in the moderate range, and 1 was in the severe range.

A total of 250 subjects in the clinical group completed both the VAS–A and the Zung SAS. Using a VAS–A cut-off score of 2.6 cm for the lower limit of inclusion to identify SAS positive subjects, an accurate hit rate of 26 of 97 (26.80 percent) of the Zung SAS negatives was obtained. A hit rate of 145 of 153 (94.77 percent) of Zung positives was obtained. There was a 71 of 97 (73.20 percent) rate of false positives and a rate of 8 of 153 (5.23 percent) false negatives. All 8 of the false negatives were in the SAS mild range.

Using a VAS–A score of 5.1 cm as the lower limit for inclusion a rate of 50 of 97 (51.55 percent) Zung SAS negatives were identified and 95 of 115 (82.61 percent) Zung SAS positives were identified. Therefore, a 47 of 97 (48.45 percent) rate of false positives and a 20 of 153 (13.07 percent) rate of false negatives was obtained using a VAS–A lower limit for inclusion of 5.1 cm. All 20 false negatives were in the SAS mild range.

A total of 237 subjects in the clinical group completed both the BDI and the VAS–D just prior to their initial session. With the BDI as the criterion measure and 2.6 cm as the VAS–D lower limit for inclusion an accurate hit rate of 24 of 67 (35.82 percent) was obtained for the BDI negatives. A hit rate of 153 of 170 (90 percent) BDI positives was obtained with the 2.6 cm lower limit for inclusion. There was a false positive rate of 43 of 67 (64.18 percent) and a false negative rate of 17 of 170 (10 percent). Of the 17 false negatives 10 were in the BDI mild range, 6 were in the moderate range, and 1 was in the severe range.

Using 5.1 cm as the lower limit score for inclusion there was an accurate hit rate of 45 of 67 (67.16 percent) BDI negatives and a hit rate of 131 of 170 (77.06 percent) BDI positives. There was a false positive rate of 22 of 67 (32.84 percent) and a false negative rate of 39 of 170 (22.94 percent). Of these 39 false negatives 25 were in the BDI mild range, 11 were in the moderate range, and 3 were in the severe range.

Visual Analogue Scales For Depression And Anxiety As Pre/Posttreatment Measures

As reported in Chapter II, a Repeated Measures Multivariate Analysis of Variance was done with the SDS, SAS, VAS–A and the VAS–D as dependent variables to identify significant pre- and posttreatment differences on these measures. The VAS–A and the VAS–D were both sensitive to the significant differences among the groups at the initial assessment as were the SAS and SDS as reported in Chapter II.

Thus, insofar as change is measured by the VAS–A and the VAS–D, the clinical group which was significantly different from the other groups by having higher scores on the VAS–A and the VAS–D prior to treatment, no longer had significantly higher scores after treatment. These findings with the Visual Analogue Scales parallel the findings with the other inventories.

With further reference to the VAS–D and VAS–A as potential scales for follow-up or repeated measures studies, for the clinical group the correlations with the criterion measures were slightly stronger at the time of follow-up (see Table 5.6). However, scales intending to measure different affects also had stronger positive correlations (i.e. the VAS–D with the VAS–A, and the SDS with the SAS) at the time of follow-up measurement. The only correlation that was not stronger at follow-up for the clinical group was the SDS with the BDI.

For the random group all correlations at the time of follow-up were weaker than at the initial measurement time. These differences by sample group also presented in Table 5.6 appear unremarkable. The correlation of the SAS with the VAS–A for the medical and vocational groups at the follow-up time were weaker as was the correlations of the SDS with the BDI for the medical group. However, for the medical group the correlations of the VAS–D with the SDS and the VAS–D with the BDI both slightly strengthened as did the correlation of VAS–D and the SDS for the vocational group. As is apparent in Table 5.6 the correlations at follow-up time of the SDS with the BDI and the SAS with the SDS for the medical group and the SAS with the SDS for the vocational group did not reach the $p. < .05$ level of statistical significance.

Proposed Briefer Screening and Assessment Inventories

According to our data, single Visual Analogue Scales have limited value in differentiating degrees of dysphoria in the upper end range. Such scales may be useful as a course screen for dysphoria in a large population presenting, for example, at a medical clinic, but they will likely add little to the further evaluation of that portion of the population that screens positive.

In keeping with the rapid assessment employed in a very brief intervention setting in which the population served usually arrives with

TABLE 5.6

SCALE WITH SCALE CORRELATIONS
BY GROUP AND TIME OF MEASUREMENT

	Initial Measurement	Follow-up Measurement
Clinical Group		
VAS-D with SDS	r=.60222, p=.0001 (n=250)	r=.68170, p=.0001 (n=83)
VAS-A with SAS	r=.58608, p=.0001 (n=245)	r=.74894, p=.0001 (n=83)
VAS-D with BDI	r=.58189, p=.0001 (n=237)	r=.82785, p=.0001 (n=81)
SAS with SDS	r=.78470, p=.0001 (n=302)	r=.80464, p=.0001 (n=94)
VAS-D with VAS-A	r=.52941, p=.0001 (n=243)	r=.71169, p=.0001 (n=83)
SDS with BDI	r=.79768, p=.0001 (n=293)	r=.78421, p=.0001 (n=91)
Random Group		
VAS-D with SDS	r=.61627, p=.0001 (n=159)	r=.50892, p=.0001 (n=117)
VAS-A with SAS	r=.65765, p=.0001 (n=160)	r=.64596, p=.0001 (n=118)
VAS-D with BDI	r=.61683, p=.0001 (n=159)	r=.57865, p=.0001 (n=117)
SAS with SDS	r=.79469, p=.0001 (n=167)	r=.78904, p=.0001 (n=124)
VAS-D with VAS-A	r=.64829, p=.0001 (n=159)	r=.59267, p=.0001 (n=117)
SDS with BDI	r=.82477, p=.0001 (n=166)	r=.80762, p=.0001 (n=122)
Medical Group		
VAS-D with SDS	r=.59386, p=.0001 (n=58)	r=.67604, p=.0001 (n=35)
VAS-A with SAS	r=.57117, p=.0001 (n=58)	r=.45046, p=.0066 (n=35)
VAS-D with BDI	r=.60442, p=.0001 (n=58)	r=.84497, p=.0001 (n=35)
SAS with SDS	r=.71420, p=.0001 (n=66)	r=.19506, p=.2473 (n=37)
VAS-D with VAS-A	r=.66501, p=.0001 (n=58)	r=.54050, p=.0008 (n=35)
SDS with BDI	r=.65429, p=.0001 (n=66)	r=.27969, p=.0936 (n=37)
Vocational Group		
VAS-D with SDS	r=.46672, p=.0002 (n=60)	r=.72219, p=.0023 (n=15)
VAS-A with SAS	r=.68779, p=.0001 (n=61)	r=.58292, p=.0226 (n=15)
SAS with SDS	r=.78942, p=.0001 (n=67)	r=.48172, p=.0588 (n=16)
VAS-D with VAS-A	r=.69043, p=.0001 (n=61)	r=.66755, p=.0065 (n=15)

substantial dysphoria, we have attempted to develop short forms of the Zung SDS and SAS, as well as a better short form of the Beck Depression Inventory than the 1972 version. To do this a stepwise discriminant analysis was performed with the inventories from the clinical group at the time of presentation for services to yield five items from each inventory that would not only correlate with the total score but would differentiate best between levels of severity (see Table 5.7). The items yielded by the fifth step from this analysis of each of the inventories were as follows (inventory item numbers in parentheses): Zung SDS: dissatisfaction (20), indecisiveness (16), tachycardia (9), appetite disturbance (5), and psycho-motor retardation (12). The five unweighted item total correlated strongly and significantly ($r. = .90$, $p. < .0001$) with the SDS total score. Zung SAS: panic (3), calmness (9), heart palpitations (10), aches and pains (7), and shaking and trembling (6). The five item unweighted total correlated strongly and significantly ($r. = .89$, $p. < .0001$) with the SAS total score. BDI: feelings of sadness (1), feelings of failure (3), feelings of guilt (5), appetite disturbance (18), and sleep disturbance (16). The five item unweighted total correlated strongly and significantly ($r. = .89$, $p. < .0001$) with the BDI total score.

We propose that validity studies be done comparing the Zung and Beck scales each with its own five item abbreviated model as described. Each item might be presented in a Likert style visual analogue scale format 10 cm in length with numbers anchoring each centimeter. This format would provide the advantage of placing scores on a 100-point scale when the total score was multiplied by 2. Such a procedure is desirable as it allows for a broader spread of scores to be obtained, and thus, there could be a finer discrimination among individuals on the basis of scores. If the abbreviated scales compare favorably they should then prove useful in the very brief treatment setting and in settings in which it is desirable to screen large groups of people for possible referral for treatment.

SUMMARY AND CONCLUSIONS

Although such inferences must be viewed with caution, the correlations of the VAS–A and VAS–D with the criterion measures from the eighteen to twenty-two year old group and the correlations from the twenty-three and older age group do not appear remarkably different. Further, the correlations between same and between different affect measures were positive, strong, and statistically significant for both age groups. The correlations were compared by age group because Gotlib (1984) has suggested that many inventories intended to measure specific affects may in fact measure general dysphoria in undergraduate age college students. Thus, the question of whether the correlations of the VAS–A and VAS–D with criterion measures differ greatly by age is important. Gotlib (1984) did not, however, conclude that the self-report instruments he was using that were designed to measure specific affective

TABLE 5.7

STEPWISE DISCRIMINANT ANALYSES RESULTS
FOR THE ZUNG SELF-RATING DEPRESSION SCALE, THE ZUNG SELF-RATING
ANXIETY SCALE, AND THE BECK DEPRESSION INVENTORY

Zung SDS

Descriptor	Item	Partial r^2	df	F	p
Dissatisfaction	20	0.4822	(3,298)	92.518	0.0001
Indecisiveness	16	0.2134	(3,297)	26.862	0.0001
Tachycardia	9	0.211	(3,296)	26.387	0.0001
Appetite Disturbance	5	0.1539	(3,295)	17.881	0.0001
Psychomotor Retardation	12	0.1512	(3,294)	17.455	0.0001
Model			(15,812)	36.918	0.0001

Zung SAS

Descriptor	Item	Partial r^2	df	F	p
Panic	3	0.4277	(3,302)	75.232	0.0001
Calmness	9	0.257	(3,301)	34.704	0.0001
Heart palpitations	10	0.1947	(3,300)	24.178	0.0001
Aches and Pains	7	0.167	(3,299)	19.986	0.0001
Shaking and Trembling	6	0.1288	(3,298)	14.690	0.0001
Model			(15,812)	37.942	0.0001

BDI

Descriptor	Item	Partial r^2	df	F	p
Feelings of Sadness	1	0.4553	(3,298)	83.021	0.0001
Feelings of Failure	3	0.2316	(3,297)	29.836	0.0001
Feelings of Guilt	5	0.2069	(3,296)	25.739	0.0001
Appetite Disturbance	18	0.1843	(3,295)	22.214	0.0001
Sleep Disturbance	16	0.1211	(3,294)	13.498	0.0001
Model			(15,823)	35.993	0.0001

states might more accurately measure general dysphoria in all age groups.

For the subjects twenty-three and older the correlations with the measures of the same affect were stronger than they were for the subjects eighteen to twenty-two years of age. However, with the measures of different affects correlations for the twenty-three and older group were for the most part weaker (the BDI with VAS–A correlation being an exception). These correlations lend support to Gotlib's (1984) conclusion that with college undergraduates self-report measures of affect in all likelihood measure general dysphoria more than they measure a specific affect. Nevertheless, the correlation of the SAS with the SDS and with the BDI, using scores from the twenty-three and older group suggests that these instruments may be largely a measure of general dysphoria in more populations than just undergraduates. These results also harken back to the conclusions of Carroll et al. (1973) regarding the questionable value of the SDS and the BDI in distinguishing those in the moderate from those in the severe range of depressive symptoms. Thus, the correlations suggest a cautionary note concerning the specificity of affect measured by the SDS, SAS, and the BDI. Specificity does appear to be more of a problem with those eighteen to twenty-two years of age than with those twenty-three and older. Concerning these issues and the relative value of the Visual Analogue Scales, it is noteworthy that the correlation of the SAS with the SDS was stronger for both age groups than the correlation of the VAS–D with the VAS–A.

With regard to the ability of the Visual Analogue Scale score to predict the corresponding Zung scale score by sample group, the VAS–D score predicted the SDS score best for the vocational group followed by the random group, followed by the clinical group, and lastly for the medical group. This may have been due for the most part to the better predictive ability of Visual Analogue Scales at the lower ends of the Zung scales. The VAS–D accounted for more of the variance in BDI scores than SDS scores. The VAS–A predicted SAS score by group in a different order (random, clinical, medical, vocational). The SDS group score best predicted by the VAS–D was the vocational group while the VAS–A predicted SAS scores least well for the vocational group. This does not appear due to the VAS–A or VAS–D ratings by the vocational group as the means and standard deviations are very close to being the same. However, on the SDS there was a greater spread of scores ($SD = 7.47$) than on the SAS (SD

= 5.87) and while the mean SAS raw score for the vocational group (31.04) is lower than the mean raw score on the SDS (35.90), both raw score means are below the cut off point for the mild level.

Although the VAS–D predicted less of the variance in SDS scores as the SDS severity level increased, the same was true of the BDI predicting SDS scores. Further, it appears that the VAS–D score may be a better predictor of SDS score than the VAS–A score is a predictor of SAS score based on the regression analyses and correlations by severity level.

Concerning the use of the Visual Analogue Scales as screening instruments to determine who would be well advised to complete a full SDS, SAS, or BDI, the time savings for large numbers of people is an obvious benefit. Both analogue scales could be completed in less than one minute while ten to fifteen minutes would be necessary for both the SDS and SAS, and about five to ten minutes for the BDI. Thus, in screening a large group such as an entering class of students a hit rate of 94.89 percent of the SAS positives could be obtained with the VAS–A using a 2.6 cm VAS–A cut-off lower limit score for inclusion taking about two minutes of each person's time. The high false positive rate of 62.50 percent seems unproblematic given the length of time to complete the VAS–A and VAS–D and the data suggest that false negatives would be in the SAS mild category. The hit rate of SDS positives using the VAS–D with a 2.6 cm lower limit score for inclusion was 83.72 percent. Again, the false positive rate of 35.04 percent seems acceptable given the brief time required to take the VAS–D and the data suggest that false negatives are likely to be in the SDS mild range.

Given that similar findings on the VAS–D and the VAS–A as on the SAS, SDS and BDI at follow-up were observed further study of the reliability of the Visual Analogue Scales as an outcome measure appears warranted. The reliability of the VAS–A and VAS–D over shorter intervals of time needs to be studied to ascertain the typical variability of scores. If the Visual Analogue Scales measure mood from moment to moment rather than more stable affective states or traits, then the VAS–D and VAS–A may still be useful screening measures as mood may highly correlate with more stable affective states.

Chapter VI

EPILOGUE: TOWARD A MODEL FOR
VERY BRIEF PSYCHOTHERAPY

JOSEPH E. TALLEY

S trupp and Binder (1984) have noted that most psychological problems and symptoms can be recast as interpersonal problems or problems one has developed in relation to others. Luborsky (1984) has described
the central task of the supportive/expressive psychotherapeutic approach
as the understanding and then the working through of a "core conflictual
relationship theme." A model of very brief psychotherapy might build
on Strupp and Binder's (1984) Time-Limited Dynamic Psychotherapy
and Luborsky's (1984) supportive/expressive approach in looking for a
core conflictual relationship theme. While it is true that little of the
"working through" aspect of treatment can be achieved in very brief
psychotherapy, it is, nevertheless, possible for a core conflictual relationship theme to be understood in terms of a formulation including how
such a theme currently operates in the client/patient's life, how to some
extent it was developed and learned (usually in the family context), and
what cues prompt the reenactment of the theme with others including
the therapist. Techniques for more rapidly identifying and working with
a theme include redecision therapy (Goulding and Goulding, 1979), the
affect bridge (Watkins, 1971), and the eliciting of early memories as
described by Binder and Smokler (1980) and Talley (1986).

Much has been made over the criteria regarding who is an appropriate candidate for brief psychotherapy (see Pinkerton, 1986, and Strupp
and Binder, 1984, for a review). The latter authors have concluded, "it is
essential to focus attention upon patients who have typically been rejected
as suitable candidates for short term psychotherapy and to explore sys-
tematically the extent to which such patients can be treated more effectively
by a well-defined, time-limited approach" (Strupp and Binder, 1984,
p. 276). They continue, "once major symptomatology is ruled out, descrip-
tions of psychopathology symptoms, complaints and so on are not par-

ticularly useful in forecasting the patient's appropriateness for this form of therapy" (p. 57). These comments appear applicable to very brief psychotherapy as well. Given that such an esteemed and experienced clinician as Wolberg (1980) has advocated that all patients be given a trial of brief psychotherapy and given the absence of studies finding very brief psychotherapy harmful to any group of persons, very brief psychotherapy might be offered initially to most seekers of treatment. A measured balance of supportive and expressive (insight oriented) interventions tailored to the individual's tolerance must be provided in order to prevent the treatment from permitting decompensation in the vulnerable. Insight may be promoted in a cautiously escalating manner so as to recognize a given individual's limits. Thus, the therapist's cautious balance between supportive and expressive techniques in the treatment, in accord with the capacity of the person receiving treatment, may be of more importance than the defining of exclusionary criteria. A judicious and flexible level of activity on the part of the therapist must be tailored to the needs of the seeker. An individual's resiliency and ability to tolerate the affects aroused by psychological exploration and by the therapist's interpretations/observations appear to be the most essential elements to assess. In short, the assessment of ego-strength done as the intervention progresses, as well as at the outset, may be the fulcrum of successful very brief psychotherapy.

Assisting the seeker of services in generating a formulation that explains, at least in part autobiographically, the problematic core conflictual relationship theme beneath the symptom or the presenting concern may result in the seeker feeling the veracity of this new view of the problem in an emotionally powerful manner. In all likelihood it leads the seeker to a feeling of increased self-understanding and to a sense of the gravity of this scenario that has been reenacted, usually with destructive consequences, and has been heretofore outside of conscious awareness. Subsequent to such an emotional realization the seeker may feel an increased potential for self control and the alteration of this pattern. Such an increase in perceived potential self control, albeit not yet accomplished, generally breeds hope, which according to the present findings is the single most critical treatment process variable in determining client satisfaction with very brief psychotherapy.

The ideas of Milton H. Erickson as described in *Hypnotic Realties* (Erickson, Rossi, and Rossi, 1976) and in *The Collected Papers of Milton H. Erickson on Hypnosis* (especially vol. IV, *Innovative Hypnotherapy*), edited by Ernest L. Rossi (1980) also include potent tools for very brief psychotherapy. Techniques are offered in these volumes for the essential processes of the fixation of attention (without which little can be accomplished), the "depotentiation of conscious sets" thus minimizing resistance, and the search within aspects of the self that have generally been either preconscious or even unconscious that when accessed can provide possibilities for a reframing of the problem. These processes may be followed by the ability to arrive at new solutions and new ways of being, in part initiated by the therapist. Suggestions by Omer (1990) on "Enhancing the impact of therapeutic interventions" may also be helpful in this regard. Once the theme or pattern has been seen and some possibilities for change have begun, very brief psychotherapy might be considered complete. However, one may be able to add the beginnings of a working through phase also.

An apt metaphor for the self-defeating or neurotic patterns that leave individuals feeling at an impasse and may prompt contacting a psychotherapist is "the Chinese monkey trap." Reportedly in regions of China a monkey of a certain species might be trapped by putting edible goodies into a very large but thin necked jar such that the monkey could freely reach in to grasp the goodies but once the goodies were held fast in the monkey's hand, the fist was too large to pass through the jar's thin neck. Thus, the monkey was stuck or trapped as it could not run well given the large jar now in tow, nor could the monkey freely use the occupied hand in climbing. Nevertheless, such monkeys would allow themselves to be caught rather than let go of the goodies—goodies that could not actually be eaten as they were still in the jar. One might imagine the monkey shaking and pulling at the jar as if the trap were external and not an internal impasse due to the monkey's own ambivalence (to anthropomorphize).

This is, at least in part, the condition of most, if not, indeed all, individuals seeking psychotherapy. A goodie is being grasped that cannot be truly had or enjoyed and the grasping is causing some discomfort or debility. However, for reasons perhaps known and unknown, letting go of the goodie and walking away without it seems impossible. Further, the dilemma or trap may not be understood as being due to an internal state of ambivalence but rather the external manifestations may be seen as the problem. Often the unpleasant emotions associated with letting go of the goodie are perceived as intolerable. Continuing in the metaphor, the task of long-term psychotherapy may be viewed as the process of working toward understanding more fully the known and conscious reasons and elucidating the presently unknown and preconscious or unconscious influences/determinants surrounding the ambivalence and consequent impasse. Subsequent tasks of long-term psychotherapy could be a working-through focused on either accepting the loss of the goodie and the associated pain or accepting the impasse indefinitely and the attending frustration.

One task of very brief psychotherapy may be viewed as the therapist helping the person-at-impasse to reconceptualize the presenting problem as the result, at least in part, of internal rather than external conflicts. While not resolving the dilemma, after completing this limited type of insight-oriented work the seeker is further along in the task of coming to resolution. Indeed, this first step is essential but is often most difficult. Another task of very brief psychotherapy might be the picking of already ripened fruit entailing a primarily supportive intervention consisting of assisting the seeker in articulating and consolidating insights already achieved and providing support, encouragement, and problem-solving while changes are being implemented. Finally, a task of very brief psychotherapy might be the beginning of work toward insight into preconscious and unconscious influences and determinants of the problem, described as the task generally reserved for long-term treatment. The tasks of brief psychotherapy can be viewed as covering the middle ground of a continuum whereby in accord with Wolberg (1980) and Rossi (1980) all seeking psychotherapy might be offered brief or very brief treatment that at times would be a prelude to longer term (perhaps more palatably called "open-ended") psychotherapy. The more insight-oriented the work in the very brief time frame, the more it would require a highly motivated (and less ambivalent), highly psychologically minded person in a state of great readiness for such work who possesses the capacity to be open to influence without being subject to decompensation.

The findings of the present study with regard to very brief psychotherapy are consistent with the general findings concerning the efficacy of psychotherapy according to Smith, Glass, and Miller (1980) in their meta-analysis of 475 controlled psychotherapy studies. In the present investigation very brief psychotherapy, like psychotherapy proper, was found to be beneficial in terms of symptom reduction and generating satisfaction with services received for all gender/age groups studied. Again, as with psychotherapy proper, there were no differences in outcome for very brief psychotherapy attributable to the gender or experience level of the therapist. Those attending more sessions within the one to seven session range in the present study felt more satisfied with services received although satisfaction was not necessarily related to a decrease in the measured symptoms of depression and anxiety.

Our findings with regard to satisfaction with very brief psychotherapy are consistent with the conclusions of studies of psychotherapy proper, concluding that outcome is more a function of client/patient attributes than a function of therapist or technique attributes and that the quality of the therapist/patient relationship is significantly determined by the client/patient factors alone (Strupp, 1980a,b,c). Thus, in the present study it was found that females eighteen to twenty-two years of age and especially those with higher BDI scores on intake and those attending only one session were more likely to be somewhat but not significantly less satisfied with services received, to feel significantly less comfortable with the counselor, to see the counselor as significantly less warm and significantly less skilled and to feel significantly less increased self-understanding than others receiving treatment. Further investigations might focus on whether the expectations of this group *vis-à-vis* treatment differ from the expectations of the other gender/age groups. Finally, our finding that the client perceiving the therapist had encouraged the belief that the client could improve the situation (the instilling of hope and a sense of control in some fashion) was somewhat of a surprise in terms of the apparent magnitude of this factor as a predictor of satisfaction. Nevertheless, Strupp and Binder (1984) have listed this variable as a "primary ingredient" among many potent nonspecific factors in psychotherapy.

In closing, three axioms of a long-time colleague are useful in guiding the process of very brief psychotherapy. They are as follows: "Never underestimate the power of denial," "Blood is thicker than therapy," and to the lament, "Sometimes it seems that in therapy one is just holding hands," the reply "Yes, but it's *how* you hold hands that matters" (W.J.K. Rockwell, personal communication, November, 1977). The first two axioms remind one of the limits that the psychotherapist must accept as inherent in all forms of psychotherapy. The third gives encouragement to the encourager by offering a counterbalancing hope that the clinician can provide something of great value.

In all likelihood attempts such as the present study to "be more scientific" will never adequately unmask such "primary ingredient, nonspecific factors." Yet closer approximations in our understanding of the main ingredients of successful treatment should prove most helpful. Our investigation demonstrates the efficacy of very brief psychotherapy in reducing symptoms of anxiety and depression and demonstrates, too that clients, on the whole, were quite satisfied with the results of very brief psychotherapy. The findings suggest that there may be some differences with regard to the process factors that promote satisfaction by gender/age groupings, however, it appears that the most fundamental factor is common across clients—the factor of encouragement.

APPENDIX A

ZUNG SELF-RATING DEPRESSION SCALE

	None or a little of the time	Some of the time	Good part of the time	Most or all of the time
1. I feel down-hearted and blue	1	2	3	4
2. Morning is when I feel the best	4	3	2	1
3. I have crying spells or feel like it	1	2	3	4
4. I have trouble sleeping at night	1	2	3	4
5. I eat as much as I used to	4	3	2	1
6. I still enjoy sex	4	3	2	1
7. I notice that I am losing weight	1	2	3	4
8. I have trouble with constipation	1	2	3	4
9. My heart beats faster than usual	1	2	3	4
10. I get tired for no reason	1	2	3	4
11. My mind is as clear as it used to be	4	3	2	1
12. I find it easy to do the things I used to	4	3	2	1
13. I am restless and can't keep still	1	2	3	4
14. I feel hopeful about the future	4	3	2	1
15. I am more irritable than usual	1	2	3	4
16. I find it easy to make decisions	4	3	2	1
17. I feel that I am useful and needed	4	3	2	1

	None or a little of the time	Some of the time	Good part of the time	Most or all of the time
18. My life is pretty full	4	3	2	1
19. I feel that others would be better off if I were dead	1	2	3	4
20. I still enjoy the things I used to do	4	3	2	1

Self-rating Depression Scale (SDS)
© William Zung, 1965, 1974. All rights reserved.
Reproduced with the permission of the author.

APPENDIX B

ZUNG SELF-RATING ANXIETY SCALE

	None or a little of the time	Some of the time	Good part of the time	Most or all of the time
1. I feel more nervous and anxious than usual	1	2	3	4
2. I feel afraid for no reason at all	1	2	3	4
3. I get upset easily or feel panicky	1	2	3	4
4. I feel like I'm falling apart and going to pieces	1	2	3	4
5. I feel that everything is all right and nothing bad will happen	4	3	2	1
6. My arms and legs shake and tremble	1	2	3	4
7. I am bothered by headaches, neck and back pains	1	2	3	4
8. I feel weak and get tired easily	1	2	3	4
9. I feel calm and can sit still easily	4	3	2	1
10. I can feel my heart beating fast	1	2	3	4
11. I am bothered by dizzy spells	1	2	3	4
12. I have fainting spells or feel like it	1	2	3	4
13. I can breath in and out easily	4	3	2	1
14. I get feelings of numbness and tingling in my fingers, toes	1	2	3	4
15. I am bothered by stomach aches or indigestion	1	2	3	4

146

	None or a little of the time	Some of the time	Good part of the time	Most or all of the time
16. I have to empty my bladder often	1	2	3	4
17. My hands are usually dry and warm	4	3	2	1
18. My face gets hot and blushes	1	2	3	4
19. I fall asleep easily and get a good night's rest	4	3	2	1
20. I have nightmares	1	2	3	4

Self-rating Anxiety Scale (SAS)

APPENDIX C

DEPRESSION AND ANXIETY VISUAL ANALOGUE SCALES

Instructions: Please cross each of the following lines once at the
place which best represents how you feel

I am not
depressed
(downhearted,　————————————————————————————————　I am as
depressed
(downhearted
blue, low)
at all
blue, low)
as I have
ever been

I am not
anxious
(tense,　————————————————————————————————　I am as
anxious
(tense,
nervous,
uptight)
at all
nervous,
uptight)
as I have
ever been

APPENDIX D

CAPS CLIENT SATISFACTION INDEX

Please respond to the following questions by rating on a scale from one to ten how true the statement is of your personal counseling experience at CAPS.

1) I understand myself better as a result of counseling.

1	2	3	4	5	6	7	8	9	10

| Not at all true | | | Somewhat true | | | Quite true | | | Extremely true |

2) The counselor helped me clarify what I wanted to get out of counseling.

1	2	3	4	5	6	7	8	9	10

| Not at all true | | | Somewhat true | | | Quite true | | | Extremely true |

3) I felt the counselor understood me.

1	2	3	4	5	6	7	8	9	10

| Not at all true | | | Somewhat true | | | Quite true | | | Extremely true |

4) I felt comfortable with the counselor.

1	2	3	4	5	6	7	8	9	10

| Not at all true | | | Somewhat true | | | Quite true | | | Extremely true |

5) The counselor seemed to be authentic or "real."

1	2	3	4	5	6	7	8	9	10

| Not at all true | | | Somewhat true | | | Quite true | | | Extremely true |

6) The counselor helped me clarify how I had been dealing with frustration.

1	2	3	4	5	6	7	8	9	10

| Not at all true | | | Somewhat true | | | Quite true | | | Extremely true |

149

7) I accomplished what I had hoped to by coming to CAPS.

1	2	3	4	5	6	7	8	9	10

| Not at all true | | Somewhat true | | | Quite true | | | Extremely true | |

8) The counselor helped me to break the problem down into smaller parts.

1	2	3	4	5	6	7	8	9	10

| Not at all true | | Somewhat true | | | Quite true | | | Extremely true | |

9) The counselor seemed to be a warm person.

1	2	3	4	5	6	7	8	9	10

| Not at all true | | Somewhat true | | | Quite true | | | Extremely true | |

10) The counselor encouraged me to believe that I could improve my situation.

1	2	3	4	5	6	7	8	9	10

| Not at all true | | Somewhat true | | | Quite true | | | Extremely true | |

11) My methods of dealing with the problems I face have changed as a result of counseling.

1	2	3	4	5	6	7	8	9	10

| Not at all true | | Somewhat true | | | Quite true | | | Extremely true | |

12) Through counseling I have become more certain of my ability to make good decisions.

1	2	3	4	5	6	7	8	9	10

| Not at all true | | Somewhat true | | | Quite true | | | Extremely true | |

13) I felt I was working together with the counselor.

1	2	3	4	5	6	7	8	9	10

| Not at all true | | Somewhat true | | | Quite true | | | Extremely true | |

14) The counselor encouraged me to discuss any feelings I might have about him/her during the sessions.

1	2	3	4	5	6	7	8	9	10

| Not at all true | | Somewhat true | | | Quite true | | | Extremely true | |

15) The counselor seemed to be a skilled counselor.

1	2	3	4	5	6	7	8	9	10

Not at all true			Somewhat true			Quite true			Extremely true

16) In summary, I am satisfied with the services I received at CAPS.

1	2	3	4	5	6	7	8	9	10

Not at all true			Somewhat true			Quite true			Extremely true

Please check either 1, 2, or 3 for the next three questions.

17) Have you sought counseling elsewhere since your experience at CAPS?
   _____ 1) Yes, at the recommendation of the counselor
   _____ 2) Yes, not due to recommendation of the counselor
   _____ 3) No

18) How does your current academic performance compare to your performance prior to coming to CAPS?
   _____ 1) The same
   _____ 2) Better
   _____ 3) Worse

19) How does the quality of your current relationships with others compare to the quality of them prior to coming to CAPS?
   _____ 1) The same
   _____ 2) Better
   _____ 3) Worse

REFERENCES

Adler, A. (1925). *Individual Psychotherapy* (P. Radin, Trans.). London: Routledge and Kegan Paul, Ltd.

Agrell, B., and Dehlin, O. (1989). Comparison of six depression rating scales in geriatric stroke patients. *Stroke, 20,* 1190–1194.

Aitken, R.C.B. (1969). A growing edge of measurement of feelings. *Proceedings of the Royal Society of Medicine, 62,* 989–996.

Alexander, F. (1946). Case B. (Depression). In F. Alexander and T.M. French (Eds.), *Psychoanalytic therapy: Principles and application* (pp. 146–155). New York: Ronald Press.

American Psychiatric Association. (1987). *Diagnostic and statistical manual of mental and emotional disorders III-R.* Washington D.C.: American Psychiatric Association Press.

Anderson, C.M., Harrow, M., Schwartz, A.H., and Kupfer, D.J. (1972). Impact of therapist on patient satisfaction in group psychotherapy. *Comprehensive Psychiatry, 13,* 33–40.

Auerbach, A.H., and Johnson, M. (1977). Research on the therapists' level of experience. In A.S. Gurman and A.M. Razin (Eds.), *Effective psychotherapy: A handbook of research* (pp. 84–102). New York: Pergamon.

Aun, C., Lam, Y.M., and Collett, B. (1986). Evaluation of the use of visual analogue scale in Chinese patients. *Pain, 25,* 215–221.

Auslander, G.K., Levav, I., and Nachmani, N. (1988). Screening for depressive symptoms among the elderly in Israel. *Israel Journal of Medical Sciences, 24,* 24–37.

Baer, L., and Surman, O.S. (1985). Microcomputer-assisted relaxation. *Perceptual and Motor Skills, 61,* 499–502.

Balch, P., Ireland, J.F., McWilliams, S.A., and Lewis, S.B. (1977). Client evaluation of community mental health services: Relation to demographic and treatment variables. *American Journal of Community Psychology, 5,* 243–247.

Ballinger, C.B., Kay, D.S., Naylor, G.J., and Smith, A.H. (1982). Some biochemical findings during pregnancy and after delivery in relation to mood change. *Psychological Medicine, 12,* 549–556.

Barron, F. (1953). Some test correlates of response to psychotherapy. *Journal of Consulting Psychology, 17,* 235–241.

Barry, J., and Fulkerson, S. (1966). Chronicity and the prediction of duration and outcome of hospitalization from capacity measures. *Psychiatric Quarterly, 40,* 104–121.

Bassi, S., Albizzati, M.G., Ferrarese, C., Frattola, L., Cesana, B., Piolti, R., and Farolfi, A. (1989). Alpidem, a novel anxiolytic drug: A double-blind, placebo-controlled study in anxious outpatients. *Clinical Neuropharmacology, 12,* 67–74.

Beaumont, G., Gringras, M., and Ankier, S.I. (1984). Trazodone and minanserin in general practice. *Psychopathology, 17,* 24–29.

Beck, A.T., and Beamesderfer, A. (1974). Assessment of depression: The depression inventory. In P. Pichot (Ed.), *Psychological measurements in psychopharmacology* (Vol 7, pp. 151–169). Basel, Switzerland: Karger Press.

Beck, A.T., and Beck, R.W. (1972). Screening depressed patients in family practice: A rapid technique. *Postgraduate medicine, 52,* 81–85.

Beck, A.T., Rush, A.J., Shaw, B.F., and Emery, G. (1979). *Cognitive therapy of depression.* New York: Guilford Press.

Beck, A.T., and Steer, R.A. (1984). Internal consistencies of the original and revised Beck Depression Inventory. *Journal of Clinical Psychology, 40,* 1365–1367.

Beck, A., Steer, R., and Garbin, M. (1988). Psychometric properties of the Beck Depression Inventory: Twenty-five years of evaluation. *Clinical Psychology Review, 8* (1), 77–100.

Beck, A.T., Ward, C.H., Mendelson, M., Mock, J., and Erbaugh, J. (1961). An inventory for measuring depression. *Archives of General Psychiatry, 4,* 53–63.

Beckham, E.E. (1989). Improvement after evaluation in psychotherapy of depression: Evidence of placebo effect? *Journal of Clinical Psychology, 45,* 945–950.

Bellack, L., and Small, L. (1978). *Emergency psychotherapy and brief psychotherapy* (2nd ed.). New York: Grune and Stratton.

Bennett, L.A. (1986). Depressive symptoms among hospitalized and posthospitalized alcoholics in Yugoslavia. *Journal of Nervous and Mental Disease, 174,* 545–552.

Bent, R.J., Putnam, D.G., Kiesler, D.J., and Nowicki, S. (1976). Correlates of successful and unsuccessful psychotherapy. *Journal of Consulting and Clinical Psychology, 44,* 149.

Bergin, A.E. (1971). The evaluation of therapeutic outcomes. In S.L. Garfield and A.E. Bergin (Eds.), *Handbook of psychotherapy and behavior change: An empirical analysis* (pp. 217–270). New York: Wiley.

Bergin, A.E., and Lambert, M.J. (1978). The evaluation of therapeutic outcomes. In S.L. Garfield and A.E. Bergin (Eds.), *Handbook of psychotherapy and behavior change: An empirical analysis* (pp. 139–189). New York: Wiley.

Berrios, G.E., Ryley, J.P., Garvey, T.P., and Moffat, D.A. (1988). Psychiatric morbidity in subjects with inner ear disorders. *Clinical Otolaryngology, 13,* 259–266.

Berry, J.M., Storandt, M., and Coyne, A. (1984). Age and sex differences in somatic complaints associated with depression. *Journal of Gerontology, 39,* 465–467.

Beutler, L. E., Arizmendi, T.G., Crago, M., Shanfield, S., and Hagaman, R. (1983). The effects of value similarity and clients' persuadability on value convergence and psychotherapy improvement. *Journal of Social and Clinical Psychology, 1,* 231–245.

Beutler, L.E., Crago, M., and Arizmendi, T.G. (1986). Therapist variables in psychotherapy process and outcome. In S.L. Garfield and A.E. Bergin (Eds.), *Handbook of psychotherapy and behavior change* (pp. 257–310). New York: Wiley.

Biggs, J.T., Wylie, L.T., Ziegler, V.E. (1978). Validity of the Zung Self-rating depression scale. *British Journal of Psychiatry, 132,* 381–385.

Binder, J., and Smokler, I. (1980). Early memories: A technical aid to focusing in time-limited dynamic psychotherapy. *Psychotherapy Theory, Research and Practice, 17,* 52–62.

Bloom, B.L. (1956). Prognostic significance of the underproductive Rorschach. *Journal of Projective Techniques, 20,* 336–371.

Bloom, B.L. (1981). Focused single-session therapy: Initial development and evaluation. In S. Budman (Ed.), *Forms of brief therapy* (pp. 167–216). New York: Guilford Press.

Bloom, L.J., and Trautt, G.M. (1978). Psychotherapists' perceptions of clients' satisfaction following termination. *Perceptual and Motor Skills, 46,* 1165–1166.

Bolon, K., and Barling, J. (1980). The measurement of self-rated depression: A multidimensional approach. *Journal of Geriatric Psychology, 137,* 309–310.

Bond, A., and Lader, M. (1974). The use of analogue scales in rating subjective feelings. *British Journal of Medical Psychology, 47,* 211–218.

Bordwell, M.B. (1989). The relationship of length of counseling to expectations about length and to satisfaction. *Dissertation Abstracts International, 50* (2), 359A.

Borg, G.A.V. (1982). Psychophysical bases of perceived exertion. *Medicine and Science in Sports and Exercise, 14,* 377–381.

Bradshaw, G., and Parker, G. (1983). Depression in general practice attenders. *Australian and New Zealand Journal of Psychiatry, 17,* 361–365.

Breuer, J., and Freud, S. (1936). *Studies in hysteria: Nervous and mental disease monograph series: No. 61,* (pp. 89–96). New York and District of Columbia: Nervous and Mental Disease Publishers Co.

Brill, N.Q., and Storrow, H.A. (1960). Social class and psychiatric treatment. *Archives of General Psychiatry, 3,* 340–344.

Brown, G.L., and Zung, W.W.K. (1972). Depression scales: Self- or physician-rating? A validation of certain clinically observable phenomena. *Comprehensive Psychiatry, 13,* 361–367.

Budman, S.H., and Gurman, A. (1983). The practice of brief therapy. *Professional Psychology: Research and Practice, 14,* 277–292.

Bugge, I., Hendel, D.D., and Moen, R. (1985). Client evaluations of therapeutic processes and outcomes in a university mental health center. *Journal of American College Health Association, 33,* 141–146.

Bumberry, W., Oliver, J.M., and McClure, J.W. (1978). Validation of the Beck Depression Inventory in a university population using psychiatric estimate as the criterion. *Journal of Consulting and Clinical Psychology, 46* (1), 150–155.

Burrows, G.D., Foenander, G., Davies, B., and Scoggins, B.A. (1976). Rating scales as predictors of response to tricyclic antidepressants. *Australian and New Zealand Journal of Psychiatry, 14,* 65–71.

Butcher, J.N., Stelmachers, Z., and Maudel, G.R. (1984). Crisis intervention. In E.B. Weiner (Ed.) *Clinical methods in psychology* (pp. 572–633). New York: Wiley.

Butler, S.F., and Strupp, H.H. (1986). Specific and nonspecific factors in psychotherapy: A problematic paradigm for psychotherapy research. *Psychotherapy, 23,* 30–40.

Byrne, D. G. (1980). The prevalence of symptoms of depression in an Australian general population. *Australian and New Zealand Journal of Psychiatry, 14,* 65–71.

Byrne, D.G., Doyle, D, and Pritchard, D.W. (1977). Sex differences in response to a self-rating depression scale. *British Journal of Social and Clinical Psychology, 16,* 269–273.

Carlsson, A.M. (1983). Assessment of chronic pain. I: Aspects of the reliability and validity of the visual analogue scale. *Pain, 16,* 87–101.

Carroll, B.J., Felding, J.M., and Blanshki, T.G. (1973). Depression rating scales: A critical review. *Archives of General Psychiatry, 28,* 361–366.

Cartwright, D.S. (1955). Success in psychotherapy as a function of certain actuarial variables. *Journal of Consulting Psychology, 19,* 357–363.

Casner, D. (1950). Certain factors associated with success and failure in personal-adjustment counseling. *American Psychologist, 5,* 348.

Cella, D.F., and Perry, S.W. (1986). Reliability and concurrent validity of three visual-analogue mood scales. *Psychological Reports, 59,* 827–833.

Chang, W.C. (1985). A cross-cultural study of depressive symptomology. *Culture, Medicine and Psychiatry, 9,* 295–317.

Chickering, A.W. (1976). *Education and identity.* San Francisco: Jossey-Bass.

Choini'ere, M., Melzack, R., Rondeau, J., Girard, N., and Paquin, M.J. (1989). The pain of burns: Characteristics and correlates. *Journal of Trauma, 29,* 1531–1539.

Claiborn, C.D., Crawford, J.B., and Hackman, H.W. (1983). Effects of intervention discrepancy in counseling for negative emotions. *Journal of Counseling Psychology, 30,* 164–171.

Cohen, B.D., Penick, S.B., and Tarter, R.E. (1974). Antidepressant effects of unilateral electric convulsive shock therapy. *Archives of General Psychiatry, 31,* 673–675.

Cooke, D. (1980). The structure of depression found in the general population. *Psychological Medicine, 10,* 455–463.

Cookson, J., and Silverston, T. (1986). The effects of methylamphetamine on mood and appetite in depressed patients: A placebo controlled study. *International Clinical Psychopharmacology, 1,* 127–133.

Crosby, A.R. (1969). The use of the self-rating depression scale after traumatic injuries. *Journal of the American Osteopathic Association, 69,* 269–270.

Davies, B., Burrows, G., and Poynton, C. (1975). A comparative study of four depression rating scales. *Australian and New Zealand Journal of Psychiatry, 9,* 21–24.

DeForge, B.R., and Sobel, J. (1988). Self-report depression scales in the elderly: The relationship between the CES–D and Zung. *International Journal of Psychiatry in Medicine, 18,* 325–338.

deJonghe, F., Swinkels, J., Tuynman-Qua, H., and Jonkers, F. (1989). A comparative study of suriclone, lorazepam and placebo in anxiety disorder. *Pharmacopsychiatry, 22,* 266–271.

DeMaio, D. and Levi-Minzi, A. (1979). Amitriptyline: Comparison of three different dosage schedules in neurotic depression. *British Journal of Psychiatry, 135,* 73–76.

Denner, B., and Halprin, F. (1974). Measuring consumer satisfaction in a community outpost. *American Journal of Community Psychology, 2,* 13–22.

Dixon, J.S., and Bird, H.A. (1981). Reproducibility along a 10 cm vertical visual analogue scale. *Annals of the Rheumatic Diseases, 40,* 87–89.

Dobson, K.S. (1989). A meta-analysis of the efficacy of cognitive therapy for depression. *Journal of Consulting and Clinical Psychology, 57,* 414–419.

Doerfler, L.A., and Richards, C.S. (1983). College women coping with depression. *Behavior Research and Therapy, 21,* 221–224.

Donnan, H.H., and Mitchell, H.D., Jr. (1979). Preferences for older vs. younger counselors among a group of elderly persons. *Journal of Counseling Psychology, 26,* 514–518.

Dorosin, D., Gibbs, J., and Kaplan, L. (1976). Very brief interventions: A pilot evaluation. *Journal of American College Health Association, 24,* 191–194.

Dratcu, L., de Costa, R.L., and Calil, H.M. (1987). Depression assessment in Brazil. The first application of the Montgomery-Asberg Depression Rating Scale. *British Journal of Psychiatry, 150,* 797–800.

Dunn, V.K., and Sacco, W.P. (1989). Psychometric evaluation of the Geriatric Depression Scale and the Zung Self-rating Depression Scale using an elderly community sample. *Psychology and Aging, 4,* 125–126.

Dyck, R.J., and Azim, H.F.A. (1983). Patient satisfaction in a psychiatric walk-in clinic. *Canadian Journal of Psychiatry, 28,* 30–33.

Edlund, M.J., and Swann, A.C. (1989). Low MHPG and continuing treatment in panic disorder. *Progress in Neuro-Psychopharmacology, 13,* 701–707.

Ehrensing, R.H., and Kastin, A.J. (1978). Dose-related biphasic effect of prolyl-leucyl-glycinamide (MIF–I) in depression. *American Journal of Psychiatry, 135,* 562–566.

Equi, P.J., and Jabara, R.F. (1976). Validation of the Self-rating Depression Scale in an alcoholic population. *Journal of Clinical Psychology, 32,* 504–507.

Erickson, E.H. (1968). *Identity, youth and crisis.* New York: W.W. Norton, Inc.

Erickson, M.H. (1980). Innovative Hypnotherapy. In E.L. Rossi (Ed.), *The collected papers of Milton H. Erickson on hypnosis* (Vol. IV, pp. xxi–542). New York: Irvington Publishers.

Erickson, M.H., Rossi, E.L., and Rossi, S.I. (1976). *Hypnotic realities: The induction of clinical hypnosis and forms of indirect suggestion.* New York: Irvington Publishers.

Eysenck, H.J. (1952). The effects of psychotherapy: An evaluation. *Journal of Consulting Psychology, 16,* 319–324.

Fabre, L.F., McLendon, D.M, and Mallette, A. (1979). A doubleblind comparison of prazepam with diazepam, chlorazepate dipotassium and placebo in anxious outpatients. *Journal of International Medical Research, 7,* 147–151.

Faravelli, C., Albanesi, G., and Poli, E. (1986). Depression: A comparison of rating scales. *Journal of Affective Disorders, 11,* 245–257.

Feifel, H., and Eells, J. (1963). Patients and psychotherapists assess the same psychotherapy. *Journal of Counseling Psychology, 27,* 310–318.

Feinberg, M., Carroll, B.J., Smouse, P.E., and Rawson, S.G. (1981). The Carroll Rating Scale for depression. III: Comparison with other instruments. *British Journal of Psychiatry, 138,* 205–209.

Fiske, D.W., Cartwright, D.S., and Kirtner, W.L. (1964). Are psychotherapeutic changes predictable?. *Journal of Abnormal and Social Psychology, 69,* 418–426.

Flegenheimer, W.V. (1982). *Techniques of Brief Psychotherapy.* New York: Jason Aronson.

Folstein, M.F., and Luria, R. (1973). Reliability, validity, and clinical application of the Visual Analogue Mood Scale. *Psychological Medicine, 3,* 479–486.

Frank, J.D. (1974). Therapeutic components of psychotherapy. A 25-year progress report of research. *The Journal of Nervous and Mental Disease, 159,* 325–342.

Frank, J.D., Gliedman, L.H., Imber, S.D., Nash, E.H., Jr., and Stone, A.R. (1957). Why patients leave psychotherapy. *Archives of Neurology and Psychiatry, 77,* 283–299.

Frank, R., Salzman, K., and Fergus, E. (1977). Correlates of consumer satisfaction with outpatient therapy assessed by postcard. *Community Mental Health Journal, 13,* 37–45.

Freud, S. (1936). Inhibitions, symptoms, and anxieties. *Psychoanalytic Quarterly, 5,* 261–279.

Freud, S. (1937). Analysis terminable and interminable. In J. Strachey (Ed.), *The Standard Edition of the Complete Psychological Works of Sigmund Freud,* v. 23, (pp. 211–253). London: Hogarth Press and Institute for Psychoanalysis.

Freyd, M. (1923). The graphic rating scale. *Journal of Educational Psychology, 14,* 83.

Friedlander, M.L. (1982). Expectations and perceptions of counseling: Changes over time and in relation to verbal behavior. *Journal of College Student Personnel, 23* (5), 402–408.

Friedman, M.J., Stolk, J.M., Harris, P.G., and Cooper, T.B. (1984). Serum dopamine-beta-hydroxylase activity in depression and anxiety. *Biological Psychiatry, 19,* 557–570.

Fuerst, R.A. (1946). Case D. (Frigidity). In F. Alexander and T.M. French (Eds.), *Psychoanalytic therapy: Principles and application* (pp. 158–162). New York: Ronald Press.

Fukuda, K. and Kobayashi, S. (1975). A study on a self-rating depression scale. *Psychiatrica Neurologia Japonica, 75,* 673–679.

Garcia-Oyola, E., and Curioso, W.I. (1989). Ranitidine plus bromazepam in the treatment of duodenal ulcer: Effect on gastric acid secretion. *Journal of International Medical Research, 17,* 55–61.

Gardner, E.A. (1983). Long-term preventive care in depression: The use of bupropion in patients intolerant of other antidepressants. *Journal of Clinical Psychiatry, 44,* 157–162.

Garfield, S.L. (1986). Research on client variables in psychotherapy. In S.L. Garfield and A.E. Bergin (Eds.), *Handbook of psychotherapy and behavior change: An empirical analysis* (pp. 213–256). New York: Wiley.

Garfield, S.L., and Bergin, A.E. (1986). *Handbook of psychotherapy and behavior change: An empirical analysis* (3rd ed.). New York: Wiley.

Gaylin, N. (1966). Psychotherapy and psychological health: A Rorschach function and structure analysis. *Journal of Consulting Psychology, 30,* 494–500.

Gelso, C.J., Mills, D.H., and Spiegel, S.B. (1983). Client and therapist factors influencing the outcomes of time-limited counseling one month and eighteen months after treatment. In C.J. Gelso and D.H. Johnson (Eds.), *Explorations in time-limited counseling and psychotherapy* (pp. 87–114). New York: Teachers College Press.

George, D.T., and Jimerson, D.C. (1986). Changes in serum chloride ion concentration following sodium lactate infusion. *American Journal of Psychiatry, 143,* 1499.

Getz, H.G., and Miles, J.H. (1978). Women and peers as counselors: A look at client preferences. *Journal of College Student Personnel, 19,* 37–41.

Giambra, L.M. (1977). Independent dimensions of depression: A factor analysis of three self-report depression measures. *Journal of Clinical Psychology, 33,* 928–935.

Gift, A. (1989). Visual analogue scales: Measurement of subjective phenomena. *Nursing Research, 38,* 286–288.

Gilligan, C.F. (1977). *In a different voice: Women's conception of the self and of morality.* Cambridge: Harvard Educational Review.

Gold, S.R., Jarvinen, P.J., and Teague, R.G. (1982). Imagery elaboration and clarity in modifying college students' depression. *Journal of Clinical Psychology, 38,* 312–314.

Goldenholz, N. (1976). The effect of sex of therapist-client dyad upon outcome of psychotherapy. *Dissertation Abstracts International, 36,* 4687B–4688B.

Goldstein, A.P. (1960). Patients' expectancies and non-specific therapy as a basis for (un)spontaneous remission. *Journal of Clinical Psychology, 16,* 399–403.

Gomes-Schwartz, B. (1978). Effective ingredients in psychotherapy: Prediction of outcome from process variables. *Journal of Consulting and Clinical Psychology, 46,* 1023–1035.

Gotlib, I.H. (1984). Depression and general psychopathology in university students. *Journal of Abnormal Psychology, 93,* 19–30.

Gottschalk, L.A., Mayerson, P., and Gottlieb, A.A. (1967). Prediction and evaluation of outcome in an emergency brief psychotherapy clinic. *Journal of Nervous and Mental Disease, 144,* 77–96.

Gould, J. (1982). A psychometric investigation of the standard and short form Beck Depression Inventory. *Psychological Reports, 51,* 1167–1170.

Goulding, M.M., and Goulding, R.L. (1979). *Changing lives through redecision therapy.* New York: Brunner/Mazel.

Greenberg, L.S. (1986). Change process research. *Journal of Consulting and Clinical Psychology, 54,* 4–9.

Greer, S., and Burgess, C. (1987). A self-esteem measure for patients with cancer. *Psychology and Health, 1,* 327–340.

Griffin, P.T., and Kogut, D. (1988). Validity of orally administered Beck and Zung Depression Scales in a state hospital setting. *Journal of Clinical Psychology, 44,* 756–759.

Grotjahn, M., and Case, C. (1946). Reactive depression. In F. Alexander, and T.M. French (eds.) *Psychoanalytic therapy: Principles and application* (pp. 155–157). New York: Ronald Press.

Haccoun, D.M., and Lavigueur, H. (1979). Effects of clinical experience and client emotion on therapists' responses. *Journal of Consulting and Clinical Psychology, 47,* 416–418.

Haggerty, J., Baldwin, B.A., Liptzin, M.B. (1980). Very brief interventions in college mental health. *Journal of the American College Health Association, 28,* 326–329.

Hamburg, D.A., Bibring, G.L., Fisher, C., Stanton, A.H., Weinstock, H.I., and

Haggard, E. (1967). Report of Ad Hoc Committee on central fact-gathering data of the American Psychoanalytic Association. *Journal of the American Psychoanalytic Association, 15,* 841–861.

Hamilton, M. (1960). A rating scale for depression. *Journal of Neurology, Neurosurgery and Psychiatry, 23,* 56–61.

Hammen, C.L. (1980). Depression in college students: Beyond the Beck Depression Inventory. *Journal of Consulting and Clinical Psychology, 48,* 126–128.

Hammen, C.L., and Padesky, C.A. (1977). Sex differences in the expression of depressive responses on the Beck Depression Inventory. *Journal of Abnormal Psychology, 86,* 609–614.

Hanfmann, E. (1978). *Effective therapy for college students: Alternatives to traditional counseling.* San Francisco: Jossey-Bass.

Hansson, L., and Berglund, M. (1987). Factors influencing treatment outcome and patient satisfaction in a short-term psychiatric ward: A path analysis study of the importance of patient involvement in treatment planning. *European Archives of Psychiatry and Neurological Sciences, 236,* 269–275.

Hapgood, C.C., Elkind, G.S., and Wright, J.J. (1988). Maternity blues: Phenomena and relationship to later post partum depression. *Australian and New Zealand Journal of Psychiatry, 22,* 299–306.

Harder, D.W., Greenwald, D.F., Strauss, J.S., Kokes, R.F., Ritzler, B.A., and Gift, T.E. (1990). Predictors of two-year outcome among psychiatric outpatients. *Journal of Clinical Psychology, 46* (3), 251–261.

Hartlage, L.C., and Sperr, E.V. (1980). Patient preferences with regard to ideal therapist characteristics. *Journal of Clinical Psychology, 36* (1), 288–291.

Hartley, D.E., and Strupp, H.H. (1983). The therapeutic alliance: Its relationship to outcome in brief psychotherapy. In J. Masling (Ed.), *Empirical studies of psychoanalytic theories* (Vol. 1). Hillsdale, NJ: The Analytic Press.

Hatzenbuehler, L.C., Parpal, M., and Matthews, L. (1983). Classifying college students as depressed or nondepressed using the Beck Depression Inventory: An empirical analysis. *Journal of Consulting and Clinical Psychology, 51,* 360–366.

Hayes, M.G., and Patterson, D.G. (1921). Experimental development of the graphic rating method. *Psychological Bulletin, 18,* 98.

Henry, W.P., Schacht, T.E., and Strupp, H.H. (1986). Structural analysis of social behavior: Application to a study of interpersonal process in differential therapeutic outcome. *Journal of Consulting and Clinical Psychology, 54,* 27–31.

Heppner, P.P., and Heesacker, M. (1983). Perceived counselor characteristics, client expectations, and client satisfaction with counseling. *Journal of Counseling Psychology, 30* (1), 31–39.

Hersh, J.B. (1988). A commentary on brief therapy. *Journal of College Student Psychotherapy, 3* (1), 55–58.

Heubush, N.J., and Horan, J.J. (1977). Some effects of counselor profanity in counseling. *Journal of Counseling Psychology, 24,* 456–458.

Hibbs, C.W. (1976). Selected factors affecting client satisfaction in a university counseling center. *Dissertation Abstracts International, 36,* 5045A.

Hickie, C., and Snowdon, J. (1987). Depression scales for the elderly: GDS, Gilleard, Zung. *Clinical Gerontologist, 6,* 51–53.

Hoberman, H.M., Lewinsohn, P.M., and Tilson, M. (1988). Group treatment of depression: Individual predictors of outcome. *Journal of Consulting and Clinical Psychology, 56,* 393–398.

Hodgson, J.W. (1981). Cognitive vs. behavioral-interpersonal approaches to the group treatment of depressed college students. *Journal of Counseling Psychology, 28,* 243–249.

Holt, R., and Luborsky, L. (1958). *Personality patterns of psychiatrists.* Topeka: The Menninger Foundation.

Howard, K.I., Kopta, S.M., Krause, M.S., and Orlinsky, D.E. (1986). The dose-effect relationship in psychotherapy. *American Psychologist, 41,* 159–164.

Ihezue, U.H., and Kumaraswamy, N. (1986). Prevalence of depressive symptoms among patients attending a general outpatient clinic. *Acta Psychiatrica Scandinavia, 73,* 395–398.

Ivanoff, J.M., Layman, F.A., and von Singer, R. (1973). Use of the Zung in identifying potential student adjustment problems. *Psychological Reports, 32,* 489–490.

Jakobsen, C.J., Blom, L., Brondbjerg, M., and Lenler, P.P. (1990). Effect of metoprolol and diazepam on preoperative anxiety. *Anaesthesia, 45,* 40–43.

Jegede, R.O. (1976). Psychometric properties of the Self-rating Depression Scale (SDS). *Journal of Psychology, 93,* 27–30.

Jegede, R.O. (1977). Psychometric attributes of the Self-rating Anxiety Scale. *Psychological Reports, 40,* 303–306.

Jones, E. (1955). *The life and work of Sigmund Freud* (vol. 1) New York: Basic Books.

Jones, E.E., Krupnick, J.L., and Kerig, P.A. (1987). Some gender effects in a brief psychotherapy. *Psychotherapy, 24* (3), 336–352.

Jones, E.E., and Zoppel, C.L. (1982). Impact of client and therapist gender on psychotherapy process and outcome. *Journal of Consulting and Clinical Psychology, 50* (2), 259–272.

Junginger, J., and Frame, C.L. (1985). Self-report on the frequency and phenomenology of verbal hallucinations. *Journal of Nervous and Mental Disease, 173,* 149–155.

Kalman, T.P. (1983). An overview of patient satisfaction with psychiatric treatment. *Hospital and Community Psychiatry, 34,* 48–54.

Karasu, T., Stein, S.P., and Charles, E. (1979). Age factors in patient-therapist relationship. *Journal of Nervous and Mental Disease, 167,* 100–104.

Kashani, J.H., and Priesmeyer, M. (1983). Differences of depressive symptoms and depression among college students. *American Journal of Psychiatry, 140,* 1081–1082.

Katz, M.M., Lorr, M., and Rubinstein, E.A. (1958). Remainer patients' attributes and their relation to subsequent improvement in psychotherapy. *Journal of Consulting Psychology, 22,* 411–413.

Kazdin, A.E. (1986). Comparative outcome studies in psychotherapy: Methodological issues and strategies. *Journal of Consulting and Clinical Psychology, 54* (1), 95–105.

Keithly, L.J., Samples, S.J., and Strupp, H.H. (1980). Patient motivation as a predictor of process and outcome in psychotherapy. *Psychotherapy and Psychosomatics, 33,* 87–97.

Kendall, P.C., Hollon, S.D., Beck, A.T., Hammen, C.L., and Ingram, R.E. (1987). Issues and recommendations regarding use of the Beck Depression Inventory. *Cognitive Therapy and Research, 11,* 289–299.

Kendell, R.E., McGuire, R.J., Connor, Y., and Cox, J.L. (1981). Mood changes in the first three weeks after childbirth. *Journal of Affective Disorders, 3,* 317–326.

Kernberg, O.F., Burstein, E.D., Coyne, L., Applebaum, A., Horwitz, L., and Voth, H. (1972). Psychotherapy and psychoanalysis: Final report of the Menninger Foundation's Psychotherapy Research Project. *Bulletin of the Menninger Clinic, 36,* 1–276.

Kinsella, G., Moran, C., Ford, B., and Ponsford, J. (1988). Emotional disorder and its assessment within the severe head injured population. *Psychological Medicine, 18,* 57–63.

Kirtner, W.L., and Cartwright, D.S. (1958). Success and failure of client-centered therapy as a function of client personality variables. *Journal of Consulting Psychology, 22,* 259–264.

Kivela, S. and Pahkala, K. (1987). Factor structure of the Zung Self-rating Depression Scale among a depressed elderly population. *International Journal of Psychology, 22,* 289–300.

Klerman, G.L., Weissman, M.M., Rounsaville, B.J., and Chevron, E.S. (1984). *Interpersonal psychotherapy of depression.* New York: Basic Books.

Knapp, P.H., Levin, S., McCarter, R.H., Wermer, H., and Zetzel, E. (1960). Suitability for psychoanalysis: A review of 100 supervised analytic cases. *Psychoanalytic Quarterly, 29,* 459–477.

Knight, R.P. (1937). Application of psychoanalytic concepts in psychotherapy: Report of clinical trials in a mental hygiene service. *Bulletin of the Menninger Clinic, 1,* 99–109.

Knight, R.G., and Thirkettle, J.A. (1986). Anxiety and depression in the immediate post-partum period: A controlled investigation of a primiparous sample. *Australian and New Zealand Journal of Psychiatry, 20,* 430–436.

Knight, R.G., Waal-Manning, H.J., and Godfrey, H.P. (1983). The relationship between state anxiety and depressed mood: A validity study. *Journal of Behavioral Assessment, 5,* 191–201.

Knight, R.G., Waal-Manning, H.J., and Spears, G.F. (1983). Some norms and reliability data for the State-Trait Anxiety Inventory and the Zung Self-rating Depression Scale. *British Journal of Clinical Psychology, 22,* 245–249.

Knudsen, P., Bjorndal, T., Johnsen, K., and Pfeiffer-Petersen, K. (1984). Zimeldine versus Nomifensine: A double-blind study of depressed inpatients. *Neuropsychobiology, 11,* 236–242.

Koss, M.P., and Butcher, J.N. (1986). Research on brief psychotherapy. In S.L. Garfield and A.E. Bergin (Eds.), *Handbook of psychotherapy and behavior change* (pp. 627–670). New York: Wiley.

Krupp, L.B., Alvarez, L.A., Larocca, N.G., and Scheinberg, L.C. (1988). Fatigue in multiple sclerosis. *Archives of Neurology, 45,* 435–437.

Kukull, W.A., Koepgell, T.D., Inui, T.S., Borson, S., Okimoto, J., Rasking, M.A., and Gale, J.L. (1986). Depression and physical illness among elderly general medical clinic patients. *Journal of Affective Disorders, 10,* 153–162.

Lambert, M.J. (1976). Spontaneous remission in adult neurotic disorders: A revision and summary. *Psychological Bulletin, 83,* 107–119.

Lambert, M.J. (Ed.). (1983). *Psychotherapy and patient relationships.* Belmont, CA: Dorsey.

Lambert, M.J., Hatch, D.R., Kingston, M.D., and Edwards, B.C. (1986). Zung, Beck, and Hamilton Rating Scales as measures of treatment outcome: A meta-analytic comparison. *Journal of Consulting and Clinical Psychology, 54,* 54–59.

Lapierre, Y.D., and Butter, H.J. (1978). Imipramine and maprotiline in agitated and retarded depression: A controlled psychiatric assessment. *Progress in Neuro-Psychopharmacology, 2,* 207–216.

Lapierre, Y.D., and Lee, M. (1976). Piperacetazine in the treatment of mixed neurotics. *Current Psychotherapeutic Research, 19,* 105–109.

Larsen, D.L. (1978). Enhancing client utilization of community mental health outpatient services. *Dissertation Abstracts International, 39,* 4041B.

Larsen, D.L., Attkisson, C.C., and Hargreaves, W.A. (1979). Assessment of client/patient satisfaction: Development of a general scale. *Evaluation and Program Planning, 2,* 179–207.

Lasky, R.G., and Salomone, P.R. (1977). Attraction to psychotherapy: Influences of therapist status and therapist-patient age similarity. *Journal of Clinical Psychology, 33,* 511–516.

Lennard, H.L., and Bernstein, A. (1960). *The anatomy of psychotherapy: Systems of communication and expectation.* New York: Columbia University Press.

Lewin, K.K. (1970). *Brief psychotherapy: Brief encounters.* St. Louis: Green.

Lindsay, W.R., and Michie, A.M. (1988). Adaptation of the Zung Self-rating Anxiety Scale for people with mental handicap. *Journal of Mental Deficiency Research, 32,* 485–490.

Lipkin, S. (1954). Clients' feelings and attitudes in relation to the outcome of client-centered therapy. *Psychological Monographs, 68,* (Whole No. 372).

Little, J.C., and McPhail, N.I. (1973). Measures of depressive mood at monthly intervals. *British Journal of Psychiatry, 122,* 447–452.

Little, K.Y. (1989). Detecting acute drug effects. *Biological Psychiatry, 25,* 645–647.

Little, K.Y., and Penman, E. (1989). Measuring sub-acute mood changes using the profile of mood state and visual analogue scales. *Psychopathology, 22,* 42–49.

Lorion, R.P. (1973). Socioeconomic status and traditional treatment approaches reconsidered. *Psychological Bulletin, 79,* 263–270.

Lorr, M. (1965). Client perception of therapists: A study of therapeutic relation. *Journal of Consulting and Clinical Psychology, 29,* 146–149.

Luborsky, L. (1984). *Principles of psychoanalytic psychotherapy: A manual for supportive/expressive treatment.* New York: Basic Books, Inc.

Luborsky, L., Auerbach, A.H., Chandler, M., Cohen, J., and Bachrach, H.M. (1971). Factors influencing the outcome of psychotherapy: A review of quantitative research. *Psychological Bulletin, 75,* 145–185.

Luborsky, L., Barber, J., and Crits-Christoph, P. (1990). Theory-based research for understanding the process of dynamic psychotherapy. *Journal of Consulting and Clinical Psychology, 58,* 281–287.

Luborsky, L., Crits-Christoph, P., Alexander, L., Margolis, M., and Cohen, M. (1983). Two helping alliance methods for predicting outcomes of psychotherapy: A counting signs vs. a global rating method. *Journal of Nervous and Mental Disease, 171,* 480–491.

Luborsky, L., Mintz, J., Auerbach, A., Christoph, P., Bachrach, H., Todd, T., Johnson, M., Cohen, M., and O'Brien, P. (1980). Predicting the outcome of psychotherapy: Findings of the Penn Psychotherapy Project. *Archives of General Psychiatry, 37,* 471–481.

Luborsky, L., Mintz, J., and Christoph, P. (1979). Are psychotherapeutic changes predictable? Comparison of a Chicago Counseling Center project with a Penn psychotherapy project. *Journal of Consulting and Clinical Psychology, 47,* 469–473.

Lundenburg, P.K. (1980). Assessment of drugs side-effects: Visual analogue scale versus check-list format. *Perceptual and Motor Skills, 50,* 1067–1073.

Luria, R.E. (1975). The validity and reliability of the Visual Analogue Mood Scale. *Journal of Psychiatric Research, 12,* 51–57.

Luria, R.E. (1979). The use of the Visual Analogue Mood and Alert Scales in diagnosing hospitalized affective psychoses. *Psychological Medicine, 9,* 155–164.

Maes, M., DeRuyter, M., Claes, R., Suy, E. (1988). Sexrelated differences in the relationship between self-rated depression and biological markers. *Journal of Affective Disorders, 15,* 119–125.

Magruder-Habib, K., Zung, W.W.K., and Feussner, J.R. (1990). Improving physician's recognition and treatment of depression in general medical care: Results from a randomized clinical trial. *Medical Care, 28,* 239–250.

Maio, D.D., Nielsen, N.P., Caponeri, M.A., Mellado, C., and Scieghi, G. (1975). Sceltae e modalita di uso dei farmaci antidepressivi in rapporto alla valutazione clinico-psicometrica dei diversi quadri clinici. *Acta Neurologia, 30,* 307–331.

Malan, D.H. (1963). *A study of brief psychotherapy.* London: Tavistock.

Malan, D.H. (1976). *The frontier of brief psychotherapy: An example of the convergence of research and clinical practice.* New York: Plenum.

Mann, J. (1973). *Time-limited psychotherapy.* Cambridge: Harvard University Press.

Master, R.S., and Zung, W.W.K. (1977). Depressive symptoms in patients and normal subjects in India. *Archives of General Psychiatry, 34,* 972–974.

Mathew, A., Mishra, H., and Kumaraiah, V. (1987). Alpha feedback in the treatment of tension headache. *Journal of Personality and Clinical Studies, 3,* 17–22.

Matsubara, T. (1985). Mental health of the aged in the depopulated areas of Japan. *Folia Psychiatrica et Neurologica Japonica, 39,* 465–471.

Matussek, N., and Hoehe, M. (1989). Investigations with the specific mu-opiate receptor agonist fentanyl in depressive patients: Growth hormone, prolactin, cortisol, noradrenaline and euphoric responses. *Neuropsychobiology, 21,* 1–8.

McClanahan, L.D. (1974). A comparison of professed counselor techniques and attitudes with client evaluations of the counseling relationship. *Dissertation Abstracts International, 34,* 5637A.

McClelland, H.A., Kerr, T.A., Stephens, D.A., and Howell, R.W. (1979). The comparative anti-depressive value of lofepromine and amitriptyline: Results of a controlled trial with comments and the scales used. *Acta Psychiatrica Scandinavica, 60* (2), 190–198.

McCormack, H.M., Horne, D.J., and Sheather, S. (1988). Clinical applications of visual analogue scales: A critical review. *Psychological Medicine, 18,* 1007–1019.

McFarlain, R.A., Mielke, D.H., and Gallant, D.M. (1976). Comparison of muscle relaxation with placebo medication for anxiety reduction in alcoholic inpatients. *Current Therapeutic Research, 20,* 173–176.

McIntyre, M.K. (1987). Client's expectations for psychotherapy: Relationship to client's satisfaction and prognostic expectations. *Dissertation Abstracts International, 47* (10), 4308B.

McKegney, F.P., Aronson, M.K., and Ooi, W.L. (1988). Identifying depression in the old, old. *Psychosomatics, 29,* 175–181.

McLean, P.D., and Hakstian, A.R. (1979). Clinical depression: Comparative efficacy of outpatient treatments. *Journal of Consulting and Clinical Psychology, 47,* 818–836.

McNair, D.M. (1974). Self-evaluations of antidepressants. *Psychopharmacologia, 37,* 281–302.

McNair, D.M., Lorr, M., Young, H.H., Roth, I., and Boyd, R.W. (1964). A three-year follow-up of psychotherapy patients. *Journal of Clinical Psychology, 20,* 258–264.

McNally, H.A. (1973). An investigation of selected counselor and client characteristics as possible predictors of counseling effectiveness. *Dissertation Abstracts International, 33,* 6672–6673A.

Mehta, B.M., Spear, F.G., and Whittington, J.R. (1980). A double-blind controlled trial of mianserian and amitriptyline in depression. *Current Medical Research and Opinion, 7,* 14–22.

Meltzoff, J. and Kornreich, M. (1970). *Research in psychotherapy.* New York, Atherton.

Merz, W.A., and Ballmer, U. (1984). Demographic factors influencing psychiatric rating scales (Zung SDS and SAS). *Pharmacopsychiatry, 17,* 50–56.

Miles, H.W., Barrabee, E.L., and Finesinger, J.E. (1951). Evaluation of psychotherapy, with a follow-up of 62 cases of anxiety neuroses. *Psychosomatic Medicine, 13,* 83–105.

Miller, S.M., and Naylor, G.J. (1989). Unpleasant tastes: A neglected symptom in depression. *Journal of Affective Disorders, 17,* 291–293.

Monk, T.H. (1989). A visual analogue scale technique to measure global vigor and affect. *Psychiatry Research, 27,* 89–99.

Moorman, J.C. (1985). The development of an integrated multidisciplinary service at Duke University. In J.E. Talley and W.J.K. Rockwell (Eds.), *Counseling and psychotherapy services for university students* (pp. 31–49). Springfield, IL: Charles C Thomas, Publisher.

Moran, P.W., and Lambert, M.J. (1983). A review of current assessment tools for monitoring changes in depression. In M.J. Lambert, E.R. Christensen, and S.S. DeJulio (Eds.), *The assessment of psychotherapy outcome* (pp. 263–303). New York: Wiley.

Mukherjee, P.K., and Davey, A. (1986). Differential dosing of trazodone in elderly depressed patients: A study to investigate optimal dosing. *Journal of International Medical Research, 14,* 279–284.

Neumann, J.K. (1981). Self-help depression treatment: An evaluation of an audio cassette program with hospitalized residents. *Behavior Therapist, 4,* 15–16.

Nietzel, M.T., Russell, R.L., Hemmings, K.A., and Gretter, M.L. (1987). Clinical significance of psychotherapy for unipolar depression: A meta-analytic approach to social comparison. *Journal of Consulting and Clinical Psychology, 55,* 156–161.

Nigl, A.J., and Weiss, S.C. (1977). A consumer analysis of campus mental health services. *Journal of the American College Health Association, 25,* 298–300.

O'Leary, A., Shoor, S., Lorig, K., and Holman, H.R. (1988). A cognitive-behavioral treatment for rheumatoid arthritis. *Health Psychology, 7,* 527–544.

Oliver, J.M., and Burkham, R. (1979). Depression in university students: Duration, relation to calendar time, prevalence, and demographic correlates. *Journal of Abnormal Psychology, 88,* 667–670.

O'Malley, S.S., Suh, C.S., and Strupp, H.H. (1983). The Vanderbilt Psychotherapy Process Scale: A report of the scale development and a process-outcome study. *Journal of Consulting and Clinical Psychology, 51,* 581–586.

Omer, H. (1990). Enhancing the impact of therapeutic suggestions. *American Journal of Psychotherapy, 44* (2), 218–231.

O'Neil, M.K., and Marziali, E. (1976). Depression in a university clinic population. *Canadian Psychiatric Association Journal, 21,* 477–481.

Orlinsky, D.E., and Howard, K.I. (1976). The effects of sex of therapist on the therapeutic experiences of women. *Psychotherapy: Theory, Research, and Practice, 13* (1), 82–88.

Orlinsky, D.E., and Howard, K.I. (1980). Gender and psychotherapeutic outcome. In A.M. Brodsky and R.T. Hare-Mustin (Eds.), *Women and Psychotherapy: An Assessment of Research and Practice* (pp. 3–34). New York: Guilford Press.

Orlinsky, D.E., and Howard, K.I. (1986). Process and outcome in psychotherapy. In S.L. Garfield and A.E. Bergin (Eds.), *Handbook of psychotherapy and behavior change* (pp. 311–381). New York: Wiley.

Orne, M. (1962). On the social psychology of the psychological experiment: With particular reference to demand characteristics and their implications. *American Psychologist, 17* (10), 776–783.

Pardes, H., and Pincus, H.A. (1981). Brief therapy in the context of national mental health issues. In S.H. Budman (Ed.), *Forms of brief therapy* (pp. 7–22). New York: Guilford Press.

Parker, G. (1985). Psychosocial predictors of outcome in subjects with untreated depressive disorder. *Journal of Affective Disorders, 8,* 73–81.

Parloff, M.B., Waskow, I.E., and Wolfe, B.E. (1978). Research on therapist variables in relation to process and outcome. In S.L. Garfield and A.E. Bergin (Eds.), *Handbook of psychotherapy and behavior change* (pp. 233–282). New York: Wiley.

Peet, M., Ellis, S., and Yates, R.A. (1981). The effect of level of depression on the use of visual analogue scales by normal volunteers. *British Journal of Clinical Pharmacology, 12,* 171–178.

Persons, J.B., Burns, D.D., and Perloff, J.M. (1988). Predictors of dropout and outcome in cognitive therapy for depression in a private practice setting. *Cognitive Therapy and Research, 12,* 557–575.

Pinkerton, R.S. (1986). Brief individual counseling and psychotherapy with students. In J.E. Talley and W.J.K. Rockwell (Eds.), *Counseling and psychotherapy with college students: A guide to treatment* (pp. 1–30). New York: Preager.

Pinkerton, R.S., and Rockwell, W.J.K. (1982). One or two-session psychotherapy with university students. *Journal of the American College Health Association, 30,* 159–162.

Piper, W.E., Azim, H.F.A., McCallum, M., and Joyce, A.S. (1990). Patient suitability and outcome in short-term individual psychotherapy. *Journal of Consulting and Clinical Psychology, 58,* 475–481.

Pishkin, V., Pishkin, S.M., Shurley, J.T., Lawrence, B.E., Loveallo, W.R. (1978). Cognitive and psychophysiologic response to doxepin and chlordiazepoxide. *Comprehensive Psychiatry, 19,* 171–178.

Price, D.D., McGrath, P.A., Rafii, A., and Buckingham, B. (1983). The validation of visual analogue scales as ratio scale measures for chronic and experimental pain. *Pain, 17,* 45–56.

Propst, L.P. (1980). A comparison of the cognitive restructuring psychotherapy paradigm and several spiritual approaches to mental health. *Journal of Psychology and Theology, 8,* 107–114.

Ray, C., and Fitzgibbon, G. (1981). Stress arousal and coping with surgery. *Psychological Medicine, 11,* 741–746.

Remington, M., Tryer, P.J., Newson-Smith, J., and Cicchetti, D.V. (1979). Comparative reliability of categorical analogue rating scales in assessment of psychiatric symptomatology. *Psychological Medicine, 9,* 765–770.

Renfroe, K.L. (1988). Effect of progressive relaxation on dyspnea and state anxiety in patients with chronic obstructive pulmonary disease. *Heart and Lung, 17,* 408–413.

Rhee, J.W., and Shin, S.C. (1978). An Ophthalmologic and psychiatric study on the headache: Chiefly on the depression, anxiety, deviations and refractive errors. *Chungnam Medical Journal, 5,* 57–66.

Riedel, H.P., Fenwick, C.R., and Jillings, C.R. (1986). Efficacy of booster sessions after training in assertiveness. *Perceptual and Motor Skills, 62,* 791–798.

Rioch, M.J., and Lubin, A. (1959). Prognosis of social adjustment for mental hospital patients under psychotherapy. *Journal of Consulting Psychology, 23,* 313–318.

Robbins, P.R., and Tanck, R.H. (1984). The Beck Depression Inventory and self-reports of behavior over a ten-day period. *Journal of Personality Assessment, 48,* 42–45.

Robinson, R.G., McHugh, P.R., and Folstein, M.F. (1975). Measurement of appetite disturbance in psychiatric disturbance. *Journal of Psychiatric Research, 12,* 59–68.

Rockwell, W.J.K., and Pinkerton, R.S. (1982). Single-session psychotherapy. *American Journal of Psychotherapy, 36* (1), 32–40.

Roethlisberger, F.J., and Dickson, W.J. (1939). *Management and the worker.* Cambridge, Massachusetts: Harvard University Press.

Rogers, C. (1957). The necessary and sufficient conditions of therapeutic personality change. *Journal of Consulting Psychology, 21* (2), 95–103.

Rogers, C.R., Gendlin, E.T., Kiesler, D.J., and Truax, C.B. (Eds.). (1967). *The therapeutic relationship and its impact*. Madison: University of Wisconsin Press.

Rosenbaum, G. (1956). Stimulus generalization as a function of clinical anxiety. *Journal of Abnormal and Social Psychology, 53,* 281–285.

Rosenbaum, M., Friedlander, J., and Kaplan, S. (1956). Evaluation of results of psychotherapy. *Psychosomatic Medicine, 18,* 113–132.

Rosenberg, S. (1954). The relationship of certain personality factors to prognosis in psychotherapy. *Journal of Clinical Psychology, 10,* 341–345.

Rosenthal, D., and Frank, J.D. (1956). Psychotherapy and the placebo effect. *Psychological Bulletin, 53,* 294–302.

Rosenthal, M.P., Goldfarb, N.I., Carlson, B.L., Sagi, P.C., and Balaban, D.J. (1987). Assessment of depression in a family practice center. *Journal of Family Practice, 25,* 143–149.

Rosenzweig, S. (1936). Some implicit common factors in diverse methods of psychotherapy. *American Journal of Orthopsychiatry, 6,* 412–415.

Rosenzweig, S. (1954). A transevaluation of psychotherapy-a reply to Hans Eysenck. *Journal of Abnormal and Social Psychology, 49,* 298–304.

Rothberg, S. (1955). Brief psychodynamically oriented therapy. *Psychosomatic Medicine, 17,* 455–457.

Rounsaville, B.J., Weissman, M.M., and Prusoff, B.A. (1981). Psychotherapy with depressed outpatients. Patient and process variables as predictors of outcome. *British Journal of Psychiatry, 138,* 67–74.

Rozenbilds, U., Goldney, R.D., Gilchrist, P.N., and Martin, E. (1986). Assessment by relatives of elderly patients with psychiatric illness. *Psychological Reports, 58,* 795–801.

Rubinow, D.R., Roy-Byrne, P., Hoban, M.C., Gold, P.W., and Post, R.M. (1984). Prospective assessment of menstrually related mood disorders. *American Journal of Psychiatry, 141,* 684–686.

Rudy, J.P., McLemore, C.W., and Gorsuch, R.L. (1985). Interpersonal behavior and therapeutic progress: Therapists and clients rate themselves and each other. *Psychiatry, 48,* 264–281.

Sargeant, J.K., Bruce, M.L., Florio, L.P., and Weissman, M.M. (1990). Factors associated with 1-year outcome of major depression in the community. *Archives of General Psychiatry, 47,* 519–526.

Saul, L.J. (1951). On the value of one or two interviews. The *Psychoanalytic Quarterly, 20,* 613–615.

Schaefer, A., Brown, J., Watson, C.G., Plemel, D., DeMotts, J., Howard, M.T., Petrik, N., and Balleweg, B.J. (1985). Comparison of the Validities of the Beck, Zung, and MMPI depression scales. *Journal of Consulting and Clinical Psychology, 53,* 415–418.

Schechter, N.L. (1985). Pain and pain control in children. *Current Problems in Pediatrics, 15,* 1–67.

Scher, M. (1975). Verbal activity, sex, counselor experience, and success in counseling. *Journal of Counseling Psychology, 22,* 97–101.

Schmidt, J.P., and Hancey, R. (1979). Social class and psychiatric treatment: Application of a decision-making model to use patterns in a cost free clinic. *Journal of Consulting and Clinical Psychology, 47,* 771–772.

Schmidt, M.M., and Miller, W.R. (1983). Amount of therapist contact and outcome in a multidimensional depression treatment program. *Acta Psychiatrica Scandinavia, 67,* 319–332.

Schneider, J.A., and Agras, W.S. (1985). A cognitive behavioral group treatment for bulimia. *British Journal of Psychiatry, 146,* 66–69.

Schnurr, R., Hoaken, P.C.S., and Jarrett, F.J. (1976). Comparison of depression inventories in a clinical population. *Canadian Psychiatric Association Journal, 21,* 473–476.

Scrignar, E.B. (1979). One-session cure of a case of speech anxiety with a 10-year follow-up. *Journal of Nervous and Mental Disease, 167* (5), 315–316.

Shapiro, J., Sank, L.I., Shaffer, C.S., and Donovan, D.C. (1982). Cost effectiveness in individual vs. group cognitive behavior therapy for problems of depression and anxiety in an HMO population. *Journal of Clinical Psychology, 38,* 674–677.

Sharpley, C.F., and Rogers, H.J. (1985). Naive versus sophisticated item-writers for the assessment of anxiety. *Journal of Clinical Psychology, 41,* 58–62.

Shaw, L., and Ehrlich, A. (1987). Relaxation training as a treatment for chronic pain caused by ulcerative colitis. *Pain, 29,* 287–293.

Siddall, L.B., Haffey, N.A., and Feinman, J.A. (1988). Intermittent brief therapy in an HMO setting. *American Journal of Psychotherapy, 42* (1), 96–106.

Siegel, S.M., Rootes, M.D., and Traub, A. (1977). Symptom change and prognosis in clinic psychotherapy. *Archives of General Psychiatry, 34,* 321–331.

Sifneos, P.E. (1972). *Short-term psychotherapy and emotional crisis.* Cambridge: Harvard University Press.

Silove, D., Parker, G., and Manicavasagar, V. (1990). Perceptions of general and specific therapist behaviors. *Journal of Nervous and Mental Disease, 178* (5), 292–299.

Silverman, W.H., and Beech, R.P. (1984). Length of intervention and client assessed outcome. *Journal of Clinical Psychology, 40* (2), 475–480.

Simons, J.A., and Helms, J.E. (1976). Influence of counselor's marital status, sex, and age on college and non-college women's counselor preferences. *Journal of Counseling Psychology, 23,* 380–386.

Smith, M.L., Glass, G.V., and Miller, T.I. (1980). *The Benefits of Psychotherapy.* Baltimore: The Johns Hopkins University Press.

Sokol, R.S., Folks, D.G., Herrick, R.W., and Freeman, A.M. (1987). Psychiatric outcome in men and women after coronary bypass surgery. *Psychosomatics, 28,* 11–16.

Sorensen, J.L., Kantor, L., Margolis, R.B., and Galano, J. (1979). The extent, nature, and utility of evaluating consumer satisfaction in community mental health centers. *American Journal of Community Psychology, 7,* 329–337.

Spencer, D.L. (1986). The interactive effects of client and helper expectations as predictors of client treatment satisfaction. *Dissertation Abstracts International, 47* (3), 1061A.

Spoerl, O.H. (1975). Single-session psychotherapy, Abstracted. *Diseases of the Nervous System, 36* (6), 283–285.

Springmann, R.P. (1978). Single-session psychotherapy in secondary male impotence. *Mental Health Society, 5* (1–2), 86–93.

Sriwatanakul, K., Kelvie, W., Lasagna, L., Calemlim, J.F., Weis, O.F., and Mehta, G. (1983). Studies with different types of visual analogue scales for measurement of pain. *Clinical Psychopharmacology and Therapeutics, 34,* 234–239.

Steer, R.A., Beck, A.T., and Garrison, B. (1986). Applications of the Beck Depression Inventory. In N. Sartorius and T.Z. Ban (Eds.), *Assessment of Depression* (pp. 123–142). Berlin: Springer-Verlag.

Steer, R.A., Beck, A.T., Riskind, J.H., and Brown, G. (1986). Differentiation of depressive disorders from generalized anxiety by the Beck Depression Inventory. *Journal of Clinical Psychology, 42,* 475–478.

Steinmetz, J.L., Lewinsohn, P.M., and Antonuccio, D.O. (1983). Prediction of individual outcome in a group intervention for depression. *Journal of Consulting and Clinical Psychology, 51,* 331–337.

Steuler, J., Rank, L., Olsen, E.J., and Jarvik, L.F. (1980). Depression, physical health and somatic complaints in the elderly: A study of the Zung Self-rating Depression Scale. *Journal of Gerontology, 35,* 683–688.

Stone, A., Frank, J.D., Nash, E., and Imber, S. (1961). An intensive five-year follow-up study of treated psychiatric outpatients. *Journal of Nervous and Mental Disease, 133,* 410–422.

Strong, S. (1968). Counseling: An interpersonal influence process. *Journal of Counseling Psychology, 15,* 215–224.

Strupp, H.H. (1980a). Success and failure in time-limited psychotherapy: A systematic comparison of two cases: Comparison 1. *Archives of General Psychiatry, 37,* 595–603.

Strupp, H.H. (1980b). Success and failure in time-limited psychotherapy: A systematic comparison of two cases: Comparison 2. *Archives of General Psychiatry, 37,* 708–716.

Strupp, H.H. (1980c). Success and failure in time-limited psychotherapy: Further evidence: Comparison 4. *Archives of General Psychiatry, 37,* 947–954.

Strupp, H.H. (1986). Psychotherapy: Research, practice and public policy (how to avoid dead ends). *American Psychologist, 41* (2), 120–130.

Strupp, H.H., and Binder, J.L. (1984). *Psychotherapy in a new key: A guide to time-limited dynamic psychotherapy.* New York: Basic Books.

Sullivan, P.L., Miller, C., and Smelser, W. (1958). Factors in length of stay and progress in psychotherapy. *Journal of Consulting Psychology, 22,* 1–9.

Tabor, A., and Jinsson, M.H. (1987). Psychological impact of amniocentiesis on low-risk women. *Prenatal Diagnosis, 7,* 443–449.

Talley, J.E. (1986). Using early memories in brief psychotherapy. In J.E. Talley and W.J.K. Rockwell (Eds.), *Counseling and psychotherapy with college students: A guide to treatment* (pp. 44–63). New York: Praeger.

Talley, J.E., Roy, E.T., and Moorman, J.C. (1986). What components of counseling work best with whom and when: A study. In J.E. Talley and W.J.K. Rockwell (Eds.), *Counseling and psychotherapy with college students: A guide to treatment.* New York: Praeger.

Talman, M. (1990). *Single-session therapy: Maximizing the effect of the first (and often the only) therapeutic encounter.* San Francisco: Josey-Bass.

Tanner, B.A. (1981). Factors influencing client satisfaction with mental health services: A review of quantitative research. *Evaluation and Program Planning, 4,* 279–286.

Turner, J.A., and Romano, J.M. (1984). Self-report screening measures for depression in chronic pain patients. *Journal of Clinical Psychology, 40,* 909–913.

Twining, T.C. (1983). Some inter-relationships between personality variables, obstetric outcome and perinatal mood. *Journal of Reproductive and Infant Psychology, 1,* 11–17.

Vredenburg, K., O'Brien, E., and Krames, L. (1988). Depression in college students: Personality and experiential factors. *Journal of Counseling Psychology, 35,* 419–425.

Wallerstein, R., Robbins, L., Sargent, H., and Luborsky, L. (1956). The psychotherapy research project of the Menninger Foundation. Rationale, method, and sample use. *Bulletin of the Menninger Clinic, 20,* 221–280.

Ward, N.G., Bloom, V.L., Dworkin, S., Fawcett, J., Narsimhachari, N., and Friedel, R.D. (1982). Psychobiological markers in coexisting pain and depression: Toward a unified theory. *Journal of Clinical Psychiatry, 43,* 32–41.

Watkins, J.C. (1971). The affect bridge: A hypnoanalytic technique. *The International Journal of Clinical and Experimental Hypnosis, 19* (1), 21–27.

Weber, D.J., and Tilley, D.H. (1981). Patients' evaluations of the mental health service at a health sciences campus. *Journal of the American College Health Association, 29,* 193–194.

White, J., White, K., and Razani, J. (1984). Effects of endogenicity and severity on consistency of standard depression rating scales. *Journal of Clinical Psychiatry, 45,* 260–261.

White, K., Pistole, T., and Boyd, J.L. (1980). Combined monoamine oxidase inhibitor-tricyclic antidepressant treatment: A pilot study. *American Journal of Psychiatry, 137,* 1422–1425.

Wilkins, W. (1973). Expectancy of therapeutic gain: An empirical and conceptual critique. *Journal of Consulting and Clinical Psychology, 40,* 69–77.

Wolberg, L.R. (1977). *The technique of psychotherapy.* New York: Grune and Stratton.

Wolberg, L.R. (1980). *Handbook of short-term psychotherapy.* New York: Grune and Stratton.

Woodward, R., and Jones, R. (1980). Cognitive restructuring treatment: A controlled trial of anxious patients. *Behavior Research and Therapy, 18,* 401–407.

Zealley, A.K., and Aitken, R.C.B. (1969). Measurement of mood. *Proceedings of the Royal Society of Medicine, 62,* 993–996.

Zetin, M., Sklansky, G.J., and Cramer, N. (1984). Sex differences in inpatients with major depression. *Journal of Clinical Psychiatry, 45,* 257–259.

Ziegler, V.W., Clayton, P.J., Taylor, J.R., Tee, B., and Biggs, J.T. (1976). Nortriptyline plasma levels and therapeutic response. *Clinical Pharmacology and Therapeutics, 20,* 458–463.

Zigler, E., and Phillips, L. (1961). Social competence and outcome in psychiatric disorders. *Journal of Abnormal and Social Psychology, 63,* 264–271.

Zung, W.W.K. (1965). A self-rating depression scale. *Archives of General Psychiatry, 12,* 63–70.

Zung, W.W.K. (1967). Factors influencing the Self-rating Depression Scale. *Archives of General Psychiatry, 16,* 543–547.

Zung, W.W.K. (1969). A cross-cultural survey of symptoms of depression. *American Journal of Psychiatry, 126,* 116–121.

Zung, W.W.K. (1971a). A rating instrument for anxiety disorders. *Psychosomatics, 12,* 371–379.

Zung, W.W.K. (1971b). The differentiation of anxiety and depressive disorders: A biometric approach. *Psychosomatics, 12,* 380–384.

Zung, W.W.K. (1972a). The depression status inventory: An adjunct to the Self-rating Depression Scale. *Journal of Clinical Psychology, 28,* 539–543.

Zung, W.W.K. (1972b). How normal is depression? *Psychosomatics, 13,* 174–178.

Zung, W.W.K. (1973a). From art to science: The diagnosis and treatment of depression. *Archives of General Psychiatry, 29,* 328–337.

Zung, W.W.K. (1973b). The differentiation of anxiety and depressive disorders: A Psychopharmacological approach. *Psychosomatics, 14,* 362–366.

Zung, W.W.K. (1974). The measurement of affects: Depression and anxiety. *Pharmacopsychiatry, 7,* 170–188.

Zung, W.W.K. (1986). Prevalence of clinically significant anxiety in a family practice setting. *American Journal of Psychiatry, 143,* 1471–1472.

Zung, W.W.K. (1987). Effect of clorazepate on depressed mood in anxious subjects. *Journal of Clinical Psychiatry, 48,* 13–14.

Zung, W.W.K., Magill, M., Moore, J.T., and George, D.T. (1983). Recognition and treatment of depression in a family medicine practice. *Journal of Clinical Psychiatry, 44,* 3–6.

Zung, W.W.K., van Praag, H.M., Dijkstra, P., and van Winzum, P. (1975). Cross-cultural survey of symptoms in depressed and normal adults. In T. Itil (Ed). *Transcultural Neuropsychopharmacology.* Istanbul: Bozak.

Zung, W.W.K., and Zung, E.M. (1986). Use of the Zung Self-rating Depression Scale in the Elderly. *Clinical Gerontologist, 5,* 137–148.

INDEX

173